In 1961, Lou Sullivan was a Catholic schoolgirl growing up in the suburbs of Milwaukee; in 1991 he was a gay man dying of AIDS in San Francisco, looking back on decades of activism and wondering if his life would be remembered. In this inspiring and deeply researched biography, Brice D. Smith offers a moving portrait of one of the U.S. LGBT community's most accomplished yet unsung leaders. He adds a long overdue chapter to queer history in recounting Sullivan's pioneering role in forging a national network of trans men, his bottomless curiosity about the transgender past, his successful crusade against the denial of transition-related health care to gay trans men like himself, and his final battles on behalf of people with AIDS. Smith's meticulous reconstruction of Sullivan's all-too-short passage through this world allows those of us living now to draw strength from the example of a long-gone man whose life is still worthy of emulation.

—Susan Stryker, Ph.D.,
Author of *Transgender History* and
Co-director of *Screaming Queens: The Riot at Compton's Cafeteria*

The immeasurable research and care given by Brice D. Smith to Sullivan's story of self-realization is a gift. *Lou Sullivan: Daring To Be A Man Among Men* is a welcome contribution to the annals of trans history, one that breaks the mold of what we have come to expect in a transgender narrative. Smith's account of Lou's self-realization takes us on a journey through the latter half of the 20th century's subcultures and activist groups—through the barriers of the established "gender professionals," into the darkness and delights of the Golden Age of the gay liberation movement, shedding light on the diversity of trans experiences. A pioneer in the distinction between gender identity and sexuality, Lou fought to be himself in a world that insisted he didn't exist. Lou transgressed the limited thinking of his era, the restrictions of his body, and even a terminal diagnosis to leave a legacy of self-determination that resounds beyond the gay FTM community he sought to empower. Smith's biography of Sullivan is essential reading for anyone interested in the history of gender.

—Rhys Ernst,
Artist & Filmmaker;
Producer of *We've Been Around* and *Transparent*

To witness Sullivan's struggle to find himself, and then watch him turn—in the face of certain death—to extend himself in the service of others, is a remarkable experience. Solidly informative and inspirational: Anyone interested in gender-related social movements, or the potential for one modest yet dedicated human being to change the world, should meet Lou Sullivan through Brice D. Smith's insightful work.

—Jamison Green,
Author of *Becoming a Visible Man*

In this path-breaking and much-awaited biography, Brice D. Smith gracefully illuminates Sullivan's tireless work as one of the most influential gender activists of the latter 20th century. Lou Sullivan helped put gay transgender men on the map in the 1980s at a time when few people were aware of transgender maleness and even fewer understood that transgender men could be gay. Smith brings Sullivan's work and writings to life, inviting us into the fascinating worlds of 1960s "counter culture," 1970s feminism and gay liberation, and 1980s health activism as Sullivan knew them. This book will find an eager audience among all those interested in gender, history, and how we can change the world. I can't wait to share it with students and friends alike.

—Finn Enke,
Professor of History and Gender and Women's Studies,
University of Wisconsin, Madison

Brice D. Smith's adept story-telling brings trans pioneer Lou Sullivan to life in this vivid biography. Thanks to the extensive personal materials that Sullivan maintained—and later archived—Smith was able to draw upon an uncommonly rich treasure trove to tell Sullivan's life story in this meticulously researched text. Such loving treatment is long overdue for one of the most influential figures in transgender history.

—K.J. Rawson,
Director of Digital Transgender Archive,
Assistant Professor of English, College of the Holy Cross

Brice D. Smith's *Lou Sullivan: Daring To Be A Man Among Men* provides an invaluable and timely service to scholars of queer history, trans people and all lovers of biographical storytelling. In this plain-spoken, carefully documented chronology, Smith offers an unsparing look at the life and times of this pioneer of gender authenticity.

From the gay liberation struggle in post-Stonewall Milwaukee to the onset of the plague years in San Francisco, Smith digs deep into the Sullivan collection in the GLBT Historical Society archives (of which he was a founding member) and other sources, walking us through Sullivan's struggles to claim his identity and sexuality as a gay man, transition as an FTM, find community and acceptance—and all the while paving the way for others to follow. I am grateful for the opportunity to walk in Lou's shoes for a little while, and gain a better appreciation for my community's history and for my FTM comrades.

—Terry Beswick,
Executive Director of GLBT Historical Society

D0221757

Lou Sullivan: Daring To Be A Man Among Men

Copyright © 2017 Brice D. Smith

All rights reserved.

ISBN: 0-9982521-1-5
ISBN-13: 978-0-9982521-1-7

New Girl Blues...or Pinks
Mary Degroat Ross

Letters for My Sisters: Transitional Wisdom in Retrospect
Edited by Andrea James and Deanne Thornton

Manning Up: Transsexual Men on
Finding Brotherhood, Family and Themselves
Edited by Zander Keig and Mitch Kellaway

Hung Jury: Testimonies of Genital Surgery by Transsexual Men
Edited by Trystan Theosophus Cotten

Below the Belt: Genital Talk by Men of Trans Experience
Edited by Trystan Theosophus Cotten

Giving It Raw: Nearly 30 Years with AIDS
Francisco Ibañez-Carrasco

For Lou

and for you

LOU SULLIVAN

TRANSGRESS·PRESS

LOU SULLIVAN

Daring To Be A Man Among Men

Brice D. Smith

ACKNOWLEDGEMENTS

First and foremost, my thanks to Lou. Thank you for the work that you did, which helped make this a world where trans people can be who they are. For the wealth of archival materials that you left behind, ensuring you would live on. And for your example, which inspired countless of us to be our authentic selves.

Thanks also to the Sullivan family, particularly Maryellen and Flame, who opened their hearts to me and opened old wounds for me. Your love for your brother is admirable and undeniable—to say the least. My condolences to Maryellen's family for your tremendous loss. One of my deathbed regrets will be not finishing this book before her death. This book meant so much to her. I pray that she trusted in its completion, and that she is now (and always) smiling down from above. Such a remarkable person, and I only experienced a bit of her love and support.

Flame—equally remarkable in your unconditional love and support—thank you for not only supporting my work on this project but for treating me like family. I will never forget how you supported me through my transition and how you spent that Christmas Eve with me going through your pictures of Lou. What a gift! Thank you also for having the courage to be a gentle man. More of us have benefited from your example than you will ever know.

A special thanks to Susan Stryker, who processed Lou's collection at the GLBT Historical Society, spent more than a decade ensuring his historical significance was known and then took a chance on passing the torch to an earnest grad student in Milwaukee. I am forever grateful to Lou for connecting us. Thank you for all that you have done for me—and for the rest of the world.

My deepest heartfelt thanks to my advisor, mentor and now-friend Merry Wiesner-Hanks, who has spent years going above and beyond and has no idea that she has done so. Thank you for all of the time, resources and encouragement that you gave me. Were it not for me, the dissertating process would have been painless. You gave me everything you could to become a successful academic and everything I needed to be a good human being. Thank you for being the amazing person you are.

Sincerest thanks to the other three members of my dissertation committee: Finn Enke, Rachel Buff and Joe Austin. I am especially thankful, Finn, for the many, many emails we sent back and forth under the auspices of my working on an article. Those emails forged an enduring friendship and went to the core of who we are. Thank you for sharing your time and your self with me.

Thank you Rachel Buff and Joe Austin. I know you're reading this, Rachel—thanks for making me a fellow avid consumer of Acknowledgements! More importantly, thank you for the innumerable times that you and Joe opened the doors of your offices and your home to me. No academics influenced me more. I loved working on my Ph.D., owed in large part to you two. My thanks to the rest of the UWM History Department for believing in me and this work, especially given that the sub-field of trans history hardly existed when I undertook this project and entered your program.

The GLBT Historical Society is one of our nation's most undervalued resources. Thank you for preserving our past—for giving us a well from which to draw inspiration now and into the future. And for your unwavering support of this project. Also, the staff at the San Francisco Public Library made hundreds—thousands?—of copies for me, for which I am deeply indebted. Were it not for your work I could not have done mine. You are all unsung heroes.

Speaking of heroes, one of the greatest of our time is Trystan Cotten, managing editor of Transgress Press. He founded Transgress Press to empower our community through books and strengthen it through charitable giving. Transgress Press was the perfect place to publish this book, both in terms of principle and execution. Thank you for believing in this work and in me, buddy.

Two other heroes who I am blessed to know are Loree Cook-Daniels and michael munson of the Milwaukee-based and nationally-recognized organization FORGE. I am humbled by your perseverance and loving generosity. The spirit of Lou lives in you, tirelessly giving of yourselves for the betterment of trans folk with no thought to personal reward. Thanking you here for your friendship, your support and your contributions to our community is the least I can do.

I also wish to mention the incredible contributions of the National Center for Transgender Equality (NCTE) and the Obama Administration to bettering the lives of trans people in this country. Thank you for seeing us, Obama Administration, and thank you for helping them to do so, NCTE.

My thanks also to Underwood Memorial Baptist Church, a beacon of hope to the marginalized since 1845. Your faith, love and community are unparalleled. And to Kara Catrelle for guiding me through my fears, loving me at my most vulnerable and teaching me how to see.

Thank you to my family. To my parents Les Smith, Chris and Danielle Hawley, who loved me unconditionally and were willing to overcome great challenges to do so. To my siblings Brooke VanWhy, Claire Hawley, Laura Stary, Tyler Smith and Savannah Smith, who know my faults better than anyone and love me anyways.

Thanks to Gideon for making my dream of becoming a dad a reality, and for making fatherhood far better than anything I ever could have imagined.

And to Carrie, whose blood, sweat and tears made this book possible. Thank you for the time that you made for me to write, for your brilliant edits and suggestions, and for your unwavering belief in me. You make me a better writer and—most important—a better person. I love you.

Finally, thank you to everyone who loved me despite and because of my being trans. I have a wonderful life and you to thank for it.

CONTENTS

INTRODUCTION

Lou Sullivan changed my life. And he continues to transform and inspire lives, despite the fact that Lou has been dead now for twenty-five years. I first met Lou in the pages of books written by the generation of trans activists and scholars who came before me. And it is my honor to now introduce you to Lou through this book.

When I met Lou in the library of the University of Wisconsin-Milwaukee (UWM), I was struggling to understand who I was and what to do with my life. The year was 2004. YouTube did not exist, Facebook was only known to Ivy League students, and I had to access the Internet through public computers. Libraries were my primary source for information, and the number of books on transgender anything took up just three feet on one shelf of the UWM library. As I flipped through these books, I was struck by the fact that nearly one-third of them noted the significance of an activist named Lou Sullivan, a gay trans man from Milwaukee who died in San Francisco in 1991 from AIDS complications.

I was captivated by Lou's heroic and haunting life. He had overcome tremendous obstacles to be who he was, devoted his life to helping others do the same, then tragically died from one of the worst diseases imaginable. I felt like I could not learn enough about Lou and feared that his contributions as a founder of the trans movement would soon be lost to the passage of time—a fate that seemed nearly as tragic as his premature death. So I decided to write Lou's biography, and enrolled at UWM as a PhD student in History to acquire the skills and resources that I felt were necessary to write a book worthy of this man. Little did I know that I was embarking upon a journey that would take twelve years—six for my PhD and another six of life experience—to bring this biography to you.

When I decided to write Lou's biography in 2004, I was trying to figure out whether or not I might be trans, and what that would mean for my life if I were. Thanks to Lou, there was a term to describe my sense of self and a definition of it that was broad enough to encompass my feelings and experiences. In 2004 that term was *transgender*. Today it is *trans*. In Lou's time it would have been *FTM* (female-to-male). The terms have become increasingly inclusive over time, owing in large part to Lou's early efforts of ensuring that *FTM* included both transvestites (people who dressed as men) and transsexuals (people who dressed as men and used medical assistance to embody maleness by transitioning). Lou experienced the power of terms to limit and liberate one's identity, and spent his life pushing the boundaries of identification, creating space for more people to find themselves and community.

I began identifying as trans and exploring what it meant for me to embody that identity. Not all trans people have the desire, need and/or means to transition, but at some point in their lives all trans people contemplate doing so. For four years I wrestled with whether or not to transition, and it was Lou who got me to ask myself the right questions. One summer night in 2008, I came upon a journal entry in which Lou recounted a letter he had written to his ex-boyfriend in 1979 regarding his desire to begin transitioning:

> Now that I'm alone, I see that, if it is true that we are all responsible for our own happiness, that we cannot expect others to fulfill us, and in the end we only have ourselves, then I better make peace with the feelings inside me. If I don't it will be the only thing on my deathbed I will regret not doing.[1]

I experienced a wave of goosebumps and asked myself, "If I were on my death bed, would I regret not transitioning?" A sea of calm passed over me as I answered "Yes."

The second question I had to ask myself was: "If Lou could do it, why couldn't I?" I feared that I could not endure—let alone overcome—the challenges of transitioning. And I feared that no one would love me if I did. But then there was Lou. A slight, soft-spoken, self-educated scholar who took on the medical establishment in a fight for his life. Or, more accurately, in a fight to live as the man he was. And a man who loved and was deeply loved in return amidst a world that told him he could not—should not—exist.

Many pleaded with Lou to write and publish his life story, and in the years after his death many more bemoaned the fact that he never did. But such an undertaking would have constrained Lou, bound him to the past when his future was knowingly limited. Instead, Lou was free to experience more, share those experiences, and record them in his journals right up to his death. When Lou died, he bequeathed to the GLBT Historical Society a wealth of research and personal effects that included photographs, video-taped interviews, letters and thirty years of journals. By leaving a record of his life, as opposed to a definitive account of it, Lou has given us the opportunity to make meaning out of his life—and death—for generations to come.

As a biographer, I found Lou's immense collection to be both exciting and overwhelming. I had more information than I could ever want—or use. I was humbled by the experience of deciding what to include and exclude, and how to create a cohesive narrative from his archive. I used Lou's journals as a touchstone to remain true to his story and spirit, and directly quoted him as much as possible to lend his voice to this work. But the sheer volume of the source material available means that what you will read in this book is only an extended glimpse into the life and significance of Lou Sullivan. And a glimpse as seen through my eyes and yours from this place and time.

If my son ever asks me why I devoted so much of my life to writing about Lou's, I will explain how the journey of writing Lou's biography coincided with my journey to become a father. Lou's biography gave my life meaning until I figured out the meaning of my life. Through Lou I found community and became a part of the trans movement. But it was because of Lou that I embraced who I am. And when I did that I was able to love myself. Once I came to love myself I was able to receive love, which came in the form of his mama. Together, our love was so great that it spilled over into the creation of him. And his birth fulfilled my dream of being a father.

But enough about me. Without further ado, here's Lou.

ENDNOTES: INTRODUCTION

1.   Lou Sullivan Journal, 3 October 1979, box 1 folder 11, Louis Graydon
      Sullivan Papers, 91-7, the Gay, Lesbian, Bisexual, Transgender (GLBT)
      Historical Society [hereafter cited as LGS Papers].

CHAPTER

PLAYING BOYS

I n June 1955, Jack and Nancy Sullivan threw a Davy Crockett-themed birthday party for their child, who turned four on June 16. That summer Disney had released the film *Davy Crockett, King of the Wild Frontier*, and Davy Crockett merchandise flew off the shelves as little boys across the country pleaded with their parents for coonskin caps and other regalia that would enable them to embody Davy Crockett. Four-year-old Lou Sullivan was no exception. His mother Nancy helped Lou into his Davy Crockett suit, and when Lou emerged from his father's den he was convinced that he was Davy Crockett. This birthday party would prove to be Lou's most memorable.[1]

Assigned female and named Sheila Jean Sullivan at birth, the joy of identifying as a man and having that identity validated left a lasting impression on little Lou. Throughout his childhood and into his early adult years Lou would try on different versions of masculinity by modeling himself after his idols. For brief moments the clothes would make the man for Lou, and he would simultaneously embody the men that he both wanted and wanted to be. But for many years the men he idolized, just like an understanding of his own identity, were just out of reach.

BEATLES AND BEATNIKS

John Eugene and Nancy Louise Sullivan, like millions of other Americans, married after World War II, bought a home, and quickly began a family. Courtesy of the GI Bill, the Sullivans were able to purchase a home in Wauwatosa, Wisconsin, a largely white suburb of Milwaukee. "Jack" and Nancy filled their home with six children in the space of nine years: Kathleen (1948), Johnny (1949), Lou (1951), Bridget (1953), Maryellen

(1955) and Patrick (1957). Jack and Nancy were devout Catholics who raised their children in the church and sent them to Catholic schools. Nancy was a homemaker and Jack owned his own trucking company.

Having five siblings meant that Lou had ready-made companions at hand while growing up. As a child, Lou most often played with Bridget and Maryellen, and as the eldest of the three, acted as ringleader. Between the ages of seven and twelve, Lou's favorite pastime was "playing boys," which entailed the three of them adopting male names and proceeding to act like boys. Lou realized early on that he enjoyed playing boys more than his sisters did, that he would continue playing boys even when Bridget and Maryellen were not around, and he only had male heroes. But Lou would also play with dolls and was by no means a stereotypical boy.[2]

For Christmas 1960 Lou received his first journal. He began journaling regularly in 1964, and would do so until his death in 1991. Adolescent Lou considered his journal his closest friend. Outside of his family, Lou found it difficult to make friends. He was shy, loved to read books, and frequently escaped into fantasy. His mother and older sister Kathleen, with whom he shared a room, began pressuring Lou to become more feminine. Between the ages of twelve and thirteen Lou was not averse to dressing femininely, and looked forward to getting his first period. Lou believed that the physical changes his body would undergo with puberty would transform him into a happy, well-adjusted woman. But on the whole puberty was disappointing, for it did not engender the psychic shift he thought it would. Furthermore, puberty ushered in societal dictates about feminine gender role behavior and a pressure to grow out of playing boys, which Lou did not want to do.

The year that Lou got his first period, 1964, was also the year of the Beatles Invasion, when John Lennon, Paul McCartney, George Harris, and Ringo Starr came to America and forever changed its cultural landscape. Lou watched the Beatles on the Ed Sullivan Show, saw their movies dozens of times, and joined the Beatles Fan Club. When Lou saw the Beatles in concert, he shrieked and sobbed uncontrollably, overcome by Beatlemania. He recorded the three days surrounding their concert in minute detail, and would remember the experience of seeing them for the rest of his life. Like millions of American girls, Lou was enamored of the Beatles, and Paul McCartney became Lou's first crush. However, for Lou the lines between desire and identification were often blurred.

Lou proudly told his journal that he was the "most Beatled kid" at school, an honor owing to the fact that he not only knew more about the

Beatles than any of his classmates, but also because he mimicked them in appearance. Through his socially-acceptable Beatlemania, Lou was able to continue playing boys. Lou spoke and wrote with a British accent like his idols, and tried to convince his mother to let him get a Beatles haircut. He also perceived a deep male love amongst the members of the Beatles and wanted to be in his own all-boy band. Lou began taking guitar lessons, to which he wore a white shirt, tie, and black slacks, like the Beatles.[3] By year's end, Lou could proclaim to his journal: "I'm not shy anymore! I don't care if people think I'm crazy, I'm gonna be myself. And guess who helped me to this. The Beatles."[4]

During puberty Lou began to have sexual fantasies about men. As a girl Lou had no reason to feel badly for thinking about men and finding them attractive, and he openly expressed his interest in boys. However, neither he nor any other female-bodied figure figured into his fantasies, which entailed men kissing, hugging and/or simply liking each other.[5] Lou channeled his sexual energy into writing stories and dreamed of becoming a writer. His stories typically involved older men helping teenage boys.

In addition to wanting to become a writer, Lou also dreamed of becoming a social worker. In fact, during Lou's early teen years he was near-obsessed with a desire to help wayward boys. "I'd like to take one of the hurt, frightened, lonely or neglected into my arms and tenderly love them and help them," he told his journal.[6] Lou never outgrew this compulsion. In later years the wayward boys would become gay men who he held in his arms and trans men who he shepherded through life.

The first wayward boy Lou knew and loved was his brother Johnney, who renamed himself Flame. While as a child Lou had been closest to Bridget and Maryellen, through his teenage years Lou was closest to his older brother Flame. Unlike Lou, Bridget and Maryellen outgrew playing boys and seamlessly moved into womanhood. Flame, on the other hand, challenged societal dictates about what it meant to be a man. At first, Lou viewed Flame as a wayward boy he wished to save, but he soon found in Flame a kindred spirit who profoundly shaped the man Lou would become.

At fifteen, Flame drank, smoked and challenged authority, but Lou knew that Flame's rebellion stemmed from feeling misunderstood and distrusting those who held positions of power. Flame was born with severe acne, and he viewed his skin as a barrier between himself and others. Because of his acne, Flame had been picked on and ostracized by his peers. He had also been subjected to radiation treatment, and as a child he had been put "on display" at a conference for the American Medical Association.[7] Flame's experiences planted within Lou a seed of distrust for the medical profession, and he could identify with Flame's experiences of his own skin—or the body he inhabited—serving as a barrier between himself and others. What Lou learned from his elder brother was to be defiant in the face of injustice while retaining a gentle heart. From Flame he also received unconditional familial love and much-needed validation—from an actual boy.

Flame not only had severe acne but, like Lou, was gender nonconforming, and Lou stuck up for his long-haired brother. Lou and Flame referred to themselves as "freaks," reclaiming the word so it lost its power to harm. They turned the meaning of the word on its head, brandishing "freak" as a badge of belonging for those who dared upset the status quo. Whereas Lou was allowed to wear masculine clothing on occasion, Flame's hair was a major point of contention with their parents, and he was eventually kicked out of the house. This double standard of accepting female masculinity while rejecting male femininity was not unique to the Sullivan household and still exists in our broader society to this day. Flame was told by his principal at Pius High School that he would have to cut his hair or find another school. He was also barred from entering CYO (Catholic Youth Organization) dances, kicked out of stores, and could not find a job, all of which saddened and bewildered Lou.[8] What was so threatening or abhorrent about altering one's own body to more accurately reflect one's sense of self? Lou's love for and identification with his brother was so strong that Flame's embodiment of masculinity came to be reflected in Lou's sense of self and the men to whom he was attracted.

As a teenager, Lou enjoyed being a girl inasmuch as boys found him attractive. Yet, when he looked at himself in the mirror, he experienced a feeling of disconnect: "I look in the mirror and say to myself, 'That's you, Sheila. That girl over there is you.' It seems so funny." [9] However, Lou's amusement often turned to frustration and fury.

> I hate being a girl, really! I have to be sheltered, I can't walk in the dark, I have to be meek and humble, I have to make a full report on what I did when gone, I have to be 'proper'. I hate that. I wish I were a boy. They have a real feeling of being someone. They can walk down a dark street like they were its king. They don't have to report or be sheltered.

> They have freedom and know what life really is. I want to,
> too. I don't want to be a girl. I hate it. I don't want it.[10]

Lou found that he received the most attention from boys when embodying stereotypical femininity, but it felt inauthentic. Lou refused to conform to mainstream gender norms "just to get some dumb boy who won't accept an individual."[11] This tension between wanting to be wanted, and frustration with feeling that he had to be someone other than his authentic self in order to be wanted, would plague Lou for his entire life.

In the fall of 1965, at the age of fourteen, Lou embraced the music and persona of his new idol, Bob Dylan. On his bedroom walls Lou replaced the pictures of the smiling, widely popular Beatles with those of the brooding, marginal Dylan, who better resembled Flame—and Lou's changing masculine ideal. Dressed like Dylan in a fur vest and bell-bottom pants, Lou would wander among Milwaukee's factories pretending he was a roamer from out-of-town. Lou yearned for Dylan's experiences and was enamored with his "complicated mind."[12] With his new infatuation for Dylan, Lou now found himself attracted to "beatniks…. Guys that think deep, I don't care how ugly they are."[13] He imagined that these guys hung out at the Avant Garde Café Espresso on Milwaukee's East Side, where he also hoped to find "the rest of [his] 'Bob Dylan side.'"[14]

The Avant Garde was a dark and dingy place with stained glass windows, lots of antiques, and mismatched furniture. "The Garde" held poetry readings, screened underground films by Andy Warhol and other beatnik artists, and featured bands on the weekends. Most importantly, the Garde offered a refuge for people like Lou and Flame who felt ostracized by mainstream society, and it served as the focal point of the counterculture in Milwaukee.[15] At the Garde, Lou found others who shared his tastes in music, literature, art and politics. He also found himself surrounded by individuals who defied prevailing gender norms in their dress and mannerisms—most obviously the long-haired men. The Garde was a place where Lou felt included and like he belonged.[16]

Several months after finding refuge at the Garde, Lou became consciously preoccupied with how he looked and what that said about who he was. Lou was not unique in being concerned about image as a teenager. What set him apart from his peers was that even on the countercultural margins he was unable to find an image with which he could wholly identify. "I wanna look like what I am but I don't know what someone like me looks like," he wrote in his journal. This conundrum led Lou to cycle through different masculinities and femininities, trying them on and then hanging them in the deep recesses of the closet he could not come out of because he did not know that it existed. During the summer of 1966, Lou's understanding of his self-image was that "when people look at me I want them to think—there's one of those people that REASONS, that is a philosopher, that has their own interpretation of happiness. That's what I am."[17] Lou decided to grow his hair "Joan-Baez style" to reflect his own interpretation of happiness, which meant growing it long and without bangs, more like the long-haired countercultural men: "I feel this's one step to lookin' the way I feel.'" [18]

Lou's mother responded to his changing aesthetic by enrolling Lou in charm school. As a tradeoff, Nancy allowed Lou to get cowboy boots, which completed his Bob Dylan outfit, under the condition that he not wear them to church or school. Cowboy boots may not have been stereotypically feminine, but they could still fall within the realm of acceptable female attire. However, for Lou the boots enabled him to embody a particular version of masculinity, and he felt transformed when he wore them. He bought a western jacket to complete what he would later refer to as his "cowboy drag," a countercultural and queer twist on the iconic American masculinity as embodied by a female-bodied Dylan idolizer.

Under the auspices of shopping, Lou took the bus downtown and to Lake Michigan's lakefront where he was able to escape into his fantasies of being a boy and delighted in the occasions in which he was heckled as one on the street. When men attempted to socially shame him with derisive catcalls, Lou remained aloof or shot them steady glares as he imagined a cowboy would. Over the next year Lou frequently noted in his journal occasions in which he wore cowboy drag, ascribing significance to otherwise mundane activities because of how differently he experienced them.[19]

In May 1967, Lou was walking along the lakefront in cowboy drag when he met a white, thinly built, long-haired boy named Don.[20] Don and Lou walked up Wisconsin Avenue in downtown Milwaukee singing "We Shall Overcome," and walked around a magic shop, the library and the museum, where they square danced to music and looked at the mummies.[21] They agreed to meet at the Garde the following night, and the day after that Don went to Wauwatosa to meet Lou's family. This time Lou wore a dress. Nancy told Lou that Don "looked like a beatnik on marijuana" and worried about what the neighbors would think.[22] But Nancy did not forbid Lou from seeing him, and Don quickly won Nancy over with displays of chivalry. A month and a half into their relationship, Don moved to

Denver, then later to San Francisco, and Lou vowed to "wait [for him] for infinity."[23]

The distance enabled Lou to put Don on a stage like the male musicians who he idolized—out of reach yet vivid in his fantasies. When Don returned from San Francisco, proposing marriage, he failed to live up to the man Lou imagined him to be. For his part, Don was disappointed to discover that Lou could not cook or sew, that he planned to write for a living, and that he would rather be a boy than a girl.[24] Lou declined Don's invitation to follow in the footsteps of the previous generation by marrying young and leading lives of socially prescribed heteronormativity. He chose instead to immerse himself in the social upheavals of the time in hopes of finding his authentic self and a partner who could meld his fantasies with reality.

BROTHERS AND HIPPIES

The Lou Sullivan who revolutionized understandings of gender and sexuality as a gay trans man with AIDS in the 1980s was born out of the cultural revolution of the 1960s. Lou came of age during the kaleidoscopic late 1960s when American society simultaneously seemed to be fracturing along lines of ideology and identification, yet also spinning toward a utopian, colorful wholeness. Like so many jewels at the end of the barrel, individuals tumbled within and among the civil rights, anti-war and countercultural movements, contained by a shared conviction that if they could turn the ways that people thought about race, war and love, the entire worldview regarding power would change. Lou, who felt marginalized from mainstream society because of his confounding gender identity, was both drawn to and shaped by these movements that sought to upset the status quo.

When Lou began his junior year of high school in the fall of 1967 after spending the summer at the Garde, he donned his same Catholic schoolgirl uniform, but teachers and classmates could see that he had changed.[25] For the next two years the "teenybopper" boys at school teased him relentlessly, to which Lou alternately responded with defiance and detachment. On the whole Lou ignored the girls at school and made no effort at friendships. In addition, Lou was bored by his classes and frustrated that "All a girl can prepare for is bein' a secretary."[26] In school Lou would "never do more than I have to or feel like," but still consistently ranked in the top twenty percent of his class.[27] From time to time Lou attempted to engage his classmates and teachers in discussions about social justice issues, including civil rights, but typically faced ridicule.

Lou found high school confining, to say the least, and doubted the utility of the white, middle-class, heteronormative instruction he received. For Lou, the activist streets were far more instructive. His unwitting quest to become a trans activist unfolded in quilt-like fashion with Lou's collecting seemingly disparate experiences and models of masculinity into a patchwork that would ultimately come together as the founder of the FTM (female-to-male) community.

One crucial piece of patchwork was Lou's experiences in Milwaukee's civil rights movement in the late 1960s and the models of masculinity he found there. He joined in the March on Milwaukee, a series of protest marches against racist housing discrimination in Milwaukee that was organized by Father James Groppi and lasted for 200 consecutive days.[28] Fr. Groppi, a white Catholic priest and native Milwaukeean, participated in the 1963 March on Washington—which was organized by gay civil rights activist Bayard Rustin—and worked with the Southern Christian Leadership Conference voter registration project led by Martin Luther King Jr. during the summer of 1965. An open housing law was finally passed in Milwaukee in April 1968, after 15,000 Milwaukeeans marched in honor of the slain Martin Luther King Jr., including Lou and his family.[29] Through marching Lou felt he could publicly express his sense of "oneness in being with all my black brothers & sisters," people who were discriminated against and ostracized because of how they looked, not unlike Flame and other long-haired men.[30] He also saw similarities between King's dedication "to love with no boundaries, peace, freedom" and the aims of the counterculture, and feared that members of the countercultural and civil rights movements alike would meet Dr. King's fate.[31]

Lou's fears seemed to be coming true when, in late October 1967, approximately twenty drunk male teenyboppers stormed the Garde and began beating up its long-haired male patrons. Lou jumped right into the fray, pulling the violent perpetrators off of their non-responsive victims and pleading with them to stop. When the horror had ended and the shock and sadness wore off, Lou was proud of how he had handled himself in his first and only fight.[32] Fearlessness in the face of injustice and an awareness of its stemming from ignorance became the hallmark of Lou's activism, from the countercultural and civil rights movements to gay liberation and the founding of the trans community.

Assaults on the Garde continued through 1968.[33] A combination of legal and extralegal measures forced the closing of the Garde by the year's end. Lou was devastated and despaired of ever finding another community to which he belonged.[34] Though he continued to be active in the counter-cultural movement, Lou would not find a sense of belonging that he had at the Garde until he found the focal point of the gay liberation movement five years later. But in the meantime there were additional pieces of patchwork to collect.

In the fall of 1969 Lou was one amongst 500,000 anti-war protesters at the 1969 Moratorium March on Washington in the nation's capital. "I'll never believe how many beautiful freaks there were," Lou wrote. "Man, the streets were loaded with them." When police tear-gassed the crowds in D.C., Lou was struck by the poise and love shown by his fellow protesters. He was especially touched when "3 freaks with water jugs & cloths" moved through the crowd and "dabbed our faces with water & told us not to rub it & that's all can be done. It was really beautiful cuz they were standing there in the gas looking for people to aid."[35] The masculinity modeled by these gentle men struck Lou with its effectiveness and extraordinariness. Little did Lou know that one day he would be party to similar acts of beautiful valor amongst strangers during the AIDS crisis, and at that time as a man among men.

Three months later, in February 1970, Lou participated in a protest organized by the Students for a Democratic Society (SDS) in Milwaukee, and the experience cemented his distrust of Establishment authority figures. The absurdly extreme measures taken by law enforcement to uphold the status quo left an indelible mark on Lou, and shored up his resiliency toward those who would attack him in defense of the status quo throughout the remainder of his life. Lou found the SDS protesters amusingly mild-man-nered, in contrast: "We started up Wisconsin Ave., loud shouts of 'Free the 8,' etc., but it was funny cuz everyone was all yelling their strength, but no one even crossed against the red light." However, after marching five blocks to the Federal Building, police in riot gear appeared and began advancing on the protesters. Lou got pushed into a large cement tree pot lining the street, and his boyfriend Mark got arrested when trying to help pull Lou out of the tree pot. When Lou refused to leave Mark, he was arrested too.

In all, fifty-one people were arrested and charged with unlawful assembly. After being detained, the police hassled them incessantly. What stuck out for Lou, though, was their conflation of law enforcement with policing gender. At one point, according to Lou, one officer said "you can't tell the boys from the girls," and another said, "Look at them! And they call us pigs!" Those arrested were also taken to the FBI Department, where Lou was shocked to discover that "the clerk had a big long report about me!" The report was generated simply due to Lou's involvement in the counter-culture.[36] Eventually all charges against the protestors were dropped but gender nonconformists remained ready targets for police harassment.

By May 1970, Lou began to think a nationwide political revolution was inevitable. Lou and Mark went to a block party in celebration of May Day where there was free music, food and alcohol. The hosts had obtained permits and everything was legal. However, as they were leaving, a police car sped into the crowd of people without any care for destruction of people or property.

> I would've never believed it. I never saw anything like it. And God, I'm so afraid. Yesterday, four students at Kent State Univ. in Ohio were shot and killed by National Guardsmen—2 guys and 2 girls. The paper said there were 1500 students protesting U.S. intervention in Cambodia, bout 300 guardsmen…. Eleven other kids were hurt.[37]

The day after writing this journal entry, May 6, 1970, approximately 3,000 students, faculty and staff from the University of Wisconsin-Milwaukee (including Lou) met for a rally and strike action, joining in a nationwide protest against the events at Kent State and the extension of United States military operations into Cambodia. Afterwards, several hundred students occupied buildings across the campus. One of the buildings was the Student Union, where students, faculty and staff held rallies, workshops and rap sessions, and staged an around-the-clock sit-in that lasted for nearly a week.[38] Six days into the occupation of the Union, Lou was sitting-in when a woman announced that the Union was surrounded by police. Lou thought, "Oh, great, this is the end. They're gonna blow us all up. I go outside and there are riot cops standing there, so I thought THIS is time for me to flee." The Milwaukee Police Department "re-took" the Union, effectively ending the campus strike. Lou returned home to find Mark had received a letter from the Selective Service wanting to know his graduation date for draft purposes.[39]

Luckily, the specter of Mark being drafted never materialized. A nationwide political revolution never materialized either, but a new consciousness about power and truth emerged, and battle lines were drawn in the social milieu. Lou's experiences in the 1960s ingrained in him a distrust of Establishment authority figures and a belief that great change could come from individuals living their truth and forming community with others who upset the status quo. The counterculture encouraged personal revelation and community organization, which would be the hallmarks of the social revolutions of the coming decades. These social revolutions would reshape our nation's understanding of what it means to be men and women and how we relate to one another socially, politically and sexually. Before he could become a leading figure in revolutionizing understandings of gender and sexuality, Lou had to understand his own gender and sexuality and experience it in relation to others.

MARK AND LOU REED

Gender identity and sexual desires may be inborn but they are undoubtedly outwardly experienced, and our sense of self as gendered and sexual beings is most intimately affected by those with whom we are most intimate. Romantic and sexual partners are in a powerful position to shape and validate our identities because of the ways in which they touch our bodies and our psyches. The lines between desire and identification had long been blurred for Lou, from the Beatles to Dylan, from the beatniks to the hippies. But his boyfriend Mark would become the first complete embodiment of Lou's desire and identification that he could touch and be touched by in return, and as a result their relationship would have a profound impact on Lou's relationship with himself.[40]

Lou's involvement in the counterculture helped him to replace the constricted, guilt-ridden proscriptions on sex from his Catholic upbringing with the tenets of free love. Lou observed that his friends would "engage in sex [because] they're very sensitive people, loving happiness, nature, love, human goodness," rather than limiting sex to a procreative act within the confines of Christian matrimony.[41] These revolutionary views on sex enabled Lou to not only admit to himself that "male homosexuals REALLY turn me on," but to also view this desire as "just natural" because an individual's sexual desires were natural in and of themselves.[42] He came to "accept sex as part of a human personality," rather than merely an act, and in doing so his desire for gay men began taking on a sense of significance for Lou.[43] For most people, including those in the counterculture, Lou's sexual attraction could be seen as heterosexual with a twist given that he was female. But Mark alone seemed to understand not only Lou's desire for gay men but to be one himself. Mark embraced Lou's gender ambiguity and encouraged his gay inclinations.

Mark was white, thinly built, long-haired and more gender ambiguous than anyone else Lou had dated. What's more, Mark was frequently read as gay due to his feminine appearance, mannerisms and demeanor. Lou met Mark at the Garde in January 1968, and the two of them shared many common interests. Mark pursued Lou for nine months, finally winning his heart by responding that Lou was the only one for him when Lou disclosed to Mark that he knew how to be a boy better than he did a girl.[45]

Jack, out of a desire to protect his daughter from heartbreak, warned Lou not to get too involved with Mark because he thought him to be homosexual. However, Jack's reading Mark as gay led Lou to like him all the more.[45] Lou recorded in detail Mark's accounts of being hit on by gay men. He also frequently recorded when others had difficulty telling whether Lou and Mark were two boys or two girls.[46] Within the first month of their relationship, Lou told Mark that he wished he were him, and spent the next ten years telling Mark how beautiful he was.[47]

When Lou graduated from high school, he and Mark rented separate rooms in the same house in Milwaukee's East Side neighborhood near Brady Street. The area was referred to as Milwaukee's Haight-Ashbury because of its head shops, record stores and countercultural scene. Mark was a student at the University of Wisconsin-Milwaukee (UWM), also located on Milwaukee's East Side, and worked in a dormitory cafeteria.

During his junior year of high school, Lou had decided against going to college, and after graduation he took a clerical position at Trade Press Publishing Company, which published business and industry magazines. On his first day of work Lou did not wear nylons and wrote in his journal that he was weaning himself off purses.[48] When Mark hitchhiked to San Francisco, Lou wore one of his shirts to work and wrote in his journal that he felt nearer to Mark in doing so.[49] Wearing the shirt of one's absent boyfriend is a socially acceptable behavior for girls. But unlike most girls, the sense of nearness engendered in Lou was more than skin-deep, for his desire was not simply to be with his absent boyfriend again but also to be him.

For nearly two years Lou and Mark essentially lived together. Lou enjoyed Mark's company and loved him deeply. In 1970, Lou thought a lot about marrying Mark and felt pressured to do so by his co-workers and family, particularly his mother Nancy. Lou wanted their relationship to be legitimate in the eyes of others and, as he became increasingly focused on getting married, he was surprised when Mark moved to an apartment two miles away, as Mark was the one who typically initiated discussions about their getting married. For his part, Lou had literal nightmares about having a baby and being married, his subconscious railing against this heteronormative trajectory.[50] The same social sanctioning that had allowed gender ambiguity within the confines of heterosexuality now threatened the safe haven their relationship had created for Lou.

The university fostered Lou's increasing curiosity in and identification with forbidden territories. In the midst of the Cold War with the Soviet Union, Lou took a job as a secretary in the Department of Slavic Languages at UWM. A perk of the job was Lou's ability to attend departmental classes, where his intelligence and enthusiasm for learning quickly won him the respect of professors.

Lou never officially enrolled as a student; he preferred to do his own independent research instead. Toward the end of 1970, Lou acquired a reading list distributed on campus by UWM's Gay Liberation Organization. He thoroughly enjoyed reading Martin Hoffman's *The Gay World: Male Homosexuality and the Social Creation of Evil* for the way it probed the gay sexual subculture.[51] Hoffman recommended John Rechy's *City of Night*, an autobiographical novel about a male hustler and his experiences in the urban "underworld," and Lou purchased it immediately.[52] "The whole story was so sad and lonesome," Lou thought, and he now found his adolescent desire to help wayward boys transposed to drag queens, of which Rechy provided "beautiful portraits" in his novel. But more than that, Lou wished to join their world, "that world I know nothing about, a serious threatening sad ferocious stormy lost world." Lou now told Mark he did not think they should marry, "thinking, as I spoke, that what can become of a girl whose real desire & passion is with male homosexuals. That <u>I want to be one.</u> That I fancy him to be one & I pretend I'm a man when we make love."[53] However, a female who imagined herself as a homosexual male was "way beyond anything [Lou had] ever read" in all of the available literature on "sexually weird people," and he was left wondering "where do I fit in"?[54]

After reading *City of Night*, Lou's desire to be a man depressed him to the point that he felt he was dying. But after two months of feeling this way, Lou "realized that I can't [be a man] so I might as well face it," and thought "if I can make myself <u>like</u> being a goddamn girl, maybe I'll feel a whole lot better."[55] Lou found he could not make himself like being a stereotypical girl, but felt he had no option but to accept that he was female. There was no framework for him to understand the conundrum of his desires for men and for being one himself. So he resigned himself to being female while traversing the boundaries of socially acceptable female behavior. Lou turned to his sister Kathleen for help, yet when they went shopping for clothes, Lou thought "that probably the best person to show me how to be a woman would be a queen as they probably got women down more than women do. It's a real ART for queens."[56] Even when pursuing an identity as a woman Lou turned to (gay) male culture, proving how significant maleness was in the identities Lou wished to construct.

Initially, Mark seemed receptive to Lou's new feminine wardrobe.[57] But at the same time Mark would comment on the attractiveness of other men and seemed more interested in reading his "Greek books" than in having sex with Lou. Lou wished that Mark would "admit to me he's gay. It'd really turn me on."[58] Lou began checking out other men too, specifically men he thought might be gay, and entertained thoughts of taking them home for the night.[59]

In 1971 Lou spent his spare time hanging out, camping and fixing cars with Mark and his male friends. "I really like it," he wrote in his journal.

> I mean, it's like an extension of when I used to play "boys" when I was younger. I like to play "boys" now. I know how to be one of the boys, I never knew how to be a <u>chick</u> & I'm Glad! Yet I think I can still be one of the guys & keep my identity as a girl, I hope, to make a pleasant combination.[60]

Lou was not simply concerned about retaining his identity as a girl in the general sense, which positioned him as the object of male desire. Lou was constructing his own unique version of what it meant to be a girl, and he appreciated that these male friends seemed to differentiate between Lou and the other females they knew—that they saw him as a girl due to his embodiment yet treated him like one of the guys.

Things were going well for Lou and Mark, who had been together for three years. Neither was interested in getting married anymore, and they referred to each other as "lovers" rather than boyfriend and girlfriend. In the spring of 1972, they decided to defy the strictures of socially-sanctioned heterosexuality and open up their monogamous relationship. One evening in a bar, Lou approached a man he found attractive and told him as much. When Lou proposed they have sex, the man was flustered and declined. "The way I felt about my approach to him," Lou wrote, "I just wanted to lay it on the line, get an answer & split," but Lou's female friends "just about died" when he told them about it, chiding him for taking the "male role."

Lou found it difficult "to play these [gender] roles," and so did Mark.[61] At one point Mark told Lou that "he feels real at ease talking to males & females he regards as males, but not when he has to talk to someone 'feminine.'"[62] Lou enjoyed what he had with Mark and was not interested in acting like a stereotypical straight woman simply to pick up another sexual partner. What Lou sought was the experience of picking up a man by acting like a man, especially like a man from Rechy's *City of Night* underworld.

One day while Lou was walking to the store, a "really good-looking [white] guy" was walking in the other direction, and when they passed each other they both looked twice. He asked Lou where he was going. Lou answered the store, asked the man where he was going, and they agreed to meet in front of the store in fifteen minutes. At Lou's apartment they ate, put on a record, "Talked about nothing," and had sex.[63] Beau left abruptly, but then showed up on Lou's doorstep two weeks later. When Beau proposed anal sex, Lou was eager to learn how, writing in his journal: "I like to make love like a man... I want to be a beautiful man making love to another beautiful man."[64]

Lou knew little about Beau and thoroughly enjoyed this (hustler) fantasy in the flesh. In addition to the gay undertones of their relationship, Beau had been to jail, asked for money after they had sex and was a "roamer." Beau was originally from Florida, and decided to stay in Milwaukee for the winter. He moved in with Lou in December 1972 and stayed for a month. Lou enjoyed telling everyone that he had a kept man.[65] After Beau moved out in January 1973, he and Lou hooked up several more times through the spring, but then Beau vanished as suddenly as he appeared. To Lou, "Beau was a lovely dream," a gay dream, and Lou never got to know him well enough as a person to dispel the aura of fantasy.[66]

Mark was not a fantasy, per se, but he increasingly became a means through which Lou could vicariously live out his fantasy of being a gay man. In late December 1972, Lou witnessed an intimate flirtatious exchange between Mark and another feminine man, which he detailed in his journal. For Lou, the experience was exciting but also highlighted his inherent limitations as a female:

No matter how I tried, I could never have joined their game. I felt a deep sadness at finally realizing I'll never have my deepest, secret dream fulfilled, ever. The guy lowered his eyelids & took Mark's hand as we left the car... I had an urge to lean over & kiss the boy as I left the car... but I knew I could never be part of the life & I had just admitted it to myself... I left the car hoping he didn't notice I was female...

Lou decided "I want to make [Mark] the lovely boy I wish I could be."[67]

After two years of thinking Mark a "latent homosexual," in January 1973 Lou wrote in his journal that "Mark has begun to 'come out'":

He told me lately he's been really getting into acting gay (he didn't come right out & say that, but it was all said & understood without using the word "gay") & he used to be afraid of being as feminine as he is, but now he's enjoying it & "if the possibility ever came up now, I don't think I could turn it down." I told him how much it turned me on & he said he knew it did. I told him that's always been my closest guarded secret & he's the only one who knows.... He said we can do such wonderful things together & we'll always be together.[68]

Lou believed it "best that I see him more often now to keep encouraging him so he doesn't lose faith in himself."[69] Now, when Mark told him stories about gay "youngmen" (Lou borrowed this term from author John Rechy), Lou thought of them in terms of potential lovers for Mark and offered not only encouragement but advice.[70] He also praised Mark's embrace of a more feminine appearance, bought him jewelry and tried helping him put on make-up.[71] Mark now made Lou think of Kathy, a drag queen in Rechy's *City of Night*, and "her ghostlike beauty."[72] Lou was blissfully incredulous to learn that Mark "wants me to be his male lover, kiss his jeweled hand, stroke his chest. But he does... he does..." and Mark's "wearing these sexy clothes and jewelry" drove Lou "mad."

For a time, the lines between desire and identification blurred for Lou in regard to Mark, just as they had with the Beatles and Bob Dylan. Lou now adopted a "new image" that consisted of wearing masculine clothing and a lot of jewelry with it—like Mark, who Lou wrote "fulfills my dreams... he is me..."[73]

Imagining himself to be Mark made for a more tangible fantasy for Lou than imagining himself to be a famous musician he had never met, let alone touched. At first, the proximity excited Lou tremendously. He had never been so near to the man he imagined himself to be. However, the realness and nearness also came with one very powerful side effect: jealousy. Lou was frustrated that, unlike Mark, he could not "dress up in female drag & be a queen" whose feminine appearance belied male anatomy and who could claim membership in the gay subculture.[74] He also envied the fact that Mark "could go to the bar any night alone & come home with a beautiful youngman."

> I wouldn't even be welcome into the bar... and even if I got in, I'd be so ashamed that I was a woman that I'd leave quickly, lost, apologetically, and want to cry in desperation. I don't even know if there was anyone that's ever felt as I do... how they coped, what they did... how do I find out what someone like me does?[75]

Lou felt that he was helping Mark discover his authentic self but neither Mark nor Lou had the means to help Lou do the same. And while Lou had never felt so authentically desired as he did with Mark, he had also never so desired authenticity. The more someone loves us for who we are, the more we want to be that person. But what did one who was born female and wanted to be a gay man do, and how did such a person identify?

One night Lou borrowed his brother Patrick's motorcycle jacket, went out to a bar with his other siblings and Mark, and had "one of the best times I've ever had!" To those at the bar whom Lou did not know, he introduced himself as Lou Reed—his "hero" who was notorious for wearing leather jackets—rather than as Sheila (his name given at birth).[76] Lou Reed's *Transformer* album, like Rechy's *City of Night*, seemed to permeate Lou's consciousness. He often quoted Reed's lyrics in his journal, most frequently from "Walk on the Wild Side," which featured a number of Rechy-like characters from the so-called urban underworld. Lou also detailed Reed's dress and mannerisms in his journal as if studying his performance of masculinity.

At the bar that night, Lou "felt super hard-guy & all drunk & don't know how it all started, but soon I was the big stud guy.... For the first time in public, I was the man hiding inside of me for so many years.... But shit, I was real!!"[77] Lou quickly purchased his own leather jacket, and envisioned himself "2 people finally coming together in peace with each other."[78] It felt real. The style differed substantially from Mark's, but more importantly it was not Mark through whom Sheila was living vicariously but rather *Lou*. The clothes had made the man, but what did that mean?

As luck would have it, the following month transsexual celebrity Christine Jorgensen came to Milwaukee, and Lou and Mark went to her lecture at UWM. In the 1950s, the extensive media coverage Jorgensen received made *sex change* a household term in the United States.[79] Now, exactly twenty years after Jorgensen returned from undergoing sex reassignment in Denmark, she remained a celebrity and was invited to join the public lecture circuit.[80] Despite the fact that Jorgensen's college lectures could draw thousands, Lou felt "hesitant to admit publicly I'm interested in this male/female thing" by attending her lecture. Unlike the vast majority who attended Jorgensen's lectures, Lou was not a mere curiosity-seeker and worried that his inward struggles might be revealed to others.

Jorgensen used her lectures to educate the public about transsexuals, and afterwards Lou noted that he found the lecture "pretty interesting."[81] The possibility of undergoing a "sex change" (or transitioning, as we say today) was appealing, but identifying as transsexual seemed out of reach. Jorgensen had transitioned from male to female in order to live as a straight woman rather than be perceived as a gay man, while Lou was a female who wanted to be perceived as a gay man. If Lou were transsexual like Jorgensen, it would have followed that Lou would transition into a straight man.

Lou was finally starting to understand and embrace his authentic self, but what was it? It seemed the closer he got to his inner truth the further he got from a recognizable identity. As Lou continued in his search for answers, he found something enduringly valuable: community.

ENDNOTES: CHAPTER 1

1. Sullivan Journal, 31 October 1965, box 1 folder 5; 1 November 1974, box 1 folder 10; 16 June 1986, box 1 folder 15, LGS Papers. Ira B. Pauly, *Female to Gay Male Transsexualism: I – Gender & Sexual Orientation* (Reno: Department of Psychiatry & Behavioral Sciences, University of Nevada School of Medicine, 1988).

2. Sullivan Journal, 6 January 1963, 10 December 1964, box 1 folder 4, LGS Papers; Pauly, *Female to Gay Male Transsexualism: I – Gender & Sexual Orientation.*

3. Sullivan Journal, 20 June 1964, 18 July 1964, 28 August 1964, 3 September – 5 September 1964, 3 December 1964, box 1 folder 4, LGS Papers.

4. Sullivan Journal, 17 November 1964, box 1 folder 4, LGS Papers.

5. Pauly, *Female to Gay Male Transsexualism: I – Gender & Sexual Orientation.*

6. Sullivan Journal, 22 December 1964, box 1 folder 4, LGS Papers.

7. Flame Sullivan, interview by author, 5 March 2006, Milwaukee, tape recording, in author's possession.

8. Sullivan Journal, 2 April 1965, 11 August 1965, box 1 folder 5, LGS Papers.

9. Sullivan Journal, 18 April 1965, box 1 folder 5, LGS Papers.

10. Sullivan Journal, 23 June 1965, box 1 folder 5, LGS Papers.

11. Sullivan Journal, 1 November 1965, box 1 folder 5, LGS Papers.

12. Sullivan Journal, 3 February 1966, box 1 folder 5, LGS Papers.

13. Sullivan Journal, 17 February 1966, box 1 folder 5, LGS Papers.

14. Sullivan Journal, 26 March 1966, box 1 folder 5, LGS Papers.

15. Flame Sullivan interview.

16. Sullivan Journal, 12 March 1966, box 1 folder 5, LGS Papers.

17. Sullivan Journal, 20 June 1966, box 1 folder 5, LGS Papers.

18. Sullivan Journal, 24 July 1966, box 1 folder 5, LGS Papers.

19. Sullivan Journal, 8 September 1966, 11 September 1966, 19 September 1966, 2 October 1966, 6 October 1966, 15 October 1966, 27 October 1966, 28 October 1966, 8 November 1966, box 1 folder 5; 3 March 1967, 24 March 1967, 5 May 1967, 23 June 1967, 24 June 1967, 14 July 1967, 8 August 1967, 14 August 1967, box 1 folder 6, LGS Papers.

20.   Don is a pseudonym.

21.   Sullivan Journal, 5 May 1967, box 1 folder 6, LGS Papers.

22.   Sullivan Journal, 7 May 1967, box 1 folder 6, LGS Papers.

23.   Sullivan Journal, 3 July 1967, box 1 folder 6, LGS Papers.

24.   Sullivan Journal, 24 June 1968, 25 June 1968, 26 June 1968, box 1 folder 8, LGS Papers.

25.   Sullivan Journal, 31 August 1966, box 1 folder 5, LGS Papers.

26.   Sullivan Journal, 22 February 1967, box 1 folder 6, LGS Papers.

27.   Sullivan Journal, 19 February 1968, box 1 folder 7, LGS Papers.

28.   Sullivan Journal, 28 November 1967, 19 December 1967, box 1 folder 6, LGS Papers. For information about the protest marches, see University of Wisconsin-Milwaukee Libraries, *March on Milwaukee Civil Rights History Project*, http://www4.uwm.edu/libraries/digilib/march/index.cfm.

29.   James Groppi Papers, 1956-1989, "Biography/History: James Groppi Papers, 1956-1978," *Archival Resources in Wisconsin: Descriptive Finding Aids*, http://digicoll.library.wisc.edu/cgi/f/findaid/findaid-idx?c=wiarchives;view=reslist;subview=standard;didno=uw-whs-mil000ex;focusrgn=bioghist;cc=wiarchives;byte=102610936; Wisconsin Cartographer's Guild, *Wisconsin's Past and Present: A Historical Atlas* (Madison: University of Wisconsin, 1998), 78.

30.   Sullivan Journal, 8 April 1968, box 1 folder 8, LGS Papers.

31.   Sullivan Journal, 5 April 1968, box 1 folder 8, LGS Papers.

32.   Sullivan Journal, 27 October 1967, 28 October 1967, box 1 folder 6, LGS Papers.

33.   Flame Sullivan interview; Sullivan Journal, 27 January 1968, box 1 folder 8, LGS Papers.

34.   Sullivan Journal, 3 December 1968, box 1 folder 8, LGS Papers.

35.   Sullivan Journal, 16 November 1969, box 1 folder 8, LGS Papers.

36.   Sullivan Journal, 22 February 1969, box 1 folder 8, LGS Papers.

37.   Sullivan Journal, 5 May 1970, box 1 folder 9, LGS Papers.

38.   Allen Ramsey, "The Student Strike and Later Protests, 1970-1975," *Vietnam War Protests at the University of Wisconsin-Milwaukee*, http://guides.library.uwm.edu/content.php?pid=85020&sid=633131.

39.   Sullivan Journal, 16 May 1970, box 1 folder 9, LGS Papers.

40. Mark is a pseudonym.

41. Sullivan Journal, 2 September 1968, box 1 folder 8, LGS Papers.

42. Sullivan Journal, 2 May 1968, box 1 folder 8, LGS Papers.

43. Sullivan Journal, 13 October 1968, box 1 folder 8, LGS Papers.

44. Sullivan Journal, 12 October 1968, 27 April 1968, box 1 folder 8, LGS Papers.

45. Pauly, *Female to Gay Male Transsexualism: I – Gender & Sexual Orientation*.

46. For examples see Sullivan Journal, 1 December 1968, 20 December 1968, box 1 folder 8, LGS Papers.

47. Sullivan Journal, 9 November 1968, box 1 folder 8, LGS Papers.

48. Sullivan Journal, 2 June 1969, box 1 folder 8, LGS Papers.

49. Sullivan Journal, 18 June 1969, box 1 folder 8, LGS Papers.

50. Sullivan Journal, 31 January 1970, box 1 folder 9, LGS Papers.

51. See Martin Hoffman, *The Gay World: Male Homosexuality and the Social Creation of Evil* (New York: Basic Books, 1968).

52. See John Rechy, *City of Night* (New York: Grove, 1963).

53. Sullivan Journal, 22 November 1970, box 1 folder 9, LGS Papers.

54. Sullivan Journal, 13 January 1971, 22 November 1970, box 1 folder 9, LGS Papers.

55. Sullivan Journal, 26 January 1971, box 1 folder 9, LGS Papers.

56. Sullivan Journal, 29 March 1971, box 1 folder 9, LGS Papers.

57. Sullivan Journal, 10 February 1971, 13 March 1971, box 1 folder 9, LGS Papers.

58. Sullivan Journal, 13 March 1971, box 1 folder 9, LGS Papers.

59. For example see Sullivan Journal, 29 March 1971, box 1 folder 9, LGS Papers.

60. Sullivan Journal, 20 July 1971, box 1 folder 9, LGS Papers.

61. Sullivan Journal, 14 April 1972, box 1 folder 10, LGS Papers.

62. Sullivan Journal, 28 April 1972, box 1 folder 10, LGS Papers.

63. Sullivan Journal, 30 October 1972, box 1 folder 10, LGS Papers.

64. Sullivan Journal, 13 November 1972, box 1 folder 10, LGS Papers.

65. Sullivan Journal, 10 December 1972, box 1 folder 10, LGS Papers.

66. Sullivan Journal, 15 January 1973, box 1 folder 10, LGS Papers.

67. Sullivan Journal, 23 December 1972, box 1 folder 10, LGS Papers.

68. Sullivan Journal, 6 January 1973, box 1 folder 10, LGS Papers.

69. Sullivan Journal, 9 January 1973, box 1 folder 10, LGS Papers.

70. Sullivan Journal, 30 January 1973, 18 February 1973, box 1 folder 10, LGS Papers.

71. Sullivan Journal, 28 January 1973, box 1 folder 10, LGS Papers.

72. Sullivan Journal, 9 January 1973, box 1 folder 10, LGS Papers.

73. Sullivan Journal, 8 February 1973, box 1 folder 10, LGS Papers.

74. Sullivan Journal, 22 January 1973, box 1 folder 10, LGS Papers.

75. Sullivan Journal, 13 February 1973, box 1 folder 10, LGS Papers.

76. Sullivan Journal, 21 April 1973, box 1 folder 10, LGS Papers.

77. Sullivan Journal, 26 February 1973, box 1 folder 10, LGS Papers.

78. Sullivan Journal, 28 February 1973, box 1 folder 10, LGS Papers.

79. Joanne Meyerowitz, *How Sex Changed: A History of Transsexuality in the United State* (Cambridge: Harvard University, 2002), 51.

80. Meyerowitz, 280.

81. Sullivan Journal, 28 March 1973, box 1 folder 10, LGS Papers.

CHAPTER

FINDING COMMUNITY

O n Monday, April 16, 1973, Lou dressed in his Lou Reed-like "leather drag" and met his friend Liz at the Gay People's Union (GPU) meeting.[1] For nearly two years GPU had held meetings every Monday night at the Eastside Community Center, a former church on Milwaukee's East Side where numerous "counterculture groups" rented meeting space.[2] Lou estimated there were thirty people in attendance that night, mostly men between the ages of twenty-five and thirty. "It was like any other club mtg 'cept they spoke so freely bout being homosexuals," Lou observed. The topic of the meeting was coming out, but unlike the other meeting attendees, Lou did not know what to come out *as*.[3]

The years 1973-1975 were a time of great excitement and discovery for Lou. In his early twenties Lou came to better understand who he might become by ruling out that which he was not. Lou graduated from trying on the masculinities of particular individuals to trying on different identities in his ongoing effort to embody who he was in a world where gay trans men supposedly did not exist. GPU and Milwaukee's gay community offered Lou a safe space for sexual experimentation, provided him with an unparalleled sense of belonging and laid the foundation for his future FTM activism.

FEMINIST? LESBIAN?

In February 1973, Lou began crossdressing full time, which included wearing men's clothes to work. Although quick to critique his long-term marriage-less relationship with Mark, Lou's co-workers largely remained silent about his new wardrobe. As they saw it, Lou's rejection of skirts and blouses was a feminist statement, and one that his university co-workers felt comfortable supporting. Skirting marriage, however, was too much for their Midwestern sensibilities; fashion could be fleeting but marriage was considered the bedrock of American society.

While most remained silent about Lou's wardrobe, Dorothy, Lou's fellow Department of Slavic Languages secretary, saw Lou's clothing as indicative of a feminist consciousness that mirrored her own.[4] Dorothy took Lou's crossdressing as a political statement that challenged gender stereotypes and inequality. Women were seen and treated as inferior to men and the fact that men and women wore such markedly different clothing meant that women's skirts and blouses could be considered signifiers of second-class status. To Dorothy and other feminists, Lou's rejection of women's clothing was a symbolic rejection of women's inferiority. By wearing men's suits, he was signaling a desire to be seen as equal to men and to show that he could do what they could do.

Calling Lou her "feminist friend," Dorothy used Lou's clothing as an invitation to engage him in what she thought would be a lighthearted dialogue on gender roles and inequality. However, their exchange (via letters) quickly evolved into a debate that mirrored the emerging conflicts over gender and gender expression between the women's and gay liberation movements.

Lou was not crossdressing to make a feminist political statement but rather to feel comfortable in his own skin. He wore men's clothing not because he identified with (feminist) women but because he identified with (gay) men. Dorothy reeled from this realization and quickly found herself engaged in a debate on gender roles and gender variance among gay men and (male) transvestites. The crux of Lou's argument was that gender equality meant creating space for all forms of gender expression, that male femininity was as valid as female masculinity and that it was hypocritical to applaud women for donning masculine signifiers while deriding men who donned feminine signifiers.

Lou assured Dorothy that "I'm not trying to deny my 'femininity'," nor denigrate women in any way. Rather, Lou confessed, "I've always thought of myself as a male homosexual." He was trying to figure out why that was and what it meant, and to do so, he told Dorothy, he was going to "get to know some gays and transvestites, see if I can learn anything about the feelings I've had."[5] Dorothy pushed Lou to embrace the tenets of feminism as a means for understanding his identity, and he pulled away. Feminism concerned itself with the status of women while all Lou could think about was men.

Lou and Dorothy's heated exchange provided a means for Lou to articulate his emerging gender consciousness, which illuminated areas for growth in feminist consciousness that would be addressed several decades later. Identifying the resonance of their debate with the larger political movements with which they identified, Lou later published his exchange with Dorothy and saw it reprinted in several contemporary gay presses. The first to publish this exchange as an article—Lou's first—was *GPU News*.

Lou went to his first GPU meeting a week after his letter exchange with Dorothy took place. He accompanied his friend Liz, whom Lou had first met as a feminine male three years prior. Now, Liz showed up at Lou's work explaining that she was "trying to get a sex-change operation" to affirm her identity as a woman. Lou disclosed to Liz that he was experiencing "an identity crisis... that the only thing I'm sure of is [that] I like real femmy guys but don't know if it's a cop-out for my desire for women." They talked for an hour and made a date to attend the Monday night GPU meeting together.[6]

At the end of Lou's first GPU meeting, where the topic was coming out, Liz introduced him to three women. These women invited Lou to the GPU Lesbian Discussion Group, which met every other Friday in various locations, usually individuals' homes.[7] Whereas Lou's university co-workers had assumed he was a feminist, initially everyone at GPU assumed that Lou was a lesbian because of his masculine gender presentation.[8] They associated his desire to be a man and his attraction to wearing men's clothing with same-sex eroticism—toward women. Lou attended the lesbian discussion group several times but struggled to identify with the women who attended because of his persistent attraction to men and (gay) male culture.

Lou increasingly distanced himself from the lesbians in GPU in an effort to differentiate his identity from theirs. However, the lines were not always easily drawn, as evidenced by an experience in which Lou was "propositioned" by a woman named Jay:

> Told her I'd never been with a woman, she said she'd make
> me feel fantastic, but there was only one requirement: that I
> didn't touch her. Why? That's just her hang-up... shit. Told
> her I don't even know if I'd want a lesbian experience...
> finally told her I consider myself a male homosexual... she

was pretty grossed out about that but I've seen her since & we're still friends.… She said she knew the first time she saw me I wasn't so butch.[9]

While Jay identified as lesbian because of her attraction to women, her interaction with Lou reveals that Jay was also deeply invested in her (female) masculine gender identity. Jay's aversion to having her genitals touched was a characteristic attributed not only to stone butches in the lesbian community, but also to transsexuals in the medical literature—a characteristic that Lou did not exhibit. Interestingly, Jay was "grossed out" by Lou's identification as a male homosexual, yet seemingly attracted to his masculinity, and Jay responded to the thwarting of her advances by criticizing the efficacy, or perhaps even the effeminacy, of Lou's masculinity.

The following week Lou decided not to attend the lesbian discussion group, making a date with Mark instead. However, hours before the group was to meet, Lou ran into Donna Utke, who led the discussion group: "she practically begged me to come as they would be discussing gay men & last week I was one of the few on 'their side.'"[10] Donna was a white forty-year-old librarian who was one of the founders of GPU, served on GPU's first board of directors and engaged in various mainstream educational outreach endeavors.[11] Lou rescheduled his date with Mark, went home and smoked two joints, "realizing it would probably turn out that I'd be battling the whole group alone."[12]

Lou's journal account of this lesbian discussion group meeting is worth quoting at length. For one thing, it is a rare record of someone articulating a trans perspective on feminism in the gay liberation movement. It also captures, through the power of personal experience and conversation, the dynamism of identity politics. Furthermore, Lou's account demonstrates his courage and intellectual acumen in the face of transphobia, which existed in practice though not yet as a concept.

> My high made me lose my inhibitions and I tied my breasts down so they wouldn't jiggle, although it did little to make them appear smaller, plus rolled up a few socks & made myself a penis, pinned it in my underwear—I was ready for them! The talk began with someone saying she disliked groups like GPU cuz it was dominated by "sexist men." One other woman tried to say they were at least trying to rid themselves of sexism. I said probably if women dominated,

or at least were in the majority, women would launch as much sexism against the men. She flatly denied this, saying she was incapable of sexism! Told her that was bullshit, that sexism oppresses men as much as women & no one could deny they are sexist just as they can't deny [their] racism. She denied it anyhow! Also she told of seeing a drag show & was lost as to why a lesbian, after the show, tipped the female impersonator in approval. She referred laughingly to the impersonator as a "shim" (she/him). Pointed out to her that she was displaying sexism right there by ridiculing transvestites. She denied it & said she just didn't understand it. I said I couldn't understand why she couldn't understand it! What's so hard to understand [about] why a man would enjoy dressing and/or appearing as a woman, or that a woman may enjoy the art with which he does it? She had no answer. Another woman said she objected to the adaptation of roles & images that women abandon as artificial... a Dorothy rap. Also, she added, they were so bad at it! I said they certainly know if they're bad at it or not, but even if they are that doesn't matter... the mere shape they are in is enough to satisfy their need.... Also, I don't remember how the topic occurred, but most everyone was shocked when it was pointed out that the majority of transvestites were heterosexual! Someone said they didn't like the idea that one's clothes should be so important to them. I got into a "long" speech that one's clothes identifies one's feeling—clothing is a means of expression &... don't you think it's possible for a transvestite, just becuz he has an identity denied him, to be a full & rich human being? The room was dead silent & I began feeling conspicuous. Someone said that's a hard question to answer & the group broke up in 15 minutes! I hung around reading a mag[azine] put out by gay men into feminism called "The Faggot Effeminists." Jay called me over where she & Donna were talking and said I was the only one around there who made any sense & she's sick and tired of bullshit, that these girls claim they aren't sexist & then ridicule transvestites, transsexuals, and everyone else not like them.

Jay left after the meeting, but Lou went with Donna to a dance at UWM commemorating the 1969 Stonewall Inn riots and birth of gay liberation. Everyone was leaving by the time they arrived, so they went to the River Queen gay bar where Lou "talked openly" about himself. According to Lou, Donna "was freaked when I told her I felt like a gay male.... Was very honest with her & told her I was feeling less afraid of exposing myself & [was] ready to get my ass kicked if that's what it would mean."[13] Rather than getting his ass kicked, Lou would find himself embraced by Milwaukee's gay community, including the exceptional women of GPU.

When Lou began attending GPU meetings in 1973, lesbian feminism was spreading across the nation. It is important to point out that while the women attending the lesbian discussion group identified as lesbians and feminists (in part upholding the saying "feminism is the theory while lesbianism is the practice"), they were not de facto *lesbian feminists*. Rather, they were open to diversity in people and perspectives, as encouraged by Lou and the GPU leadership, and as a result, demonstrated a more expansive and empathetic version of feminism than lesbian feminism.

Lesbian feminism encouraged separatism for women's empowerment—even separation from the gay liberation movement. However, while the lesbian discussion group met separately from the main GPU meetings, they remained part of the broader organization. Lesbian feminism also advocated lesbianism as a response to the patriarchal institution of heterosexuality, but these Milwaukee women understood lesbianism not as a political choice but rather an inherent way of being. Another tenet of lesbian feminism was a critique of female masculinity as simply reinforcing patriarchy, but the lesbians in GPU worked to include people like Jay and Lou. And finally, lesbian feminism vilified trans people for how they supposedly reinforced gender stereotypes. In the words of the popular yet controversial Janice Raymond, "All transsexuals rape women's bodies by reducing the real female form to an artifact, appropriating this body for themselves."[14] Lou encouraged those in the lesbian discussion group to rethink their views before they reached such an extremist position as Raymond's, and he would later do the same for the broader GPU membership.

This meeting of the lesbian discussion group was just the beginning of Lou finding his voice and helping to create an inclusive space within GPU. Whereas many gay organizations across the nation divided over ideological differences on gender, GPU overcame differences to retain its trans and lesbian members and all were provided with a richer understanding of sexual orientation, gender, gender identity and gender expression as a result.

GAY PEOPLE'S UNION (GPU)

Lou loved the general GPU meetings, which he enthusiastically attended every Monday night. Lou became an official member of GPU on May 7, 1973, which made him feel that he belonged—that he was a part of Milwaukee's gay community. His experiences in GPU also taught Lou invaluable community organizing skills that he would later use in founding the FTM community, including organizing and executing meetings, networking, producing newsletters and—perhaps most importantly—employing an all-inclusive identity category that welcomed many disparate individuals into the fold.

Milwaukee's Gay People's Union was officially incorporated in November 1972, but its roots can be traced back to the Gay Liberation Organization (GLO) at the University of Wisconsin-Milwaukee (UWM), where Lou worked. GLO was the first gay organization in Milwaukee, and approximately seventy-five individuals attended the first GLO meeting, including students, faculty, staff and non-university-affiliated members of the broader community, all of whom shared "the realization that GAY IS GOOD!"[15] GLO formed in the early months of 1970, and was one of hundreds of gay liberation organizations that sprang up around the country after the movement-galvanizing Stonewall riots in New York's Greenwich Village the previous year. GLO brought together numerous individuals under the umbrella *gay*, many of whom would go on to become prominent community activists.

In the winter of 1970-1971, a group of GLO members began working on a weekly radio show called *Gay Perspective*. The show initially aired on a popular underground progressive rock radio station in Milwaukee and was later picked up by the campus station WUWM.[16] *Gay Perspective* was the first regularly scheduled scripted gay radio program in the nation, and its early producers were Alyn Hess, a white landscape architect in his early forties, and Eldon Murray, a white stockbroker also in his early forties.[17] According to Eldon, neither he nor Alyn "had any special skills of any kind," but both were well read, hard working, deeply dedicated to gay liberation and (perhaps most importantly) openly gay.[18] With the success of *Gay Perspective*, Alyn and Eldon quickly found themselves at the forefront of the gay liberation movement in Milwaukee, and in time their work would bring them well-deserved national recognition.

The initial airing of *Gay Perspective* in February 1971 coincided with the GLO renaming itself the Gay Peoples Union (GPU). At the conclusion of the spring semester GPU ceased to be a UWM organization, and while the UWM campus was largely vacated during the summer, GPU could claim an active membership of fifty individuals.[19] Over the years GPU continued to collaborate with LGBT students and other members of the UWM campus community. While various organizations at UWM and throughout Milwaukee came and went, GPU was a mainstay for the next two decades. A core group of dedicated activists that included Alyn and Eldon set about institutionalizing the gay community in Milwaukee.

In reclaiming and reconstructing the history of the gay liberation movement, historians have focused almost exclusively on the east and west coasts of the United States, suggesting by omission that the movement only existed on the geographical margins of this country. But in the Upper Midwest industrial city of Milwaukee, GPU provided a consistent meeting space outside of the bars, engaged in educational outreach to the mainstream community and worked with the police and government officials on legal reform. GPU also hosted social events like film screenings, dances and sporting contests, and networked with other gay organizations across the country.

GPU quickly became an internationally recognized organization in the gay liberation movement, in part because of its monthly newsmagazine *GPU News*.[20] The onset of gay liberation ushered in an explosion of publications. Many were short-lived, and the majority of them were published on the coasts, but Milwaukee's *GPU News* (1971-1981) was a noteworthy exception.[21] When GPU members decided to publish a newspaper, they elected the assertive and ever-opinionated Eldon Murray as *GPU News* editor. *GPU News* included articles, editorials, book and film reviews, fiction and poetry, and it covered local, national and international news that was relevant to the gay community and the gay liberation movement.

From its inception, *GPU News* concerned itself with representing "the views of the entire gay community," reflecting GPU leaders' notion that *gay* was an all-inclusive category of identification that encompassed gays, lesbians, bisexuals, transvestites and transsexuals.[22] GPU's inclusiveness resulted in a heterogeneous community that created space for dialogues across differences. It also created space for someone like Lou to explore who he was, feel supported in his journey, and know he was part of a greater whole.

GPU leaders clearly considered trans people part of the community. For instance, in the first issue of *GPU News*, "transvestism and transsexualism" were listed first among the "programs that need to be prepared" for the GPU radio show *Gay Perspective*.[23] Later that month, Eldon produced a well-researched program on *Gay Perspective* that included a cross-cultural historical account of crossdressing, and an interview with local female impersonator Winnie Storm in which Eldon and Winnie discussed transvestites (who wore gender-atypical clothing as a means of gender expression), transsexuals (who modified their bodies to permanently live as the gender with which they identified) and female impersonators (who engaged in cross-gender performance for entertainment purposes). When Eldon introduced the show by saying "on this program we will discuss… the fine art of female impersonation, or the drag queen: a gay perspective," it was not tongue-in-cheek.[24] And the following year, in December 1972, Eldon's *GPU News* editorial stated:

> It has been, by-and-large, the gay transvestites who have been the first to resist periodic scourges against the gay community. They have used their already jeopardized position in society to raise a banner of resistance to tyranny as they did in the Stonewall Riot of 1969. Few minority life-styles have produced as many examples of an equally courageous caliber. Transvestites, condemned, ignored, and misunderstood, have paradoxically exerted an influential power far in excess of their numbers.[25]

Though Eldon did not specifically state as much, *transvestites* most assuredly referred to those born male. There was nothing in the gay discourse about female transvestites—those born female who wore men's clothes were simply identified as lesbians. That is, until Lou joined GPU and began publishing in *GPU News*.

TRANSVESTITE? TRANSSEXUAL?

Shortly after joining GPU, Lou was inspired to publish the exchange he had with his feminist co-worker Dorothy in *GPU News*. The article itself was largely an exploration of ideas about gender identity and expression, but for Lou it served as a form of coming out. In the article Lou did not come out as a particular identity because he still was not sure how to identify, but he did disclose that he was a female who felt like and thought of himself as a male homosexual.

Before publishing the article, Lou shared it with Mark. Mark had long served as Lou's sole confidant and source of validation, and their mutual gender non-conformity had intimately bound them. But the publication of this article made Mark realize that he did not share Lou's desire to find an identity that matched his gender expression, especially not if it entailed public declarations of marginality. They differed in their respective self-understandings of gender non-conformity, a sentiment about which Mark felt ambivalent because he had once felt intimately bound to Lou through what he considered their secret understanding of one another.[26] Unfortunately, Lou seemed oblivious to the fact that while he was actively engaged in discerning and embodying a publicly-recognizable identity, his partner was trying to overcome—or at the very least keep private—his unconventional desires and expressions.

Lou also ended up sharing his article with his mother before it was published. Lou had not intended to come out to Nancy at this time nor in this way, but she surprised him one Sunday when he visited his parents' house. Out of the blue Nancy told Lou that she and his younger sister Maryellen had read an article about "a girl who had a sex-change to a man." When Nancy said that "if they'd've had those in her day, she'd've definitely thought of doing it," Lou opened up and confided in his mother about how he felt and showed her his article. Nancy was supportive, telling Lou that if he decided to get gender confirmation surgery one day she would "be behind [him] all the way." But Lou did not "think I'm to that point yet."[27] For Lou, transitioning seemed like a strong future possibility—after he had thoroughly researched his identity options and determined which one best suited him.

Two days after this conversation with his mother, Eldon invited Lou to his house where they talked about the article and Lou's identity. Lou and Eldon quickly forged a lifelong friendship built upon a shared affinity for research, writing and community organizing. Eldon unquestionably welcomed Lou as a member of the gay community and helped Lou explore whether he might be a transvestite or transsexual. According to Lou, Eldon loved his article and

> [s]aid when he read the part where I said I felt like a male homosexual, he just about flipped & thought that's one of the weirdest things & it's really way-out. Told him I knew that better than anyone! He told me stories of some transvestites he knew & lent me the transsexual book.[28]

"The transsexual book" was *The Transsexual Phenomenon* by Dr. Harry Benjamin.

Dr. Benjamin popularized the term *transsexual*, and his book remains *the* transsexual book to this day. Unlike the majority of his colleagues, who pathologized trans people and wanted to "cure" them through psychotherapy, Benjamin empathized with people who were trans. He had worked with both transsexuals and transvestites for seventeen years and wrote the book to explain transsexuality not only medically, but also legally, socially and historically. Dr. Benjamin argued that it was the responsibility of doctors to help trans people live in the gender that corresponded with their gender identity. Gender identities could not be changed, but the bodies of trans people—and the views of society—could. Benjamin validated his patients' identities and provided the means for more trans people to embody their identities both directly and indirectly. He did so indirectly because his findings inspired a cadre of health providers to specialize in the diagnosis and treatment of transsexuality and eventually led to the formation of the Harry Benjamin International Gender Dysphoria Association, which professionalized trans research and medical and therapeutic services for trans people.

Lou "just read & read the transsexual book." But as he finished *The Transsexual Phenomenon*, which Benjamin concluded with a chapter on "The Female[-born] Transsexual," Lou began crying and feared that he would "always be like I am—a symbol of mangled, violated sex. Destroyed in a strange way..." whether he physically transitioned or not.[29] Lou identified strongly with the subject matter of Dr. Benjamin's book though he never specifically described Lou's situation. Benjamin paid scant attention to those born female, for less than 15% of his subjects identified as female-to-male (FTM) transsexuals, and he claimed female transvestites were "rare and of somewhat doubtful reality" because they could fulfill their desire to wear men's clothing without being too conspicuous.[30] In terms of sexual orientation, Benjamin wrote that FTM transsexuals "fall deeply in love with normal or homosexual girls, often those of a soft, feminine type. Besides wanting to be lovers, they want to be husbands and fathers."[31] Lou's desires were not mirrored by these characterizations. Unfortunately, even this most accurate, comprehensive and empathetic source of information on gender identity did not validate his.

In *The Transsexual Phenomenon*, Dr. Benjamin devoted a great deal of attention to explaining the difference between transsexuality and transvestism. Whereas today people like Lou would simply identify as trans, at the time, they were compelled by experts—who shaped public perception—to be either a transvestite or transsexual. "Both can be considered symptoms or syndromes of the same underlying psychopathological condition," Benjamin explained, "that of a *sex or gender role disorientation and indecision*. Transvestism is the minor though the more frequent, transsexualism the much more serious although rarer disorder."[32] The most obvious distinction Benjamin made between the two was that a transsexual wanted "corrective surgery, a so-called 'conversion operation,'" while a transvestite "requests nothing from the medical profession, unless he wants a psychiatrist to try and cure him."[33] Lou could relate to the idea of having "sex or gender role disorientation and indecision," but he was not particularly interested in "corrective surgery" at that point, and he was attracted to (gay) men.

Lou began spending a lot of time at the UWM library, to which he had unlimited access as a university employee. In his research Lou found many articles and books on transsexuality, transvestism and gender identity in general and read everything he "could get [his] hands on."[34] Lou had approached the literature with a mix of anticipation and apprehension: "Don't know what my research will lead me to but I'm ready."[35] Ultimately, for all of his effort, Lou's research led him nowhere. Compared to their male counterparts, there was little information on (largely socially acceptable) female gender non-conformity, and Lou found no mention anywhere of individuals born female who identified as gay men.

Invalidated by the so-called experts, Lou sought validation from Milwaukee's gay community. Lou first consulted Liz, who had not only taken him to his first GPU meeting, but was also the only person Lou knew personally who identified as transsexual. Liz told Lou that the fact that he fantasized being male while having sex was an important indicator of Lou's gender identity, and she offered him tips on being read as male. Liz suggested that Lou buy an "elastic panty-girdle" to bind his breasts, and "She said I have a chance to look male but that I'd always look like a 16-year-old boy [without injecting testosterone] cuzza my fair skin, no beard, etc." Liz took Lou to the Riviera "drag bar," where she introduced him to the belly dancer from whom she got *her* information about feminizing hormones and surgeons who did genital reconstructive surgeries. Upon meeting the belly dancer, Lou found her "super-convincing and beyond me!" Lou, who had never seen a drag show before, "felt right at home!"[36]

Lou also felt right at home in GPU when his first article appeared in *GPU News*—the one stating that he had always thought of himself as a male homosexual. This article served as Lou's official coming out to the members of GPU and the broader gay community—or at least to those who read *GPU News*—and it was well received. While Lou had repeatedly defended (primarily male) transvestites, drag queens and gay men, he had never officially come out as anything, and only anecdotally informed others that he had always considered himself a gay man. Even at the time of the article's publication Lou was still unsure about what identity category to embrace. Eldon titled Lou's article, "A Transvestite Answers a Feminist," thus identifying Lou as a transvestite, and Lou did not object.[37]

Several days after Lou's article appeared in print, Eldon called Lou and asked him to contact Liz, saying "he has someone we'd probly both like to meet." Lou cancelled his breakfast plans with Mark to meet Elizabeth Farley, who was visiting from Minneapolis. Lou, Liz, Eldon and Elizabeth went to lunch, and then to Eldon's home where he recorded the interview with Elizabeth for peer counseling purposes. In his journal, Lou described Elizabeth as a "44-year-old 'woman' who's really a man passing in society as a woman for 23 years without any operation or other medical aid."[38] The challenges Elizabeth faced and her determination to live authentically despite the costs would have a profound and lasting impact on Lou.

Elizabeth Farley, who was white, identified as a woman before she knew anything about transsexuals. In 1950, at the age of nineteen, Elizabeth left her small Virginia town for New York City to "become a woman."

> Not on the transsexual basis of today. It was not available at that time and I had never even heard of such a thing. That was a pipe dream as far as anybody that I knew at that time was concerned…. I just decided that I would go away and become a woman as far as dress, looks, and work.

When Christine Jorgensen became a media sensation in 1953 and *sex change* became a household term, Elizabeth thought about taking hormones and undergoing surgery, but it was too expensive and required going overseas. Luckily for Elizabeth, standards for legal documentation were lax at the time, and at 5'2" and less than 100 pounds, she was able to attain a Social Security card stating she was female because she was easily read as such.

Elizabeth's associates were predominantly straight and never knew that she was assigned male at birth. When dating straight men Elizabeth had to be "very, very careful… but I played the role which was popular at that time, thank heavens, moral situations being what they were in those days," which meant that she resisted their sexual advances without arousing suspicion. "There's been many times that I've had very attractive dates that

I was dying to tell," Elizabeth acknowledged. "I didn't for fear I'd have my head handed back to me, or get stabbed in the back or get choked to death or something." Due to her embodiment and the lack of knowledge about trans people, Elizabeth believed that the only way that she could live as a woman was by "holding [herself] back" sexually. As with many trans people at the time, Elizabeth's physical embodiment hindered her ability to experience sexual intimacy.

Occasionally she moved between the straight and gay worlds. In gay bars Elizabeth would "make it my business to be known" as a trans person, not wanting to "pull the wool over anyone's eyes," because to her "that would be tricking my own kind & I don't do that sort of thing." But in the 1950s,

> most of the gays seemed to be reluctant to invite me to their homes... because of the tremendous publicity that Christine Jorgensen received... because of fear that I might be found out by one of their straight friends and the whole thing would blow up in everybody's face.

Though she now chose to lead a "quiet life" and primarily associated with straight people, she was received affectionately by the Twin Cities' drag community and believed that "Gays accept almost everybody."[39]

TRANS INCLUSION

Unfortunately the acceptance about which Elizabeth spoke was about to change. Across the country trans people were coming under fire that year. In fact, trans historian Susan Stryker identifies 1973 as "a low point in U.S. transgender political history."[40] Four years earlier, the Stonewall Inn riots had been instigated by those most frequently targeted by the police for harassment: gender non-conformists, people of color, low-income people. It was this particular rebellion that ignited the gay liberation movement, and this event that served as the basis for Gay Pride celebrations. But by 1972, the Gay Liberation Front (GLF), which formed days after the riots and aimed to transform society through dismantling heterosexism, capitalism, racism and sexism, had ceased operations. The GLF was unable to overcome its internal divisions, primarily the division over whether to prioritize issues specific to homosexuality or to incorporate a broader spectrum of political issues. After four years, the gay liberation movement had foregone the revolution in favor of organizations and had settled into a gay community that by and large eschewed intersectional ideology in its struggle to define itself on the basis of sexual orientation.

Whereas a movement is defined by what it does, a community is defined by what it is, or more accurately, who it includes (or excludes). When the gay community sought to identify and establish itself in 1973, a nationwide debate over trans inclusion ensued that seemed to come to a head with a number of 1973 Gay Pride celebrations throughout the country. In San Francisco, two separate Gay Pride events were scheduled that year because the community was divided over the inclusion of drag queens, whom feminists and their gay male supporters deemed offensive to women.[41] And at the New York Gay Pride rally commemorating the Stonewall Inn riots that she helped instigate, Puerto Rican-American street queen Sylvia Rivera had to fight her way onto the stage to speak.[42] A group of lesbian feminists distributed flyers outlining their opposition to people like Rivera for female impersonation—regardless of how they actually identified—and Rivera had fallen out of favor with a number of white, middle-class, gender conforming gay male activists. Although Rivera helped launch the movement and its earliest organizations, she was subsequently excluded from the gay community.[43] This particular injustice is a dark moment in history that the LGBT community continues to struggle to overcome to this day.

Then, as now, the gay community did not exist as some singular homogeneous entity. Lou's experiences with GPU highlight the fact that *the* gay community was actually comprised of many local communities. Further, while *the* gay community, on a national scale, was engaged in a debate over trans inclusion, this debate was also carried out within local communities, and the outcomes were by no means the same everywhere. GPU leaders demonstrated themselves to be favorable toward trans inclusion within the Milwaukee gay community and encouraged others to be the same. Sylvia Rivera was one of the people Eldon lauded to *GPU News* readers, and rather than preventing trans people from speaking, GPU gave them platforms to do so through news coverage and meetings. And during its own debate over trans inclusion in the summer of 1973, Milwaukee's lesbians and gay men came to a different conclusion than their counterparts in New York and San Francisco as to whether or not drag queens were offensive to cisgender (or non-transgender) women.

In 1973 Milwaukee held its "first significant Gay and Lesbian Pride Celebration," and invited Del Martin to host the festivities.[44] On two fronts it made sense why GPU invited her. For one, she was a movement veteran.

Martin was one of the women who in 1955 had founded the Daughters of Bilitis, considered the first lesbian rights organization in the United States. The Daughters of Bilitis and its counterparts, the Mattachine Society and ONE, Inc., gave birth to the gay liberation movement's predecessor: the homophile movement. In defining itself as a movement, gay liberation by necessity had to distance itself from the homophile movement, and the gay liberation movement's new activists rejected what they considered the conservatism of the homophile movement, which emphasized assimilation and gender conformity.[45] As an organization, GPU bridged the homophile and gay liberation movements. The older members of GPU were quite familiar with the role that the homophile movement had played in advancing a minority group consciousness, and saw gay liberation as a continuation of the homophile activists' political efforts.

As an organization, GPU also strove to bridge the gay liberation and women's movements. The second reason it made sense that GPU invited Del Martin to host the Pride festivities is because its leaders wanted to incorporate a feminist consciousness into their organization and she was a well-known feminist. However, Martin was not simply a feminist and a lesbian (like many GPU members), but a *lesbian feminist* who advocated lesbians' separatism from the gay liberation movement, in part, because of the movement's embrace of gender non-conformity. "The exaggerations of the switching (or swishing) of sex roles has become the norm in the public eye," Martin said. "While we were laughing at ourselves we became the laughingstock and lost the personhood we were seeking."[46]

Not coincidentally, shortly after Martin's visit, GPU members debated whether or not to move forward on holding a drag ball with trans performers. Lou suddenly found himself again defending drag queens and trans women (the two were conflated in these early conversations regarding trans inclusion), only this time he was primarily confronting GPU's gay men. Lou's "heart started beating real fast" at the GPU meeting when "A few guys argued against [holding the ball] cuzza the old jive rap that drag oppresses <u>women</u> by promoting stereotyped looks." Liz spoke up first, explaining that crossdressing was a means of individual self-expression rather than a performance of stereotypes with the intention of oppressing or degrading women. Then Lou followed by saying that crossdressing is liberating because seeing a drag queen or trans woman "who's 100% better in what is supposed to come natural to me" made him realize that females are not inherently feminine, nor are males inherently masculine.[47] GPU listened to Lou and Liz and decided to host the drag ball, which would draw more than 350 people.[48] Lou wore a tuxedo to the ball and "got compliments all over how good I looked," but, he wrote, "The thing I was most happy about was everyone included me in on everything & were so so nice."[49]

According to Lou, after the meeting regarding whether or not to hold the ball, a woman in her mid-30s came up to him, disclosed that she was a male transvestite, and said she was "glad to hear someone sticking up for TVs [transvestites]."[50] For his part, Lou was grateful that trans people themselves were not the only voices speaking up for trans people in GPU.

The inclusion of trans people in GPU was an ongoing process that required the fortitude and compassion of its trans members and their allies. For Lou, GPU president Alyn Hess was the embodiment of compassionate fortitude. After a meeting one night, Lou found himself feeling uncomfortable and alone, for he did not identify with the women in the group nor did he feel permitted to identify with the men. Alyn approached Lou, wondering why he was being uncharacteristically standoffish, and Lou told him "I'm beginning to think I don't belong anywhere, that I feel I'm the biggest pervert there is." Alyn sat down next to him. As a group of lesbians formed around them, Alyn "talked about the plight of transvestites and transsexuals, all the while squeezing my hand." Alyn further endeared himself to Lou as an ally when he "Told of a man who had an operation to be a woman, then after awhile found she didn't want men and so was wondering how to meet lesbians." Lou "wanted to yell out, 'That's how I am, too,'" but hesitated to do so.[51]

At the time, Lou was equally hesitant to admit to himself and to his fellow GPU members that he wanted to transition. However, GPU leaders not only accepted trans people like Lou, but "felt the gays have a lot to learn by far-out cases like ours."[52] Before long the rest of GPU's membership shared this sentiment, and their acceptance went a long way toward Lou's acceptance of himself.

Lou continued to attend GPU meetings every Monday night, and at least once a week he assisted with the publication of *GPU News* by typing, typesetting and doing whatever else was needed. Lou often socialized with GPU members in the bars and participated in many GPU social activities. In the fall of 1973, Eldon and Alyn encouraged Lou to run for a leadership position in GPU, and he ran for secretary—uncontested.[53] And by November of that year, Lou was GPU's contact person for anyone seeking information about transvestism. "I've never felt such acceptance before," Lou wrote in his journal. "I've never been in a group like that—I mean like in high school, even grade school, I was always left out of things & at GPU I feel so wanted. People accept me as a female TV, even tho there's really not spozed to be such a thing."[54]

Lou's quest for other transvestites who were female and/or "heterosexual" like him resulted in several disappointing encounters. Lou counseled transvestites referred to him by the lesbians and gay men volunteering with the GPU hotline, but the majority of transvestites Lou knew identified as (male) drag queens.

Lou may have been the only female transvestite he knew, but there were a number of ways in which he could identify with (male) transvestites. For one thing, the medical literature described transvestites' crossdressing in terms of eroticism, which Lou could comply with because he felt sexual and sexually attractive crossdressing and presenting as masculine. Dr. Harry Benjamin and many of his colleagues asserted that the litmus test for differentiating between transvestites and transsexuals was the desire for a "conversion operation." At the time, though, Lou was not interested in genital reconstructive surgery. His disinterest stemmed from his research showing that the construction of a fully functional penis was surgically impossible, and the prevailing belief that a penis was what made a man.

Perhaps the most important reason that Lou identified with (male) transvestites was the fact that though their membership was contested within the broader gay community, their identities were recognized and accepted within that same community. Interestingly, Lou was emphatic about the inclusion of transvestites in the gay community, though he knew from his research that the medical world asserted that most transvestites were heterosexual. That transvestites were largely identified as heterosexual was one of the means by which Lou could identify with the medical definition of transvestism because its categorization of transvestites as largely heterosexual accommodated Lou's simultaneous masculine identification and attraction to men.

Lou may not have been homosexual due to his current body and—as a result—his current embodiment of desire, but he was gay in the all-inclusive GPU sense of the word. Lou drew on his experiences with GPU for his second *GPU News* article, "Looking Toward Transvestite Liberation." In the article, Lou treated the strife over trans inclusion as a call to arms for members of the gay community to combat sexism and liberate feminine males. He concurred with the gay community's feminists that gay liberation should not only be about sexual liberation, but liberation from oppressive sex-role expectations as well. However, whereas feminists "[had] done much to change the societal role of women," there was not yet a comparable movement to change the societal role of men.[55] Lou encouraged feminists to ally with transvestites "to obtain changes in laws and in societal attitudes, promoting acceptance of both the woman who desires traditionally 'masculine' attitudes and the man who desires traditionally 'feminine' attitudes."[56] For Lou, feminists denigrated (male) transvestites, yet both were engaged in a common endeavor to illuminate gender as a social construction.

In "Looking Toward Transvestite Liberation," Lou articulated concepts that would be popularized by Judith Butler and other theorists twenty years later—concepts that laid the foundation for queer theory. "The crux of the argument between the transvestite and the feminist seems to lie in… symbols," or gender signifiers, which are bad when they "trap a woman into believing these symbols are her personality," and that their loss results in her loss of identity. But the transvestite separates the symbol from the woman, and "uses feminine symbols to liberate himself from his sex-role stereotype just as the feminist uses masculine symbols to liberate herself."[57] Furthermore, if women could truly detach themselves from the feminine symbols, transvestites would simply be establishing themselves as feminine men rather than being seen as furthering stereotypes of women. But first sexism had to be eradicated in order to allow the existence of feminine men.[58]

Lou's article on transvestite liberation was reprinted in *Female Impersonator* and Detroit's *Gay Liberator*, which had also published his article "A Transvestite Answers a Feminist."[59] Someone with *Gay Liberator* told Lou that his article "provided considerable insight & information" that had been used for "a ½ hr television special about gay liberation & gay lifestyles" and "deserves much wider publication."[60] Lou sent his article to two "women's" publications, *Playgirl* and *Ms*, both of which declined to publish it. While his ideas were rejected by national women's organizations, Lou was nonetheless accepted by the women in GPU, the majority of whom were feminists and honored his wish "to be treated like a gay male."[61]

In finding community Lou was able to begin giving voice to the experiences of trans people. But gay liberation activists alone did not make up the gay community, nor would they have thought to claim as much. While activists may have been the mouthpiece of the community, its breeding grounds were the bars.

Gay Bars, Gay Sex

In September 1973, Mark moved to Berkeley to attend graduate school at the University of California. Throughout the summer Lou dreaded Mark's leaving, but a week after he had gone Lou realized that he felt a certain sense of relief and freedom. As he wrote in his journal, "Mark's leaving has kind of released me from having to think about him."[62] On one hand, when Lou and Mark went to straight bars together, Mark would occasionally flirt with other men, and then he and Lou would go home and have passionate sex. Lou loved when they went out and Mark "camped it up" while Lou played "real butch." In general Lou felt that "we make a pretty strange-looking couple: Mark very feminine and me very masculine. We really have a gay relationship—I don't know how else to describe it." However, on the other hand, when Lou took Mark to the River Queen, one of a number of gay bars in downtown Milwaukee, Mark was nervous and uncomfortable. "He told me it really felt weird to be in a place where everyone is after your body," and when Lou suggested that they frequent the River Queen, "Mark said he was scared to cuz sooner or later he'd have to get picked up," which exasperated Lou.[63]

Although Mark had continued to check out men with Lou, to talk of taking a male lover, and on occasion appeared to enjoy dressing femininely for Lou, he did so to please and titillate his partner. He did not share Lou's drive to understand his identity and never went to GPU meetings. In fact, the more Lou became involved with GPU the more time Mark spent with a college student girlfriend who was straight and cisgender. Lou was bewildered by the seriousness of Mark's relationship with this high femme who seemed to be Lou's polar opposite. However, as Mark saw it, her femininity "[kept] things balanced off" for him given Lou's masculinity, and Mark assured him that Lou met other needs that no one else could.[64] Now that he was gone, Lou no longer worried about Mark's college student girlfriend or about how his identity and behaviors affected Mark.

Though Lou felt relieved when Mark left, he also missed him. They would soon be celebrating their five-year anniversary and were as sexually active with one another as ever. Lou felt lonely in his absence. "I have to go to bars often if I'm to find myself a boy to sleep with," he wrote after

Mark left. "In times [that] I can't, I can become a boy to sleep with. But it's so much nicer with a real one."[65]

With Mark in California, Lou longed for both a sex partner and a companion, which he quickly found in his new "fine youngman" friend Charles, whom Lou described as "gorgeous... he looked a <u>lot</u> like a dancer, had that classic, statue face & body." In fact, Charles was a white ballet dancer from New York who was in town dancing with the Milwaukee Ballet Company and staying at the local YMCA. Lou and Charles locked eyes at a GPU meeting, and when Charles left after the meeting, Lou rushed out after him: "I don't know why but he just struck me as not being untouchable like most gay guys, I guess from that stare we had." Lou caught up to Charles, who was "on his way to Juneau Park to have some sex" when Lou approached him and asked, "You wouldn't happen to be bi, would you?"

> He said he hasn't gone to bed with a girl in 5 or 6 years. I felt like saying as far as I'm concerned if he went with me he wouldn't be breaking his record, but didn't. He said, "Well, OK, let's give it a try."... [At Lou's apartment] he said "I feel like I'm in high school—I don't know what to do!... [Charles] freaked at my elastic band to flatten my breasts... & was freaked by my jockey shorts... [but] we fucked superbly.... He said, "Oh, you're really fun! I'm really glad you're so fun cuz being a homosexual I'm really scared of girls."

Lou felt like the "impossible [had] happened.... I still can't believe that I could do it—get a gay man & make love to him."[66]

Over the next several months Lou and Charles became intimate friends. But more than that, because Charles was nearly ten years older than Lou and the first gay man that he had had a sexual relationship with, Charles became Lou's mentor. And Lou was an eager apprentice. Charles taught Lou how to have anal sex and other tricks of the trade, and he provided Lou with detailed reports of his sexual exploits with other men. Sexually and socially Charles made it easy for Lou to believe he was a boy. When they went out to the bars they danced, were affectionate with one another, and checked out men together. Charles encouraged Lou to pick up men and to be a gay man himself.

In the fall of 1973 Lou began going out to the gay bars multiple times during the week, usually with Charles. They frequented the River Queen and the Factory, which featured a DJ and light show in the days before disco and consistently took out a full-page ad in *GPU News*. After a few drinks at the bar, Lou "let my fantasies take over so much I was shocked they weren't a reality."[67] In the bars, dressed in his leather jacket, Lou was no longer Sheila the female transvestite but *Lou*. He would check out men with Charles, talk to friends from GPU, flirt and dance with drag queens and gay men, and was occasionally successful at picking up men. However, despite the joys of sleeping with gay men, at times Lou would become depressed and feel guilty, thinking "I have to make boys be heterosexual to have sex with them."[68]

Unlike Elizabeth Farley, Lou would not—could not—forego sex for the sake of his gender identity. Nothing made Lou feel more like a man than having sex with a gay man, for gay men were attracted to other men and bedding gay men validated his gender identity. Both Lou and Elizabeth felt safe disclosing their embodiment to gay men, but just as Elizabeth feared straight men would react violently to having gay sex with her because of her male genitalia, Lou was concerned that having sex with gay men could only be rendered heterosexual due to his female genitalia. But Lou still found gay men to be receptive sexual partners. Unfortunately, his friend Liz did not find female sexual partners to be so receptive. Lou saw Liz's advances consistently rebuffed by women, whether they be lesbian or straight, with the exception of one woman who implied "they could be lovers after Liz's operation."[69]

In Liz, Lou had a friend who was born male and identified as lesbian, and in Charles a friend who was a cisgender gay man, and though he valued their friendship, Lou could not wholly identify with either of them. Lou yearned to know that there was someone else just like him.

Lou wanted to cultivate a particular masculine image, one increasingly associated with the leather and S&M gay subculture, but also more generally hard-guy butch. Out at the bars one night, Lou ran into "a tall queen" who

> complimented me saying he <u>loves</u> the way I walk & he saw me walking on the street & asked his friends if I was a boy or girl (they told him girl) & he just thinks I'm so cool & he'd love to ride on the back of my motorcycle if I had one. Told him he wasn't too bad himself & if I had a cycle I'd

like him on the back too. He said REALLY?? It was really an ego-booster.

Later that night, Lou went with Charles and Charles's new boyfriend Jeffrey to the Wreck Room, Milwaukee's "gay leather S&M bar."

> I've always been scared to go there, being a girl, but once inside [I] wasn't. Mostly older guys in motorcycle & cowboy getup & no one paid much attention to me. And after a while I began seeing how un-hard the whole scene was. Like they had some kind of raffle & all the hard guys were looking at their ticket to see if they won & then they announced everyone with a motorcycle cap or a cowboy hat on could get a free drink. How high school! I just leaned up against a wall acting hard & it was fun. We're all girls pretending we're big shot boys! HA HA.[70]

In March 1974, Charles moved back to New York. Lou and Charles had not had sex since December 1973 when Charles began dating Jeffrey, but they still remained close and Lou was saddened by his departure. Two days before Charles left, he, Jeffrey and Lou drove ninety miles to Chicago to attend the opening party for the Gay Broadway Baths. Charles introduced Lou to everyone as Lou (instead of Sheila), and Lou wrote "I got as far into a gay bath as I possibly could, being what I am." Lou toured the baths during the party, but when they opened for business at midnight, he and Charles waited in the lobby for Jeffrey. Sitting in the lobby, "This one kind of cute but too chunky guy stood in his towel on the other side of the hall cruising me hard," but Lou only stared back as they were leaving. Charles and Lou both knew the bath owner, who was able to get them free rooms at a gay rooming house for the rest of the night. No one seemed to suspect that Lou was born female.[71]

Two weeks later Lou and Jeffrey returned to Chicago for the weekend. On Friday night they went to the Gold Coast, "the heavy Chicago S&M (sadism/masochism) bar," where an older man begged to be Lou's slave. Of the Gold Coast, Lou wrote: "Sure can't see why the place has such a horrendous reputation—I guess maybe just the presence of S&M'ers is freaky to some. Not me." The following night Lou and Jeffrey went to "THE place, The Machine," which had dance floors on two levels and "yummy boys!!!" There Lou met and went home with a "cute little David Bowie" who "looked like he wasn't real—not of this world" because of his clothing, hair, make-up and eyes. Lou thought it fitting that he worked at the computer company IBM, "a place as out of reality as he." Lou had been attracted to men who adopted the glitter/glam rock style before, finding their flamboyance to be feminine and sexy, and often detailed their gender presentation in his journal. Lou was familiar with the "glitter crowd" in Milwaukee because they frequented the same bars that he did. Many of its members identified as bisexual. Interestingly, while Lou read this "sweet pretty" man in Chicago as David Bowie, he read Lou (in his leather drag) as Suzi Quatro, a glam rock star who was popular in Europe. Lou returned to Milwaukee "<u>so</u> high from the weekend," particularly because of the "fleeting angel" with whom he had spent the night.[72]

READY FOR A CHANGE

Lou's sexual escapades did nothing to diminish his love for Mark, and he spent many months yearning to see him again. He only saw Mark once in the space of ten months, when they spent Christmas together in Berkeley. Lou was excited when, during the course of his Christmas visit, Mark decided he would quit graduate school and move back to Milwaukee that summer. However, as summer approached, Lou began to worry about Mark's return to Milwaukee. Lou feared that Mark "would bring back my past to haunt me" and that he would have to give up the life he had led for the past year.[73]

Lou feared that he would lose himself in Mark, and in the process lose the fun and excitement of the gay community. To assuage his fears, Mark told Lou that in the months after seeing him at Christmas he had begun "dressing to the hilt & going to the bars all the time." However, once he returned to Milwaukee, Mark suddenly seemed hesitant to do either. Rather than picking up on the fact that Mark had simply been telling Lou what he wanted to hear, Lou decided that Milwaukee made Mark "closety," and wondered whether "NY may be just what we need to really come out together."[74] Lou and Mark quickly booked a flight to visit Charles and Jeffrey in New York, and also discussed the possibility of moving there.

New York had held a special fascination for Lou the past year, since he first read John Rechy's *City of Night*. "[I] remember how, a little over a year ago I was so alone, desperately trying to find where I fit in this gay world—where I knew I belonged somehow. And how, grasping in the dark, I knew I had to go to NY."[75] During their visit, Lou and Mark "saw gay NY": "Went to 12 gay bars including leather & glitter ones, to a gay movie & to the cruisy gay area of Central Park twice. Saw the hustlers in Times Square (where <u>were</u> they all??), to the gay dance at the Firehouse Community Ctr, saw the Stonewall Inn."[76] Lou wrote that he even passed as a gay man several times. Later, Lou and Mark "hit some of the bars in the Village," saw Holly Woodlawn, "one of Andy Warhol's super-star drag queens, do a night club act," and went to "<u>the</u> drag bar here, the Gilded Grape, advertised as the 'most decadent spot in the world'."[77] But on the whole, Lou was disillusioned with New York. "It wasn't all as exciting or different as it had been cracked up to being…. It was fun & new to be in a place like Times Square where all the lights are, etc., but not worth moving out there & giving up what I have in Milwaukee."[78]

Mark did not share Lou's sentiment. Lou did his best to integrate Mark into Milwaukee's gay community by taking him to gay bars and inviting him to GPU-related activities. Lou introduced him to everyone he knew and wrote that they all "loved him," but Mark insisted that they were Lou's friends and wanted to move. Sensitive to Mark's feelings, Lou decided a change could be good. Though Lou had little first-hand experience with San Francisco, he knew it had a gay bar scene and agreed to move there the following summer.[79]

One of the primary reasons that Lou had been apprehensive about Mark's return to Milwaukee was because he desperately wanted to be Mark's male lover but feared that Mark would not accept him as a "youngman."[80] A month after he moved back to Milwaukee, they went to the River Queen one night, and Mark poured his beer out in front of Lou. Lou took it as "a public display of his rejection of me." He confronted Mark, saying "no one else had this problem of accepting me in the gay world. Everyone accepted me as a boy except him." Lou was shocked when Mark replied, "I know you're a boy. I know that better than anyone," because it was "the first positive thing he's said that way."[81]

Lou was further encouraged when Mark told him that he liked when Lou was mistaken for a boy and people thought they were a gay couple.[82] Emboldened, Lou told Mark that he was contemplating a "sex change." According to Lou, Mark did not want him to do it, but also acted supportively, saying "that if I did get it he'd still… be my lover. I was so surprised & pleased he said that so seriously & lovingly." However, Mark told Lou "that he has an identity problem in the gay-straight sense" in that "while he really likes boys & they turn him on, he knows he'll always be impotent with them." Lou responded by saying that what he found most appealing was undergoing top (chest reconstructive) surgery. Mark "really was attracted to the idea," Lou wrote in his journal, saying Lou would be like a boy with girl's genitalia.[83]

When Lou began thinking seriously about accessing gender confirmation services, he started spending more time than usual with Liz, who talked about her gender identity with him. Liz had begun attending individual and group therapy sessions at a gender program in Chicago, and encouraged Lou to contact them. Lou believed Liz was "pretty together & I know how hard she dissuades people she thinks are phonies."[84] He "drafted a letter asking to talk to someone about my transsexual fantasies, etc.," but did not mail it for nearly a month because he was "a little scared they'll tell me things I don't want to hear."[85] Liz urged Lou "to see someone professional," so Lou sent a letter to Liz's psychiatrist. Liz told Lou that her psychiatrist:

> [W]ouldn't try to take anything away from me or do anything I don't want—such as give me exercises so I'll get to like my breasts better. Yek! She says he'll only ask me what I want & then hold me to it. I told her no way am I going to be able to go in there & tell him I want to have my breasts cut off & for him to help me be a femmy homosexual! But she said he will.[86]

Liz and Lou believed that transsexuals could simply decide what kind of gender transition they wanted. Despite the lack of medical research on female-to-male transsexuals who identified as gay, Liz and Lou believed that he would be diagnosed as transsexual. After years of struggling to understand his identity, Lou now feared that a medical professional would confirm his suspicions that he was transsexual and that he and his life would dramatically change as a result. Mark told Lou to "remember that this psych doesn't know any more than I do" and that "I shouldn't seek to fit myself into a definition of 'what I am'." [87] Mark found it "good & commendable" that Lou "felt like I didn't FIT anywhere." Lou summed up their conversation as follows:

> [I] said the only crowd I feel relaxed in is the gays & I can't be 40 yrs old & still hanging around them & he asked why not? He was so logical, I realized I was building it all up in my mind. Why not indeed! I said I should maybe stop reading all I do on the gender identity subject & he said no, keep on, he feels I'm doing something really valuable.

> Told him I like the gays so much that I wish I was more like them—the old problem of wanting <u>to be</u> that which you admire.[88]

While Mark may have seemed logical to Lou, his logic misled both of them as to the reason Lou wanted to be more like gay men.

The idea that Lou simply wanted to be that which he admired could explain why he dressed up and pretended he was the Beatles and Bob Dylan in his youth. They were extremely popular rock stars worthy of admiration. They were also individual people. However, Lou did not want to be one particular gay man, nor were there any out gay celebrities to emulate. He did not want to be a gay man because he admired gay men. Rather, he admired gay men because he wanted them and wanted to be a gay man himself.

With the help of his friends in Milwaukee's gay community, Lou had never been closer to finding his true identity. But Mark was subconsciously trying to lead Lou into a no-man's land of repressed desire. When the psychiatrist responded to Lou's letter by simply saying "I should probably see someone, but the drift of the letter was he'll see me if I pay," Lou thought "Fuck 'm."[89] He did not need to see nor want to pay for a psychiatrist. Yet, two weeks later Lou found himself thinking about "those damn hormones" and how "The changes would be so erotic to me…"[90]

Lou often wrote in his journal that year about wanting to get top surgery and wanting to go on testosterone. These entries were almost always accompanied by Lou's describing how he fantasized about being Mark's male lover. On one occasion, Mark said to Lou that "he always told people he has a 'man,' that he can't call me his girlfriend. That he wanted me to be his boyfriend & seduce & fuck him. I began thinking: hormones, hormones, I want them so bad, I could be his man then, it would be true then."[91]

Lou "[kept] thinking when we go to California I'll get ahold of Stanford's Gender Clinic there, one of the best."[92] He had learned of the Stanford University Gender Dysphoria Program through his extensive research into transsexuality and transvestism. Lou deeply believed he was transsexual, and assumed that the experts at Stanford's clinic would diagnose him as being transsexual, accept him into their program, and begin administering hormone therapy. However, he also had fears of how Mark might react to his transitioning, and about how the benefit of a transsexual diagnosis meant that Lou would be absolved of any responsibility for the discomfort it may cause Mark. In other words, he would have to transition, per the doctors' diagnosis. Stanford's proximity to San Francisco may not have been the reason for their upcoming move, but Lou definitely viewed it as an added perk.

In fact, Lou had no clear reason at all for moving other than Mark's unhappiness in Milwaukee and Lou's adventuresome spirit. Lou was simply up for a change and wanted Mark to be happy. Moving to San Francisco was a huge risk for Lou. He and Mark had no jobs lined up nor did they have a place to live. They also didn't know a soul in the city. Lou was leaving his close-knit family and a community that embraced his female body, brilliant mind and gay male soul. His friends in GPU were devastated by his moving, but sent Lou off with a round of applause at his last GPU meeting. Eldon was especially sad, telling Lou that he would not only miss his work on *GPU News*, but also miss him as a good friend. On the upside, the worldly and well-connected Eldon assured Lou that "I should have no problem applying for jobs wearing a suit cuz 'everyone' in SF is gay." Lou was excited to learn that although the city was smaller than Milwaukee, it had "<u>100</u> gay bars & that's only the <u>bars</u>!"[93] San Francisco was becoming a gay mecca.

For months Lou and Mark looked forward to their move with great anticipation. But on the eve of their departure Lou began to have second thoughts. In his journal Lou confessed feeling "a little scared of the gay community in SF, that they won't accept me like I've been here because I'm straight and female."[94] He quickly cast his insecurities aside and donned the confidence and charisma he had developed over the past two years. Lou had grown tremendously with the love and support of Milwaukee's small, anything-goes gay community. He was moving to the largest gay community on earth, which must be teeming with opportunities. *And* he would be just miles away from the most reputable gender program in the world.

On July 19, 1975, Lou jumped on the train with Mark for their two-day trip to San Francisco... heading straight for what would unfortunately become "the most tormenting stage of [Lou's] life."[95]

ENDNOTES: CHAPTER 2

1. Sullivan Journal, 17 April 1973, box 1 folder 10, LGS Papers.

2. Eldon Murray, interview by author, 19 January 2006, Milwaukee, tape recording, in author's possession. Groups at the East Side Community Center included a babysitting co-op and film club, Wholesome Foods Parlor, Industrial Workers of the World, Multi-Cultural High School, and Gay Action Youth. See East Side Community Center to Eldon Murray, 21 September 1972, box 1 folder 14, Milwaukee Mss 240 (Gay Peoples Union Records, 1971-1984), University of Wisconsin-Milwaukee Libraries, Archives Department [hereafter cited as GPU Records].

3. Sullivan Journal, 17 April 1973, box 1 folder 10, LGS Papers.

4. Lou used "Dorothy" as a pseudonym for his co-worker in Sheila Sullivan, "A Transvestite Answers A Feminist," *GPU News* (August 1973): 9-11, 14. Reprinted as Lou Sullivan, "A Transvestite Answers A Feminist" in *The Transgender Studies Reader*, ed. Susan Stryker and Stephen Whittle (New York: Routledge, 2006), 159-164.

5. Sullivan, "A Transvestite Answers A Feminist," 164; See also Sullivan Journal, 7 April 1973, box 1 folder 10, LGS Papers.

6. Sullivan Journal, 12 April 1973, box 1 folder 10, LGS Papers.

7. Sullivan Journal, 17 April 1973, box 1 folder 10, LGS Papers.

8. Eldon Murray interview.

9. Sullivan Journal, 23 June 1973, box 1 folder 10, LGS Papers.

10. Sullivan Journal, 1 July 1973, box 1 folder 10, LGS Papers.

11. Articles of Incorporation of Gay Peoples Union, Inc., box 1 folder 2, GPU Records. For more on Donna Utke, see Don Schwamb, "Donna Utke," *Wisconsin GLBT History Project*, http://www.mkelgbthist. org/people/peo-u/utke_donna.htm. See also Milwaukee Mss 233 (Donna Utke Papers, 1971-1991), University of Wisconsin-Milwaukee Libraries, Archives Department.

12. Sullivan Journal, 1 July 1973, box 1 folder 10, LGS Papers.

13. Ibid.

14. Janice Raymond, *The Transsexual Empire: The Making of the She-Male* (New York: Teachers College Press, 1994): 104.

15.	University of Wisconsin-Milwaukee Registration of Campus Organizations, 22 April 1970, and Gay Liberation Organization (GLO) Statement of Purpose and Principle, 23 June 1970, at "Gay Liberation Organization at UWM (GLO-UWM)," *Wisconsin GLBT History Project*, http://www.mkelgbthist.org/organiz/act_pol/gay-lib-org.htm.

16.	*Gay Perspective* radio programs can be accessed online via "The Gay Peoples Union Collection," *University of Wisconsin Digital Collections*, http://digicoll.library.wisc.edu/GPU/.

17.	Alyn Hess qtd. in Sue Burke, "Milwaukee Has 1st Gay Radio Program, Newspaper in Early 1970s," *Wisconsin Light* (9 February 1989 – 22 February 1989): 12.

18.	Eldon Murray interview. For more on Eldon Murray, see Don Schwamb, "Eldon Murray," *Wisconsin GLBT History Project*, http://www.mkelgbthist.org/people/peo-m/murray_eldon.htm. See also Milwaukee Mss 256 (Eldon Murray Papers, 1938-2007), University of Wisconsin-Milwaukee Libraries, Archives Department. For more on Alyn Hess, see Don Schwamb, "Alyn Hess," *Wisconsin GLBT History Project*, http://www.mkelgbthist.org/people/peo-h/hess_alyn.htm.

19.	Steven M. Brondino and Jamakaya, "Panel 6: 1971," Milwaukee Pridefest exhibit, *History in the Making: Milwaukee's Gay and Lesbian Community*, Milwaukee, Wisconsin, June 1997.

20.	In 1975 *GPU News* circulation neared 1,700 with subscribers throughout the United States, Canada, United Kingdom and Western Europe. See "Financial Report for Fiscal 1975" in *Gay Peoples Union, Inc. Annual Report for 1975*, box 1 folder 1, GPU Records.

21.	Rodger Streitmatter, *Unspeakable: The Rise of the Gay and Lesbian Press in America* (Boston: Faber and Faber, 1995), 87, 117.

22.	"G.P.U. Publishes New Newspaper," *GPU News* (October 1971): 1.

23.	"Gay Perspective Now Aired 8:30 P.M.," *GPU News* (October 1971): 5.

24.	"Drag and Female Impersonation," *Gay Perspective* (28 October 1971), box 3 audio 16, GPU Records. Accessible via http://digital.library.wisc.edu/1711.dl/GPU.

25.	"Editorial," *GPU News* (December 1972): 2.

26.	Sullivan Journal, 16 May 1973, box 1 folder 10, LGS Papers.

27.	Sullivan Journal, 31 May 1973, box 1 folder 10, LGS Papers.

28.	Ibid.

29.   Ibid.

30.   Harry Benjamin, *The Transsexual Phenomenon* (New York: Warner, 1966), 178, 47.

31.   Benjamin, 180.

32.   Benjamin, 31.

33.   Benjamin, 27.

34.   Sullivan Journal, 17 July 1973, box 1 folder 10, LGS Papers.

35.   Sullivan Journal, 7 July 1973, box 1 folder 10, LGS Papers.

36.   Sullivan Journal, 13 July 1973, box 1 folder 10, LGS Papers.

37.   Sullivan Journal, 8 August 1973, box 1 folder 10, LGS Papers.

38.   Sullivan Journal, 13 August 1973, box 1 folder 10, LGS Papers.

39.   Interview with Elizabeth Farley, 11 August 1973, box 1 folder 15, GPU Records.

40.   Susan Stryker, *Transgender History* (Berkeley: Seal, 2008), 101.

41.   Stryker, *Transgender History*, 101-102.

42.   Sylvia Rivera, "Queens in Exile: The Forgotten Ones," in *Genderqueer: Voices from beyond the Sexual Binary*, ed. Joan Nestle, Clare Howell and Riki Wilchins (Los Angeles: Alyson, 2002), 82.

43.   Benjamin Shepard, "Sylvia and Sylvia's Children: A Battle for a Queer Public Space," in *That's Revolting!: Queer Strategies for Resisting Assimilation*, ed. Mattilda, a.k.a. Matt Bernstein Sycamore (Brooklyn: Soft Skull, 2004), 99-100.

44.   Steven M. Brondino and Jamakaya, "Panel 9: 1973," *History in the Making.*

45.   Elizabeth A. Armstrong, *Forging Gay Identities: Organizing Sexuality in San Francisco, 1950-1994* (Chicago: University of Chicago, 2002), 67.

46.   Sullivan Journal, 13 July 1973, box 1 folder 10, LGS Papers.

47.   Ibid.

48.   "GPU Ball...," *GPU News* (February/March 1974): 14-15, 29.

49.   Sullivan Journal, 12 February 1974, box 1 folder 10, LGS Papers.

50.   Sullivan Journal, 13 July 1973, box 1 folder 10, LGS Papers.

51.   Sullivan Journal, 17 July 1973, box 1 folder 10, LGS Papers.

52.   Sullivan Journal, 13 August 1973, box 1 folder 10, LGS Papers.

53. Sullivan Journal, 9 December 1973, box 1 folder 10, LGS Papers; Gay Peoples Union, Inc. Business Meeting Minutes for 3 December 1973, box 1 folder 12, GPU Records.

54. Sullivan Journal, 13 November 1973, box 1 folder 10, LGS Papers.

55. Sullivan, "Looking Toward Transvestite Liberation," *GPU News* (February/March 1974): 22.

56. Sullivan, "Looking Toward Transvestite Liberation," 23.

57. Sullivan, "Looking Toward Transvestite Liberation," 22.

58. Sullivan, "Looking Toward Transvestite Liberation," 23.

59. Sullivan Journal, 22 March 1974, 1 April 1974, box 1 folder 10, LGS Papers.

60. Sullivan Journal, 10 September 1974, box 1 folder 10, LGS Papers.

61. Sullivan Journal, 15 July 1974, box 1 folder 10, LGS Papers.

62. Sullivan Journal, 16 September 1973, box 1 folder 10, LGS Papers.

63. Sullivan Journal, 7 July 1973, box 1 folder 10, LGS Papers.

64. Sullivan Journal, 2 April 1973, 9 April 1973, box 1 folder 10, LGS Papers.

65. Sullivan Journal, 16 September 1973, box 1 folder 10, LGS Papers.

66. Sullivan Journal, 18 September 1973, box 1 folder 10, LGS Papers.

67. Sullivan Journal, 30 November 1973, box 1 folder 10, LGS Papers.

68. Sullivan Journal, 30 October 1973, box 1 folder 10, LGS Papers.

69. Ibid.

70. Sullivan Journal, 18 January 1974, box 1 folder 10, LGS Papers.

71. Sullivan Journal, 22 March 1974, box 1 folder 10, LGS Papers.

72. Sullivan Journal, 10 April 1974, box 1 folder 10, LGS Papers.

73. Sullivan Journal, 24 June 1974, box 1 folder 10, LGS Papers.

74. Sullivan Journal, 10 July 1974, box 1 folder 10, LGS Papers.

75. Sullivan Journal, 19 July 1974, box 1 folder 10, LGS Papers.

76. Sullivan Journal, 29 July 1974, box 1 folder 10, LGS Papers.

77. Sullivan Journal, 26 November 1974, 6 December 1974, box 1 folder 10, LGS Papers.

78. Sullivan Journal, 29 July 1974, box 1 folder 10, LGS Papers.

79. Sullivan Journal, 27 December 1973, 19 August 1974, box 1 folder 10, LGS Papers.

80. Sullivan Journal, 17 May 1974, box 1 folder 10, LGS Papers.

81. Sullivan Journal, 5 August 1974, box 1 folder 10, LGS Papers.

82. Sullivan Journal, 26 September 1974, box 1 folder 10, LGS Papers.

83. Sullivan Journal, 19 August 1974, box 1 folder 10, LGS Papers.

84. Sullivan Journal, 1 October 1974, box 1 folder 10, LGS Papers.

85. Sullivan Journal, 10 September 1974, box 1 folder 10, LGS Papers.

86. Sullivan Journal, 1 October 1974, box 1 folder 10, LGS Papers.

87. Ibid.

88. Sullivan Journal, 16 October 1974, box 1 folder 10, LGS Papers.

89. Ibid.

90. Sullivan Journal, 1 November 1974, box 1 folder 10, LGS Papers.

91. Sullivan Journal, 23 December 1974, box 1 folder 10, LGS Papers.

92. Sullivan Journal, 8 November 1974, box 1 folder 10, LGS Papers.

93. Sullivan Journal, 5 May 1975, box 1 folder 11, LGS Papers.

94. Sullivan Journal, 9 May 1975, box 1 folder 11, LGS Papers.

95. Sullivan Journal, 4 August 1975, box 1 folder 11, LGS Papers; Lou, "FTM Male Box," *FTM* 15 (April 1991) in *FTM Newsletter, 1987-1992*, ed. Martin Rawlings-Fein (San Francisco: FTM International, Inc., 2005), 90.

Lou journaled on a regular basis for thirty years—from the age of ten until his death in 1991.
(Lou Sullivan Papers, Courtesy of GLBT Historical Society)

Sullivan siblings on the front stoop of their Wauwatosa, WI home in 1960. Clockwise from top left: Lou, Flame, Kathleen, Bridget, Maryellen and Patrick. (Courtesy of Flame Sullivan)

1964 school picture taken while Lou was a student at a private Catholic middle school.
(Lou Sullivan Papers, Courtesy of GLBT Historical Society)

1964 "self portrait" Lou took in a photo booth while wearing a Beatles-style hat.
(Lou Sullivan Papers, Courtesy of GLBT Historical Society)

Lou in "cowboy drag" during his Bob Dylan phase. Taken in 1966 on the steps of his family home. (Lou Sullivan Papers, Courtesy of GLBT Historical Society)

Sullivan siblings in 1970. Clockwise from top left: Bridget, Patrick, Maryellen, Lou, Flame and Kathleen.
(Lou Sullivan Papers, Courtesy of GLBT Historical Society)

Lou before attending the 1974 GPU drag ball. He and another trans person convinced the GPU leadership to hold the ball on the grounds that cross-dressing is liberating as opposed to degrading.
(Lou Sullivan Papers, Courtesy of GLBT Historical Society)

In 1975, Lou had difficulty finding employment in San Francisco when he went to job interviews dressed in a suit and tie.
(Courtesy of Flame Sullivan)

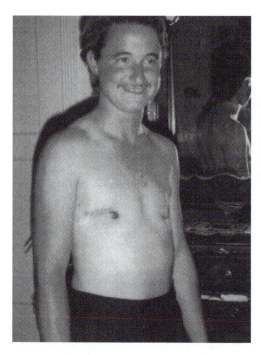

After undergoing top surgery with Dr. Falces in 1980, Lou shared photos of the results with other FTMs. (Lou Sullivan Papers, Courtesy of GLBT Historical Society)

For Lou, one of life's greatest pleasures was feeling the sun on his smooth, masculine chest. Here he is picnicking with friends at Golden Gate Park in 1981. (Courtesy of Flame Sullivan)

Lou considered 1982 the best year of his life. He easily moved through the world as a "youngman," enjoyed his job at ARCO Engineering and lived happily with his partner Keith in their Haight-Ashbury flat.
(Courtesy of Flame Sullivan)

Lou was shocked when he received his AIDS diagnosis in January 1987. He did not think he was at risk because he had a relatively small number of sexual partners and because he was trans. Lou dedicated the remainder of his life to helping other trans men and ensuring everyone knew that gay FTMs existed.
(©Mariette Pathy Allen; Lou Sullivan Papers, Courtesy of GLBT Historical Society

By 1989, Lou hardly recognized himself in the mirror. One of Lou's concerns about wasting syndrome was locating muscle in his thigh for testosterone injections.
(Courtesy of Flame Sullivan)

Dr. Lin Fraser, Dr. Paul Walker, Lou and Jamison Green at the 1990 ETVC event honoring Lou's contributions to the trans community.
(Courtesy of Flame Sullivan)

1990 Lou with FTMs in San Francisco.
(Courtesy of Flame Sullivan)

Lou's 1990 book signing for *From Female to Male: The Life of Jack Bee Garland* at A Different Light bookstore.
(Lou Sullivan Papers, Courtesy of GLBT Historical Society)

1990 Lou with FTMs in Seattle.
(Courtesy of Flame Sullivan).

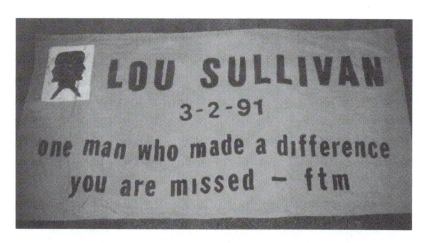

In a dedication ceremony on August 11, 1991, this panel made for Lou on behalf of the FTM organization he founded became part of the Names Project AIDS Memorial Quilt. (Lou Sullivan Papers, Courtesy of GLBT Historical Society)

CHAPTER

3

UNMOORED

L ou left Milwaukee confident and courageous, excited for adventure.
The support Lou found in Milwaukee's gay community had anchored
him and shored up his identification. He was moving to a city with
more gay bars, more gay organizations, more gay men—more of everything
that Lou loved. And he was moving with the person he loved most. When
Lou returned home to Milwaukee for a visit, it was not surprising that he
had changed dramatically, but it *was* surprising that he had changed for the
worse. Lou was almost unrecognizable to his Milwaukee friends, not just
because he now wore women's clothing but because of his complete lack of
self-confidence.[1]

Lou would later remember the years between 1975 and 1978 in San
Francisco as encompassing "the most tormented stage of [his] life."[2] He had
set sail with Mark to America's gay mecca only to capsize under the weight
of their relationship. Whereas in Milwaukee Mark had been one aspect
of Lou's life—albeit a very important one—in San Francisco he became
Lou's whole life. Without a supportive crew like he had in Milwaukee, Lou
quickly found himself lost at sea in San Francisco. The constants in his life
remained Mark and his desire to transition, but the tension between the
two left him feeling like a drowning man. It would take the rediscovery of
community, along with a great deal of struggle, loss and heartache, for Lou
to realize that he had to let go of Mark in order to save himself.

THE GREAT GAY MIGRATION AND TRANS TENDERLOIN

When Lou disembarked from the train in San Francisco in the summer
of 1975, filled with excitement and anticipation, it was like stepping into
another world. He was amazed at "how many queeny men there are just

mingling in the masses <u>all</u> <u>over</u>!... It's as tho we just blend in!"[3] Unbeknownst to Lou and Mark, they had moved to San Francisco at the same time that tens of thousands of gay men across the country were doing the same, during what is now called the "Great Gay Migration."[4]

Gay liberation had given rise to a new identity consciousness, and set in motion a massive "sexual migration" as individuals increasingly identified themselves as gays and lesbians and sought the company of others like them. They moved to large cities reputed to have well-developed gay subcultures, cities like New York and San Francisco.[5] New York may have been the so-called birthplace of gay liberation due to the Stonewall riots of 1969, but in the 1970s San Francisco held greater appeal for gay migrants, making it the premier destination of the Great Gay Migration. Some migrants were drawn to the temperate climate. Others felt "the scene" was more advanced in San Francisco than New York, for long before Stonewall, San Francisco had already seen decades of gay activism, and its thriving bar culture was over a century old.[6] What is undeniable is that the 1970s were San Francisco's gay heyday, as thousands of gay migrants created an explosion of gay organizations, both nonprofit and commercial, and the nation's first gay neighborhood.[7]

Reputation alone could not sustain the 1970s' Great Gay Migration to San Francisco, however. Thousands of migrants would not have been able to set up residence without jobs and living accommodations, both of which were offered by postindustrial San Francisco. Unlike cities in the nation's Rustbelt like Milwaukee, San Francisco was able to transition from a city based on manufacturing and commerce to one centered on finance, real estate and advanced business services. As a result, its demographics shifted, with retreating blue-collar workers replaced by white-collar workers migrating to San Francisco. Included among them were thousands of gay men who not only reshaped the face of San Francisco's workforce, but the face of its neighborhoods as well.

Throughout the 1960s, North Beach (the home of the 1950s' beats movement) and the Tenderloin/Polk Gulch area had been the geographic centers of San Francisco's gay community. But by the time Lou and Mark arrived in San Francisco, the geographic center of the gay community was shifting west to the Castro, which would become the nation's first gay neighborhood. The first gay bar opened on Castro Street in the late 1960s amidst great furor. But as the neighborhood's Irish Catholic inhabitants increasingly moved out, either following their blue-collar employers to places like Oakland or moving out to the suburbs as part of the nationwide exodus of heterosexual middle-class whites from U.S. cities, gay men willingly moved in and took advantage of the well-maintained cheap housing and gentrified the neighborhood.[8]

Lou and Mark knew that the Castro was a gay neighborhood but never discussed the possibility of moving there. Instead, Lou and Mark took the first apartment that they found—a studio apartment in San Francisco's Tenderloin district—and inhabited the fringes of San Francisco's gay community. The Tenderloin area had been a prostitution zone since the 1910s, where those engaging in sex trade included drag queens and female impersonators.[9] For decades the Tenderloin was inhabited by those who either could not afford to live elsewhere or, as in the case of (primarily MTF) trans people, were prevented from doing so.[10] The Tenderloin was one of San Francisco's poorest and most densely populated neighborhoods, constituting half of what was once known as San Francisco's central-city ghetto.[11] As a result of urban renewal, many of its MTF residents were increasingly displaced by new residents (like Lou and Mark) seeking the last remaining affordable housing in downtown San Francisco. MTF residents were pushed out on the streets, crammed into residency hotels, or pushed out of the Tenderloin altogether, but the Tenderloin's drag bars continued to flourish as they had for decades.[12]

Though Lou would frequent the Tenderloin's drag bars, he was unaware that the new neighborhood he lived in was the site of some of our nation's earliest trans organizing and activism, which began with the Compton's Cafeteria riot in the summer of 1966. In fact, few people knew of this precursor to the Stonewall riots, in which MTFs, gay hustlers and other sex workers fought back against police harassment, until it was reclaimed by historians in the 21st century and immortalized by Susan Stryker's film *Screaming Queens*.[13] The Tenderloin was also home to COG (Conversion Our Goal), the first known transsexual peer support group in the country, which was formed in 1967 and attracted MTF transsexual sex workers.[14]

When Lou moved to the Tenderloin, he knew nothing of the neighborhood's history of harassment and resistance, nor had he ever experienced the kind of employment discrimination that led many of the Tenderloin's residents to resort to work in the sex trade. However, he would quickly come up against the limits of San Franciscans' embrace of their city's newest migrants, and in time would build upon the city's history of trans organizing to help it become a trans mecca.

"THIS IS SAN FRANCISCO!"

Their first month in San Francisco, Lou and Mark only half-heartedly looked for jobs as they became acquainted with their new home. But as Lou intensified his search, he became increasingly frustrated when two months passed without his securing employment. Postindustrial San Francisco was full of new white-collar clerical positions, and Lou had never had a hard time getting a job before. He went in for a number of interviews for secretarial positions armed with glowing recommendations and an impressive skill set—dressed up in his best men's suit.

For years Lou had crossdressed while working as a secretary in Milwaukee and assumed he would have no problem doing the same in the more "progressive" San Francisco. However, potential employers called him in for interviews, took one look at him and then told him they had changed the job requirements. When interviewers looked at him strangely, Lou assumed they took him for snobby since he had worked at a university. After several disappointments, Lou finally learned at one interview why he was being turned down. The job supervisor told Lou that he would be perfect for the job if he did not dress so masculine, and was shocked that no one had bothered to tell Lou of this "problem" before. Lou was stunned: "Can they really care that much what I wear?... I've been applying so nonchalantly thinking all these people want is a top-notch secretary & as long as you don't smell like piss they don't care what you look like. This is San Francisco!"[15] But it seemed employment for gender transgressors was confined to the stage or the streets, and that an important qualification for secretaries remained that they be satisfying to—or at the very least comfortable for—the heterosexual male gaze.

Lou turned to the gay community for help. Whereas in Milwaukee all support services began and ended with GPU, a larger LGBT population and more decades of organizing experience meant that San Francisco both needed and could sustain several support services organizations. Lou began with the Society for Individual Rights (SIR), which was GPU's San Francisco counterpart. SIR was older, bigger, better known, and able to offer more services to the local gay community than Milwaukee's GPU, including employment assistance.[16] SIR's employment assistance could not overcome the challenges presented by Lou's gender presentation, however.

The employment counselor at SIR was unable to help Lou get a job, for while the places to which Lou was referred were open to hiring lesbians, they wanted their female employees to appear feminine. The employment counselor hired Lou to do temporary work with SIR's referral service, and Lou decided to try his luck with the California State Employment Service. Lou applied for two jobs, but the state agency's interviewer took one look at him and, rather than sending Lou to the two jobs for which he had applied, the interviewer gave him the phone numbers of several organizations that he recommended Lou contact for "help & advice." Lou "felt so upset, desperate, helpless" that he called one of the places and was referred to the Center for Special Problems.[17]

The Center for Special Problems was a unit of the San Francisco Public Health Department that began providing services for transsexuals in the late 1960s. During President Lyndon B. Johnson's War on Poverty, the Tenderloin area was declared an antipoverty district under the federal Equal Opportunity Act, which made funds available for community development.[18] In the fall of 1966, the Central City Anti-Poverty Program Office opened, which included an office for Sergeant Elliott Blackstone, San Francisco Police Department's liaison to the gay community. One day MTF Tenderloin activist and COG organizer Louise Ergestrasse entered Blackstone's office, handed him a copy of Dr. Harry Benjamin's *The Transsexual Phenomenon*, and demanded that he do something for "her people."[19] Blackstone began working closely with Dr. Benjamin, and contacted the Center for Special Problems—"a radical enclave in the San Francisco Department of Public Health"—about providing services for transsexuals.[20] Soon the Center was offering group support sessions, psychological counseling, hormone prescriptions and referrals for the Stanford University Gender Dysphoria Program.[21]

In October 1975, Lou went to the Center for Special Problems nearly frustrated to tears because of his problems finding a job. Lou had never met with medical professionals to discuss his gender identity and was pleasantly surprised by his interaction with a therapist and staff psychologist there. In a letter to his mother about the meeting, Lou recounted how

> they didn't think I was that strange & [said] sooner or later I'll hit a place that doesn't think I'm strange either…. Sure made me feel good that these 2 couldn't seem to find anything mental about me & they seemed amazed at my 'adjustment' to my predicament.

They even invited him to attend their transsexual group meetings, but Lou wanted to focus on getting a job first.[22]

Less than two weeks later Lou, dressed in suit and tie, interviewed for a position as secretary at Wilson Sporting Goods and was hired on the spot.[23] According to Lou, the office manager who hired him told Lou that he "learned in the army to live & let live," and only asked that Lou not wear a tie to work. Lou agreed and also took his lunch in the "Ladies Lounge" in order to avoid tension among the other employees, but made no effort to engage with his stereotypically feminine female co-workers.[24]

In fact, Lou hardly engaged with anyone but Mark. Lou and Mark went to the gay bars and discos, but Lou did not pick up anyone or make any friends. Nor did Lou mind, for he and Mark were very happy together until the spring of 1976. Unfortunately, their relationship took a turn when Lou's desire to physically transition resurfaced. Mark responded by dating a beautiful, feminine cisgender woman.[25] Both felt hurt and betrayed, feelings exacerbated by the fact that they had been each other's whole world for nearly a year. Neither wanted to break up, but something had to change. Lou moved out and focused on developing a social life outside of Mark in hopes of improving the situation. This had more or less done the trick years earlier. When Lou branched out beyond Mark, getting involved in Milwaukee's GPU and broader gay community, it relieved the impossible pressure placed on them to satisfy all of each other's needs. And Lou was much happier when he felt that he belonged in a community.

Lou had been welcomed by Milwaukee's gay community with open arms, and in San Francisco's gay community he hoped to recapture the happiness, friendship and sexual fulfillment he had had as a female trans-vestite in Milwaukee. However, Lou did not feel welcome in this new gay community. He went to the gay bars and enjoyed cruising, dancing, and buying drinks for "vanishing angels in the night," but never went home with anybody.[26] When Lou joined 120,000 others in celebrating San Francisco's 1976 Gay Pride at the end of June, he thought the parade was "spectacular"—unlike anything he had ever seen before. But Lou ended up crying because "I felt so deeply that they are my people" yet believed "I can never be accepted as one of them," because membership in the gay community at that time was for cisgender gay men.[27] What Lou was finding was that the large number of LGBT people in 1970s San Francisco led to the formation of distinctly separate gay, lesbian and trans commu-nities rather than an all-encompassing, inclusive gay community like in Milwaukee.

Feeling unwelcome in the gay community, Lou explored the trans community to see if he could find a home there. He called the Center for

Special Problems to ask about the transsexual group he had been invited to join a year ago while he was struggling to find a job. Lou spoke with a different therapist this time, and she encouraged him to meet with her rather than the group, which was comprised exclusively of MTFs. Lou had had such a positive experience with therapists at the Center before that he agreed to work with her one-on-one, unwittingly delaying his opportunity for community.[28]

Lou told Mark that seeing this "counselor for transsexuals" would help him to decide once and for all whether or not he was transsexual. However, his journal entries and correspondence with family and friends revealed Lou's belief that the therapist would simply confirm that he was transsexual, and wrote that when he imagined what it would feel like to transition, "a kind of tranquility flow[ed] thru me."[29] Lou had come to feel that it was important he do whatever he could to live comfortably, and had never before felt so sure that transitioning from female to male would enable him to do so.[30]

Before seeing the therapist, Lou thought through the benefits and drawbacks of transitioning thoroughly. He worried about erasing his female past, and realized how difficult life could be without a male past—without having experienced "all the subtle & typical male growing up occurrences." Lou questioned whether transitioning would make his life any different than it already was, and whether he could make it on a day-to-day basis. He worried that sexual encounters with gay men might be out of the question because he would not have typical male genitals, and feared getting beat up by heterosexual men because he would "come off like the screaming swishy faggot." But Lou concluded that his present situation had just as many drawbacks. He was tired of taking (female hormonal) birth control pills, tired of binding his chest (which hurt his back and made it difficult to breathe), and he was tired of having a woman's voice. Most importantly, Lou was tired of feeling "like an imposter."[31]

Two days before his first therapy session—"like an angel sent just for me!"—an article titled "Sex Change Uproar in Emeryville" appeared on the front page of the Saturday edition of the *San Francisco Chronicle*. The article detailed the plight of FTM high school teacher Steve Dain, who was facing employment discrimination because he had physically transitioned on the job.[32] Lou was overjoyed "[at] the thought there was <u>someone else</u> like me!" He immediately sat down and penned Dain a letter:

For the past 3 years I've described myself as a female-to-male transvestite & have lived 24 hours a day in men's clothing. I retain my female identity, but I can & do pass off & on in public. For 3 years I have tried in vain to locate a female with similar feelings. All this time I have fantasized switching over, but in the past several months I cannot rid myself of the intense desire to do so.... I've sought professional advice on the subject & will begin meeting a counselor on a weekly basis.... However, my greatest desire at present is to be able to meet with & talk to someone who has gone through this change. I so badly need peers &, as I am sure you know, there aren't a hell of a lot of F→Ms around.... [P]lease know that just being made aware you exist has made me feel less a screwball.

In his letter Lou included a brief history of his identity formation, desperately seeking Dain's validation of his gay FTM identity.

Dain responded to Lou's letter right away, saying he would love to meet with Lou as soon as things settled down in his own life. Lou read his letter over and over, and came to realize that "my biggest hang-up is my lack of self-confidence, lack of respect for my own judgment & my inability to make a decision that will affect my whole life. I am plagued by fear of the unknown future, tho I know in my heart I feel the same way now as I did 10 years ago." Dain told Lou that he was glad he was seeking professional counseling "so that at least you can share your deep concerns in confidence—but remember only you will be able to answer the questions you ask of yourself—so listen for your answers as you share your feelings with your counselor!"[33] Dain and Lou both knew that if Lou's therapist diagnosed him as transsexual, then Lou would be able to get the medical treatment he needed to masculinize his body. But Dain cautioned against over-reliance on clinical authority, urging Lou to listen to himself more than his therapist. Dain's advice made a lasting impression on Lou and would eventually serve him well down the road.

Lou often re-read his journals. Looking at his past experiences through the lens of transsexuality, Lou could identify enough cues to suggest he was transsexual. However, Lou's story differed from the archetypal transsexual narrative because of his enduring attraction to men.[34] In his first therapy session at the Center for Special Problems, Lou cautiously weighed every word. His therapist asked a series of questions that Lou found unsettling, and in the end explained she was trying to determine why Lou was inter-ested in transitioning and whether it was worthwhile for him to do so. She told Lou she had to admit that it was not a "typical reaction" for one to want to become male, and especially a gay male. At the time, Lou felt that his wanting to transition was all that mattered and that what the therapist deemed Lou's reason for wanting to transition was irrelevant.[35]

Two months after he began seeing a therapist at the Center, Lou submitted a fourteen-page application to the Stanford University Gender Dysphoria Program, located just thirty-five miles away in Palo Alto. In applying to the Stanford program, Lou was seeking assistance from what was then the largest university program performing gender confirmation surgeries. When Lou mailed off the application, he found himself exhausted from months of being consumed by the idea of transitioning. He felt as though he had already made up his mind to transition and prayed that Stanford would help him.[36] Lou believed Stanford would diagnose him as transsexual and hoped Mark would support him in transitioning, because it would be treatment for a medical diagnosis rather than a lifestyle choice.

ANDROGYNE ADRIFT

Stanford, however, did not respond to Lou. One of the things that the Center for Special Problems offered transsexuals was referrals to the Stanford program. Lou listed his therapist as the professional person involved in his efforts to "cross-live" who referred him to the program.[37] But there is no record of Lou's therapist giving him a positive referral to Stanford's program. She did, however, ask Lou what he would do if Stanford turned him down. And when he began second-guessing himself, Lou's therapist latched onto the notion that Lou's desire to transition stemmed from his internal misogyny and encouraged Lou to get to know more women.[38]

Lou's therapist also fueled his fears of losing Mark by focusing on how Mark felt about Lou's self-identification. Lou clung to the hope that he and Mark could "form a good gay love," but they continually fought over Lou's desire to transition.[39] Mark, whom Lou had fallen in love with for under-standing his gender non-conformity, was now determined to use as much of his influence as possible to stop Lou from transitioning. Mark threatened to break up with Lou if he transitioned because Mark now knew without a doubt that he was straight. He had tried being gay and thought he might be, only to realize that he was a feminine straight man. Mark wanted to be with Lou but could not be with a man.

When it came to Lou's transitioning, Mark had gone from hesitant to resistant to offensive. When Lou told him that he had sent an application to Stanford, Mark accused Lou of pursuing a physical transition in order to become a celebrity, and claimed Lou was fraught with self-hatred.[40] Mark claimed that Lou's gender "ambiguity" was one of the few things that made him interesting.[41] Mark even told Lou that he would not be able to have any sort of relationship with him if he transitioned, not even a friendship, because Lou would never be a man but rather a "mutilated… Frankenstein."

According to Lou, Mark did not feel like he was asking Lou to choose between himself and their relationship, but Lou felt like Mark was presenting him with an ultimatum.

> [Mark] said he didn't feel that [transitioning] was really me, that I was losing sight of where fantasy ends & reality starts. It was all sounding like the only way was for us to split up. That the switch was the only logical thing for me & severing his ties with the female me, thus severing us, was the only thing he could do.

The idea of losing Mark, his best friend, lover and kindred spirit, devastated Lou, and he felt that he would be a fool to let Mark go. Lou's therapist encouraged him to smooth things over with Mark, but the only way he could do so was by giving up his pursuit of transitioning. As a result, Lou decided against physically transitioning and tried to repress his desires. He told himself that he could never be a "real man" anyway, because "in my heart I know I am a nothing."[42]

In November 1976, after his near break-up with Mark, Lou visited Milwaukee for the first time since moving to San Francisco. He was welcomed back warmly in GPU and the gay bars. Lou immediately felt as if he had never left and wondered why he had.

When Lou returned to San Francisco, Mark told him that he had had sex with a cisgender woman during the time they had been arguing about Lou transitioning. According to Lou, Mark slept with this woman "just to make sure he could still do it."[43] Mark's ability to find sexual self-assurance through his gender embodiment contrasted painfully with the ways that Lou's femaleness foreclosed the possibility of finding validation of his sexual and gender identity from cruising gay men. Lou sank into a deep depression and despaired over his feeling of isolation:

[E]verywhere I look I see nothingness, no bridge to cross over. The gays—but how are they to accept me? How do I fit in? The feminists—…they won't embrace me. The lesbians—but I like men… The straights—no way. The transvestites—they're all male → female… I can't relate to <u>anyone</u>…. I feel so lonely & just want to kill myself.[44]

Lou also felt as if he had let himself down by not following through on his desire to be male. "I had failed," he wrote in his diary. "I had wanted so badly to be a man and I failed."[45]

Lou summarized the experiences of countless trans men then and now when he told his therapist that as a man he felt whole on the inside but uncomfortable on the outside, and as a female he felt freer to relate to others because he was more socially identifiable but felt empty on the inside.[46] At his therapist's suggestion, Lou began attending women's group therapy at the Center. Parroting his therapist, Lou explained to the group that the reason for his being there was that he changed his mind about transitioning after realizing that his desire to transition was really his desire to run away from the female within him, and that he needed to "rediscover" himself and meet strong women with whom he could identify.[47] Rounding out his female self-empowerment regimen, Lou purchased a number of women's magazines and a copy of *Our Bodies, Our Selves*—also at his therapist's suggestion. He continued to feel confused, lost and depressed, but at least now Lou was no longer suicidal.[48]

Throughout 1976 Lou's therapist had dissuaded him from transitioning, deliberately avoided recommending the Center's transsexual group therapy sessions to Lou, and encouraged him to foster relationships with women. She also worked to help Lou become his own kind of woman, which Lou struggled with. Lou decided he had to go to the feminine extreme (i.e., wearing make-up and a dress) to assure himself and others that he was in fact female before he could inhabit his own version of femaleness.[49] Lou had embraced the notion of not being a stereotypical male, but struggled to understand which non-stereotypically female behaviors were socially acceptable. And yet, Lou found reinforcement for presenting himself as more feminine from the women he befriended in the support group, his co-workers and Mark.[50] Mark, perhaps fearing Lou would resume thinking about transitioning, always wanted Lou to wear dresses, and when he looked especially feminine, Mark was highly complimentary.

While Lou renegotiated his relationship with his female body, his gay sexual desires went unchanged. As Lou's confidence increased, he began attracting men again, but his increasing self-confidence caused turmoil in his relationship with Mark, who found it threatening. To cope with their fighting, Lou hid in his gay sexual fantasies. Lou developed a long-term crush on a man he regularly conversed with on the bus (whom he referred to as his "Cutie on the Bus"), imagining him a gay man. For months he occupied Lou's thoughts and masturbatory fantasies, in which he imagined them as gay lovers.[51] Lou's affair with his "Cutie on the Bus" never extended beyond imagination, and he often felt that thinking about sex was much better than actually having it, in large part because when he thought about having sex he imagined himself having sex with men as a man. When Lou did have sex with men, he found them unable to fulfill his fantasies because they did not see him as male.

Lou continued to think about his identity, religiously saving newspaper articles about FTM teacher Steve Dain and taping them into his journals. At this time Dain embodied a secret desire that Lou could not even admit to himself. He had been the only one to validate Lou's desire to become male, but he was too removed from Lou's personal life. No one and nothing else validated Lou's desire to transition—including his therapist, partner, friends and the medical literature on FTM transsexuality.

So Lou continued to identify as a transvestite. While he now mostly wore women's clothing, Lou did not entirely forego crossdressing. For him, crossdressing was the outward manifestation of his "maleness" and he was striving to bring his male and female "sides" into harmony. However, Lou feared Mark's rejection if he saw him crossdressed so was cautious around him.[52] Mark had gone from finding Lou's crossdressing interesting and titillating, to fearing it was indicative of Lou's desire to transition, to thinking it was a "perverted," unnatural urge that Lou should control.[53] Since moving to San Francisco, Mark felt he had overcome or grown out of the gender ambiguity of his youth, and believed Lou could and should do the same.

In fact Lou did find his identity as a transvestite to be tenuous and unfulfilling, but not for the same reasons Mark did. Living in the Tenderloin, Lou was surrounded by other crossdressers, but he did not feel a sense of community with them. Lou badly missed organizational work for the gay community and how fulfilling it had been for him. He waged a constant battle against his desire to be a gay man, but Lou now believed that he could not and would never be what he most desired. Lou worried about his lack of self-identity and sense of purpose since deciding to remain female.

He felt disconnected from his body and less self-aware. On the upside, Lou now felt bolder and more positive than he had since moving to San Francisco two years prior.[54]

Increasing his self-confidence was the most important gain Lou had made in therapy. Lou learned that he could interact with others whether dressed like a man or a woman, and eventually learned how to stand up for himself, especially with Mark. He knew now that he could control his own identity even if he did not know what his identity was. Lou did not feel therapy could help him anymore, and—against her wishes—decided to stop seeing his therapist.[55]

The main reason Lou stopped therapy was because he no longer had the desire to transition. Trying to sort this out was the reason he began therapy at the Center for Special Problems in the first place. For Lou, this therapy had not served as a means to transitioning. Instead, it led him to rethink his identification. Lou assured his therapist that he would continue going to women's group therapy sessions for female companionship and emotional support, but in reality, Lou came to rely upon his sister Maryellen, who had left Milwaukee and the rest of the Sullivan clan to join Lou in San Francisco.[56]

For the next several months, Lou and Mark's relationship was better than it had been in years. They went to shows and partied together, and agreed not to have sex with or date anyone else. Lou kept his lingering desire to be male secret, no longer sharing his internal struggle about the matter with Mark. However, Lou confessed to his journal his sense of emptiness from being unable to crossdress, and that he was trying to have Mark fill that emptiness.[57] Lou was often jealous that Mark still had a life of his own, whereas Lou did not—because he was only doing and being what Mark wanted.

It was Lou's old gay Milwaukee friends Eldon and Charles who assured him that he did have a life of his own, and told Lou that he held a unique perspective on the world. Charles acknowledged that Lou's experiences could be painful, but also enthralling. He told Lou that he was a specialist in an area that few people knew anything about (female transvestites and transsexuals), and encouraged Lou to share his knowledge with others through writing, lectures and social outreach.[58] Lou especially valued Eldon's sage advice:

> Accept yourself for where YOU are. Don't worry about trying to be someone else. You are unique and beautiful.

Being true to yourself isn't easy for anyone, but if you can keep from rollercoaster heights and depths of emotions (which I think you do well)—if you can understand that life is a constant battle and that being truly human calls for some pain as well as joy to allow for growth, if you can learn patience—real growth as a human is slow—you will find all the things you are and achieve much of what you want. Those of us who love you don't doubt for a moment that you can!—that you will![59]

In February 1978, Lou received a letter from Eldon and *GPU News* informing him that they had given permission to reprint his article "Looking Toward Transvestite Liberation" in *The New Gay Liberation Book*.[60] Lou was astounded to realize that his article would appear alongside articles by such famous authors as Gore Vidal, Christopher Isherwood, William Burroughs and John Rechy, and felt as high as the first time he did hashish.[61] The inclusion of his work validated Lou's developing belief that he did have a unique perspective to offer, and that his scholarship could be a valuable form of activism.

NOT ALONE

In May 1978, still paying lip service to his female self-empowerment regimen, Lou picked up a local women's paper. In it he saw a "TV/TS meeting for women" listed in the local events calendar. Which women? Who's a woman? Lou wondered. He could not resist. Even though he figured the Golden Gate Girls group would be primarily composed of heterosexual male transvestites, Lou decided to go to the meeting.[62] His suspicions were correct, but Lou was nonetheless impressed with how the "middle-aged TVs" talked about their complex identities, and he hoped they could help him figure out how to keep his "2 halves separate."[63]

At that same initial meeting, Lou also witnessed the group vote to extend membership to female-to-males and change their name to Golden Gate Girls/Guys (GGG/G).[64] Lou was anxious to attend the next meeting, where he would get to meet the individual who had prompted the vote. After doing so, Lou wrote to Eldon, telling him ecstatically that at long last he had found someone like him—another female transvestite, who went by Emmon.[65]

Lou referred to Emmon by his chosen name and pronouns, as was standard practice for GGG/G members. The two kept eyeing one another during their first GGG/G meeting together, and when it was over Lou summoned up the courage to introduce himself. Lou found Emmon extremely easy to talk to. Sizing him up, Lou decided that Emmon had a more butch job (swimming pool plumber) than he (secretary), but that Lou was much more experienced and "bold" than Emmon. For example, when Emmon went shopping he pretended to be a woman buying clothes for her son, and feared getting read as an FTM if he got any alterations done. Lou assured Emmon that salespeople would rarely risk confronting him and making a scene even if they found him suspicious.

The icing on the cake was the fact that Emmon did not crossdress in order to attract women. In fact, like Lou, Emmon was attracted to men. "God, Eldon. I'm not alone," he wrote. "Everyone's just hiding. This closet even has toilet paper stuck in the keyhole!"[66] But alas, finally meeting another female who identified as a transvestite attracted to men was not a cure-all for Lou's identity struggles.

Mark was against his attending GGG/G meetings, claiming the meetings were bad for Lou.[67] Lou had always been susceptible to Mark's influence, but he continued to go to the meetings despite Mark's objections, which held more power when Lou's self-confidence was down and he felt isolated. During Lou's periodic bouts of depression over his identity, he felt Mark was the only thing he had to live for and that he would be nothing without him. Lou's thinking this way further isolated him from others. But in GGG/G Lou had once again found community, and the meetings provided a venue in which he could be Lou—not Sheila. Over time, Lou would take over the writing and publication of *Gateway*, GGG/G's monthly newsletter, and be appointed Treasurer.

GGG/G not only provided a venue for personal growth, but community growth as well. GGG/G gave Lou the means to begin laying the groundwork for what would become an international FTM network. Lou reached out to other (predominantly MTF) trans organizations throughout the United States and Canada trying to locate others on the FTM spectrum. He was particularly interested in finding FTMs who identified as gay men or female transvestites—as he did. Initially Lou came up empty-handed, though he did receive some interested replies to his identification as a female transvestite and requests for articles. These included a personal invitation from Dr. Virginia Prince to publish an article in *Transvestia* magazine, the first long-running trans-oriented periodical in the United States, which Lou described as being "famous."[68]

Gradually, Lou's networking led him to several people who were assigned female at birth and identified as transvestites and/or gay men. These correspondences were invaluable to Lou, and he began building an international FTM network to connect with and ease the isolation of others. To all of his correspondents Lou emphasized the importance of coming out as FTM. According to Lou, it made him crazy to think about how many others were hiding scared because no one thought they should exist. Lou, who had been involved with the gay liberation movement in Milwaukee and who identified strongly with gay men, equated coming out as a female transvestite with coming out as gay: expressing one's identity in a public way would enable female transvestites to have greater self-confidence and encourage others to come out as well, thus eradicating their invisibility. "If these male TVs and gay guys can be so out about what they like," Lou wrote, "why can't we?" [69]

However, it was difficult for Lou to be truly out while in a relationship with Mark. He had a strong desire to crossdress more frequently, but Lou limited his urges because he did not want to cause trouble with Mark. Mark and Lou had been together ten years, and Lou knew that they were both proud of being together for so long. In Lou's opinion, he and Mark had been getting along really well lately. Although he disagreed with Lou's crossdressing, Mark had "given" him the space to "indulge" in crossdressing on his own once in a while and to pursue his scholarly and social interests in transvestism. [70]

Lou tried to give hope to his new FTM friend Emmon, who doubted he would ever find love as a female transvestite. Lou did so by telling Emmon that even though Mark was very much against his transitioning, he "put up" with Lou's crossdressing. [71] And Lou assured Emmon that while he (Lou) had picked up a number of men while crossdressing, Emmon looked "ten times better" than he did. [72] Mentoring Emmon provided Lou with more special occasions for crossdressing, and he hoped to boost Emmon's confidence by going out crossdressed with him to gay bars. Lou decided to play it safe, taking Emmon to a few of his "regular gay men's bars" on Polk Street. These bars were in Lou's neighborhood and he knew the men there. They saw him there with Mark every Saturday and knew that Lou was female. But what Lou really wanted was to go to the Castro where no one knew he was female. [73] For the time, this remained a fantasy and an unrealizable one, so long as he was a transvestite and only modified his clothing, not his body.

Lou began consciously extending his transvestite identity beyond the confines of the trans community. He regularly went out dressed in men's clothing to punk concerts, gay bars and discos, and varied his style according to the venue. Lou dabbled in the Bay Area punk scene, drawn to its anti-establishment ethos much like he had been drawn to the 1960s counterculture in Milwaukee. Dressing for punk concerts in his leather jacket, white T-shirt and black pants was reminiscent of Lou's days in Lou Reed drag.[74]

For a while Lou was satisfied dressing like a man and going to the gay bars and discos where he cruised men and pretended to be "like all the other guys there." But he avoided talking to the men for fear that they would discover he was female and ruin the illusion.[75] As Lou became increasingly comfortable in his identity, he went out in a suit and tie in hopes of finding a bisexual man. Lou believed that bisexual men were his best option, because if they were attracted to males they would find his crossdressing and demeanor attractive yet not be repelled by his female embodiment. Unfortunately Lou's attempts were unsuccessful. Nonetheless, they were far superior to his experiences of picking up men at straight bars when he was not crossdressing.[76] Lou found his sexual liaisons with "straight-o's" largely unsatisfying, and often turned off potential heterosexual partners with his aggression and experimental side. He found these sexual encounters to be one-sided, and would not only encourage the men to expand their horizons, but also to be more considerate of their sexual partners.[77]

After attending a Golden Gate Girls/Guys dinner party one Saturday night, Lou went out to the bars on Polk Street alone and got hit on by a drunken, white, middle-aged, cisgender gay man. Lou shocked the man by telling him that he was female and felt complimented by the man's attraction. However, once he revealed his female embodiment, the man was no longer interested. Lou boldly assured him that he would not have gone to his place anyway because the man was not "fem" enough for him.[78] Unfortunately, when Lou finally mustered up the courage to go to the Castro crossdressed he was met with the same reaction. He would cruise men or be cruised by them only to be rejected once they "discovered" his female body.

Lou really wanted his identifying as a female transvestite to be the end-all be-all. But Lou could not shake the feeling that he was settling for a female transvestite identity. Because what he really wanted was to fully embody maleness. After deciding to forego transitioning, Lou stopped corresponding with Steve Dain, but he still yearned for an FTM transsexual with whom to identify, as evidenced by a revealing book review he published.

Though Lou had now lived in San Francisco for several years, he continued publishing trans-related pieces in *GPU News*. One such piece was a review of *Emergence: A Transsexual Autobiography.*[79] A picture of the book's cover was included with the review. On the top of the cover it read: "The first complete female-to-male story." The cover included a picture of the book's author, Mario Martino. According to Lou's review, he wanted the book "to present a human being I could understand and really feel, a believable progression of what led to the desperate decision of surgery, and the differences the change made in the author's life—not more lines of delusion." Lou was disheartened because he felt the book focused on the author's sexual attraction to women (which was very much in accord with the existing medical literature on FTM transsexualism) rather than a "confused body image." Lou was left wondering why Martino had physically transitioned, feeling like he never adequately explained his reasons.[80]

For years now Lou had wrestled with the idea of transitioning and knew that doing so would come at a great cost—losing Mark. Transitioning had come at a great cost to Martino, too, but he had done it and harbored no regrets. Lou wanted to know why Martino transitioned to see if he could identify with the reason(s) and be compelled to transition himself. He was looking for a formula—for a diagnosis—yet discovering that it is ultimately a matter of individual knowledge. Yes, transsexuals shared certain identifiable commonalities, but what ultimately set them apart from transvestites and other gender transgressors was the decision to transition. While they had no control over wanting to transition, transsexuals could only move forward if they decided to.

TRAGEDY AND CLARITY

In the early morning hours of October 19, 1978, Lou was awakened by Maryellen pounding on his apartment door, informing him that their brother Patrick had been in a terrible motorcycle accident and was not expected to make it through the night. Lou's first reaction was "that this is just another Sullivan freak-out exaggeration." He called his parents, who were understandably upset, but the "clincher" was when he spoke with Flame. Flame was so upset that Lou understood how serious the situation was. For the next few days, Lou repeatedly looked to Flame who, despite years of being a misunderstood outcast, ended up serving as the family's fortress of emotional strength during the tragedy.[81]

When Lou moved to San Francisco, Patrick was still in high school. After graduating from high school, Patrick began hanging out with Flame, and the two developed a close relationship similar to the one Flame and Lou had shared during their days at the Garde. The night of the accident, Patrick, Flame and Flame's best friend Bert had been out partying at a bar and then decided to leave. Flame usually rode on the back of Bert's motorcycle, but for some reason that night Patrick gave Flame his car keys and told him he was going to ride with Bert. Bert was going some 60-80 miles per hour down a city street when he hit a car broadside. Nearly every bone was broken in Bert's body, and one broken bone severed an aorta, which quickly killed him. Patrick, who had catapulted over the top of the car and landed on his head, was brain-dead and on life support.

Lou and Maryellen were met at the airport by their mother, grandmother and eldest sibling Kathleen, who told them that they were waiting for Lou and Maryellen to see their brother one last time "before they pulled the plug." They went to the hospital, said their goodbyes, and the hospital was supposed to turn off the respirator the following day. However, taking Patrick off life support turned into a three-day fiasco. Patrick was an organ donor, and the hospital informed the Sullivans that state law required that an individual have a flat EEG reading for twenty-four hours before taking them off of life support. For three days the hospital refused to honor the family's wishes to take Patrick off life support, until they realized that their EEG machine was broken.[82] The *Milwaukee Journal* ran a front-page article about the family's ordeal. According to the article, the Sullivans "lived with the uncertainty born of an age in which technology allows—and so necessitates—technical definitions of death," and outlined their experience of waiting "for science to surrender."[83]

The Sullivans' experience with taking Patrick off life support would have challenged anyone's faith in medical professionals. However, it would help give Lou the conviction to stand up against gender program experts and to revolutionize the diagnosis and treatment of transsexuality. The seeds of distrust for medical authority had been planted in Lou by Flame's being put on display at the American Medical Association as a child with severe acne, by the hypocrisy of establishment authority figures revealed to him during his countercultural days, and by his letter from FTM Steve Dain encouraging him to trust himself over the gender professionals. Lou's distrust now germinated in light of the experience of being unable to take

Patrick off of life support due to medical ignorance, and it would soon grow into outright defiance. Eventually the right conditions enabled Lou's deep-seeded distrust to blossom into a compassionate desire to educate medical professionals. By the time of his own death, Lou would plant the seeds of patient-centered care for trans people. For now, Patrick's death would bring many things into stark relief for Lou.

When Lou returned to San Francisco after Patrick's funeral, he remained in a state of shock for a long while. It all felt like a bad dream. Lou knew that it would be a long time before he stopped thinking of Patrick and death. A week after returning to San Francisco, Lou sent Flame a Lou Reed album and a letter for his birthday:

> Even out here, I still can't seem to get [Patrick] off my mind. I know now what they mean about the spirit staying with us after someone dies…. It makes me feel that that's what happens when you die: you watch all the people you knew and suddenly you understand why they do what they do, what it is that makes them want to live, and you finally love them. I feel like I'm carrying [Patrick] around in my heart, that he's letting me know he loves and understands me.[84]

The tragedy of Patrick's death rekindled Lou's relationship with Flame, who now told him that Lou was the closest thing to a brother that he had remaining.[85] Patrick's death also reconfigured Lou's understanding of his family, as the center of power shifted from his parents (more specifically his mother) to the Sullivan children. For a time the Sullivan siblings discussed the idea of Lou and Maryellen moving back to Milwaukee and making their father's trucking business a family business. Instead, Flame, Bridget and their respective families moved out to San Francisco, where they all lived for several years.[86]

Lou found no consolation for his grief in Mark, who froze up in the face of vulnerability when Lou needed warmth and compassion.[87] To make matters worse, when Lou returned from Milwaukee, Mark informed him that he had spent quite a bit of time with his co-worker while Lou was gone, and implied that he was developing feelings for her. At the time, Lou was too emotionally drained to deal with this, but three weeks later it became apparent that things were getting serious between her and Mark, and Lou was infuriated. He felt like there was no excuse for this relationship because things had been going so well between them. Lou reasoned that Mark's relationship two years earlier had been somewhat excusable since he had been crossdressing regularly and considering transitioning. But Lou had given up his transitioning pursuit and respectfully kept his crossdressing life separate from Mark. Mark, who had admonished Lou about controlling his desire to be male, now told Lou that he was simply powerless over his feelings for his co-worker. Lou could not imagine continuing to endure Mark's intense long-term relationships with others for the rest of his life, and Mark told Lou that he did not like being with a transvestite. Mark did not want to break-up, but Patrick's death made Lou think "that we just don't have that long to spend our time hurting each other," and ended their eleven-year relationship.[88]

Over the next eight months others would report to Lou how torn up and miserable Mark was over their break-up. Lou maintained an intense passion and longing for Mark, but he had come to the important realization that a relationship with Mark came at the cost of "denying myself"—not just his desires, but his self.[89] Lou thought back on the reasons why he had decided not to transition in 1976: "(1) because I was too unsure of myself to take on that major change, (2) I hadn't reconciled my female-male conflict, & (3) because Mark said he would leave me & I didn't believe I could go on in life without him."[90] In Lou's estimation, now none of these reasons held true anymore. Lou had broken up with Mark, had come to realize that his male and female sides were not at odds with each other, and now had the self-confidence and desire to make this transition. "If I am ever going to do anything with my life that I can be proud of," Lou resolved, "it must be my success at living full time as a youngman."[91]

When Lou informed him of his decision to transition, Mark tried to talk Lou out of it again. But this time his opinions held no sway. As he told Mark,

> Now that I'm alone, I see that, if it is true that we are all responsible for our own happiness, that we cannot expect others to fulfill us, and in the end we only have ourselves, then I better make peace with the feelings inside me. If I don't it will be the only thing on my deathbed I will regret not doing.[92]

ENDNOTES: CHAPTER 3

1. Sullivan Journal, 10 November 1976, 11 November 1976, box 1 folder 11, LGS Papers.

2. Lou, "FTM Male Box," *FTM* 15 (April 1991) in Rawlings-Fein, 90.

3. Sullivan Journal, 4 August 1975, box 1 folder 11, LGS Papers.

4. See Kath Weston, "Get Thee to a Big City: Sexual Imaginary and the Great Gay Migration," *GLQ: A Journal of Lesbian and Gay Studies* 2 (1995): 253-277.

5. John D'Emilio, "Gay Politics, Gay Community: San Francisco's Experience," in *Making Trouble: Essays on Gay History, Politics, and the University* (New York: Routledge, 1992), 86-88.

6. Benjamin Heim Shepard, *White Nights and Ascending Shadows: An Oral History of the San Francisco AIDS Epidemic* (London: Cassell, 1997), 22-23. See also Nan Alamilla Boyd, *Wide-Open Town: A History of Queer San Francisco to 1965* (Berkeley: University of California, 2003).

7. Armstrong, 113.

8. Randy Shilts, *The Mayor of Castro Street* (New York: St. Martin's Press, 1982), 82; Robert W. Bailey, *Gay Politics, Urban Politics: Identity and Economics in the Urban Setting* (New York: Columbia University, 1999), 291; Armstrong, 124.

9. Boyd, 43-44.

10. Stryker, *Transgender History*, 66.

11. Members of the Gay and Lesbian Historical Society of Northern California, "MTF Transgender Activism in the Tenderloin and Beyond, 1966-1975: Commentary and Interview with Elliot Blackstone," *GLQ: A Journal of Lesbian and Gay Studies* 4.2 (1998): 367 n1.

12. Stryker, *Transgender History*, 69.

13. Stryker, *Transgender History*, 70, 72, 64. See also *Screaming Queens: The Riot at Compton's Cafeteria*, DVD, dir. Victor Silverman and Susan Stryker (San Francisco: Frameline, 2005).

14. Meyerowitz, 230; Stryker, *Transgender History*, 75.

15. Sullivan Journals, 14 October 1975, box 1 folder 11, LGS Papers.

16. On SIR and the services it provided to San Francisco's gay community, see Boyd, 227-231.

17. Sullivan Journal, 23 October 1975, box 1 folder 11, LGS Papers.

18. Meyerowitz, 231; Bailey, 288.

19. Stryker, *Transgender History*, 75; Members, 352.

20. Members, 358; Meyerowitz, 230.

21. Stryker, *Transgender History*, 75-76.

22. Sullivan Journal, 23 October 1975, box 1 folder 11, LGS Papers.

23. Sullivan Journal, 3 November 1975, box 1 folder 11, LGS Papers.

24. Sullivan Journal, 14 November 1975, box 1 folder 11, LGS Papers.

25. Sullivan Journal, 9 March 1976, 14 May 1976, box 1 folder 11, LGS Papers.

26. Sullivan Journal, 11 July 1976, box 1 folder 11, LGS Papers.

27. Sullivan Journal, 28 June 1976, box 1 folder 11, LGS Papers.

28. Sullivan Journal, 27 July 1976, box 1 folder 11, LGS Papers.

29. Sullivan Journal, 5 August 1976, box 1 folder 11, LGS Papers.

30. Sullivan Journal, 27 July 1976, box 1 folder 11, LGS Papers.

31. Sullivan Journal, 5 August 1976, box 1 folder 11, LGS Papers.

32. Carolyn Anspacher, "Sex Change Uproar in Emeryville," *San Francisco Chronicle* (7 August 1976): 1

33. Sullivan Journal, 21 August 1976, box 1 folder 11, LGS Papers.

34. On reading one's past through a transsexual filter, refiguring one's life according to pre-existing transsexual narratives and clinicians' measuring subject narratives against the narratemes of an archetypal transsexual narrative, see David Prosser, *Second Skins: The Body Narratives of Transsexuality* (New York: Columbia University, 1998), 104, 117, 124.

35. Sullivan Journal, 21 August 1976, box 1 folder 11, LGS Papers.

36. Sullivan Journal, 12 October 1976, box 1 folder 11, LGS Papers.

37. Sheila Sullivan, Application for Stanford University Gender Dysphoria Program, 17 October 1976, box 1, folder 1, LGS Papers.

38. Sullivan Journal, 6 September 1976, box 1 folder 11, LGS Papers.

39. Sullivan Journal, 19 October 1976, box 1 folder 11, LGS Papers.

40. Sullivan Journal, 16 October 1976, box 1 folder 11, LGS Papers.

41. Sullivan Journal, 21 August 1976, box 1 folder 11, LGS Papers.

42. Sullivan Journal, 24 October 1976, box 1 folder 11, LGS Papers.

43. Sullivan Journal, 14 November 1976, box 1 folder 11, LGS Papers.

44.   Sullivan Journal, 26 November 1976, box 1 folder 11, LGS Papers.

45.   Sullivan Journal, 23 January 1977, box 1 folder 11, LGS Papers.

46.   Sullivan Journal, 24 January 1977, box 1 folder 11, LGS Papers.

47.   Sullivan Journal, 19 December 1976, box 1 folder 11, LGS Papers.

48.   Sheila Sullivan to Liz Marshall, 31 December 1976, box 3 folder 110, LGS Papers.

49.   Sheila Sullivan to Liz Marshall, 24 April 1977, box 3 folder 110, LGS Papers.

50.   Sullivan Journal, 23 January 1977, 5 April 1977, 10 November 1977, box 1 folder 11, LGS Papers.

51.   Sullivan Journal, 6 February 1977, 20 April 1977, 29 May 1977, box 1 folder 11, LGS Papers.

52.   Sullivan Journal, 29 May 1977, 24 June 1977, 13 November 1977, box 1 folder 11, LGS Papers.

53.   Sullivan Journal, 26 May 1978, box 1 folder 11, LGS Papers.

54.   Sullivan Journal, 7 August 1977, box 1 folder 11, LGS Papers.

55.   Sullivan Journal, 10 July 1977, 28 August 1977, box 1 folder 11, LGS Papers.

56.   Sullivan Journal, 7 August 1977, 28 August 1977, box 1 folder 11, LGS Papers.

57.   Sullivan Journal, 4 December 1977, box 1 folder 11, LGS Papers.

58.   Sullivan Journal, 23 February 1978, box 1 folder 11, LGS Papers.

59.   Sullivan Journal, 8 March 1978, box 1 folder 11, LGS Papers.

60.   See Sheila Sullivan, "Looking Toward Transvestite Liberation," in *The New Gay Liberation Book: Writings and Photographs about Gay (Men's) Liberation*, ed. Len Richmond with Gary Noguera (Palo Alto: Ramparts Press, 1979), 147-153.

61.   Sullivan Journal, 23 February 1978, box 1 folder 11, LGS Papers.

62.   Sullivan Journal, 26 May 1978, box 1 folder 11, LGS Papers.

63.   Sullivan Journal, 14 May 1978, 26 May 1978, box 1 folder 11, LGS Papers.

64.   Sullivan Journal, 11 May 1978, box 1 folder 11, LGS Papers; see also box 4 folder 165, LGS Papers.

65. In the summer of 1999 Emmon was bludgeoned to death in his home. His murder remains unsolved. Emmon's last name was Bodfish, and he is included on a spreadsheet of victims compiled for Transgender Day of Remembrance memorial services. See "Statistics and Other Info," *International Transgender Day of Remembrance*, http://www.transgenderdor.org/?page_id=192.

66. Sullivan Journal, 26 May 1978, box 1 folder 11, LGS Papers.

67. Sullivan Journal, 4 July 1978, box 1 folder 11, LGS Papers.

68. Sullivan Journal, 14 February 1979, box 1 folder 11, LGS Papers. For more on *Transvestia*, see Stryker, *Transgender History*, 53-54, and Meyerowitz, 181-182.

69. Lou Sullivan to FTM, 8 August 1979, 4 September 1979, box 2 folder 49, LGS Papers.

70. Sullivan Journal, 7 September 1978, 21 September 1978, 16 October 1978, box 1 folder 11, LGS Papers.

71. Sullivan Journal, 26 May 1978, box 1 folder 11, LGS Papers.

72. Sullivan Journal, 21 September 1978, box 1 folder 11, LGS Papers.

73. Sullivan Journal, 7 September 1978, 21 September 1978, box 1 folder 11, LGS Papers.

74. Sullivan Journal, 19 December 1979, box 1 folder 11, LGS Papers.

75. Lou Sullivan to FTM, 4 September 1979, box 2 folder 49, LGS Papers.

76. Sullivan Journal, 8 July 1979, box 1 folder 11, LGS Papers.

77. Sullivan Journal, 12 May 1979, box 1 folder 11, LGS Papers.

78. Sullivan Journal, 18 July 1979, box 1 folder 11, LGS Papers.

79. See Mario Martino with harriet, *Emergence: A Transsexual Autobiography* (New York: Crown Publishers, 1977).

80. Sheila Sullivan, "Review: Emergence: A Transsexual Autobiography by Mario Martino with Harriet. Crown Publishers, Inc. New York, 1977. $10," *GPU News* (February 1978): 17-18.

81. Sullivan Journal, 23 October 1978 to 1 November 1978, 6 November 1978, box 1 folder 11, LGS Papers; Flame Sullivan interview.

82. Sullivan Journal, 23 October 1978 to 1 November 1978, box 1 folder 11, LGS Papers.

83. Ron Elving, "Science Delayed Grief, but Lent Comfort, Too," *The Milwaukee Journal* (24 October 1978): 1.

84. Sullivan Journal, 6 November 1978, box 1 folder 11, LGS Papers.

85. Sullivan Journal, 10 September 1979, box 1 folder 12, LGS Papers.

86. Sullivan Journal, 6 March 1979, 21 August 1979, box 1 folder 12, LGS Papers.

87. Sullivan Journal, 27 November 1978, box 1 folder 11, LGS Papers.

88. Sullivan Journal, 23 October 1978 to 1 November 1978, 21 November 1978, 27 November 1978, 7 January 1979, 11 March 1979, box 1 folder 11, LGS Papers.

89. Sullivan Journal, 11 March 1979, box 1 folder 11, LGS Papers.

90. Sullivan Journal, 11 September 1979, box 1 folder 11, LGS Papers.

91. Sullivan Journal, 10 September 1979, box 1 folder 11, LGS Papers.

92. Sullivan Journal, 3 October 1979, box 1 folder 11, LGS Papers.

CHAPTER

TRANSITIONS

B reaking up with Mark empowered Lou to follow his "own dreams, regardless of ANY ONE else's opinions."[1] On September 10, 1979, Lou went to a Golden Gate Girls/Guys meeting wearing a chest binder and sporting a new "boy's haircut." He had done some serious soul-searching that day and concluded: "I KNOW myself & who I am." He was a gay man named Lou.[2] Lou had agonized for years over the decision to transition. He now experienced the euphoria of embracing who he was and the excitement of bringing himself into being.

The next two years brought about great changes in Lou's life as he experienced one transition after another. Lou physically transitioned with hormones and top surgery and emerged as a leader of the trans community, which was transformed by the growing presence of FTMs. Lou transitioned from being a secretary to having one, and he changed neighborhoods, moving out of the trans Tenderloin and into the macho Mission. Lou also fell in love with a man who was willing to change his sexual orientation because he loved Lou. But it is doubtful that any of this would have been possible had the medical establishment not gone through a transition of its own. Reputable physicians received authorization to treat trans people outside of gender programs, and Lou was in a position to both take advantage of and advance this change.

DYSPHORIC STANDARDS

When Lou decided to stop fantasizing about transitioning and make it a reality, the first people he reached out to were his friends at Golden Gate Girls/Guys. He knew they would support any decision regarding his trans identification and that they would be a great source of information.

Attending a GGG/G meeting right after making his decision also provided Lou with much-needed validation.

At the meeting, Lou spoke at length with psychotherapist Lin Fraser and Georgia, GGG/G president, about his desire to begin physically transitioning. When Lou told Georgia that he wanted to go through a "reputable clinic" such as the one at Stanford, she told him to forget it. Lou wanted to go to a "reputable clinic" because he was all too familiar with the horrors that could befall people at the hands of hack jobs. However, university-based programs would not touch Lou with "a 10 foot pole," Georgia cautioned, because he did not have the "typical transsexual story" they wanted to hear.[3]

Because of his involvement in the trans community and his knowledge of the medical discourse on transsexuality, Lou worried that Georgia was correct about the gender programs. He did not fit the archetypal trans-sexual profile because he was attracted to men and identified as gay. After six years of researching FTM transsexuality, he found no literature on gay FTMs. Transsexuality was ostensibly about reconfiguring one's body to align with his/her gender identity; it was about one's relationship with one's own body. Yet, gender professionals' heteronormative bias meant that sexuality—or the relationship between one's body and another's—could become a deciding factor in the diagnosis and treatment of transsexuals.

Medical professionals had to differentiate between transsexuality and homosexuality in order to legitimate transsexuality as a disorder in its own right. In the early 1970s, gay liberationists challenged the homophobia of the medical profession and lobbied psychiatrists to acknowledge that homosexuality was not a disorder. Psychiatrists were open to this discussion because attempts at curing homosexuality had been largely unsuccessful. As a result, homosexuality was removed from the 1974 edition of the American Psychiatric Association's *Diagnostic and Statistical Manual of Mental Disorders* (*DSM-III*). Meanwhile, psychiatrists lobbied to get "gender identity disorder" (now gender dysphoria) added to the *DSM*, and collaborated with surgeons, endocrinologists and other medical profes-sionals to open gender programs to treat individuals they diagnosed as transsexuals.

In 1966, the same year that Harry Benjamin published *The Transsexual Phenomenon*, the first gender program was opened and initiated a move to give professional legitimacy to the diagnosis and treatment of transsex-uality. The opening of the Johns Hopkins gender program ushered in an era of centralizing the diagnosis and treatment of transsexuality in university-based programs. Medical and psychotherapeutic professionals believed transsexuals could be better served through these gender programs than through relationships transsexuals established with surgeons and endocrinologists.[4] These programs were the primary means for transsexuals to access hormonal and surgical treatments in the 1970s.

Gender professionals considered themselves pioneers administering a great service to a dysphoric population forced to live homosexual lives. Driven by the desire to transform their bodies to align with their gender identity, many transsexuals simply told authorities at the gender programs what they wanted to hear rather than chance disclosing any seemingly aberrant thoughts, feelings or experiences that might prevent them from accessing transitioning services. Sadly, this repetitious catering to the medical definition of transsexuality resulted in transsexuals inadvertently reinforcing the medical experts' authority and heteronormative biases in transsexual diagnosis and treatment.

Interestingly, although there was nothing in the medical literature about gay FTMs, neither was there was anything specifically stating that gay sexual orientation meant one was not transsexual. In fact, Lou met all of the diagnostic criteria identified in the Standards of Care and by the Stanford University Gender Dysphoria Program, so technically he should have been accepted into Stanford's program despite identifying as gay.

The Standards of Care (SOC) codified the methods of diagnosis and treatment implemented by the gender programs over the previous decade.[5] The SOC had been drafted by six experts in the field, including psychotherapist Paul Walker, whom Lou would later meet, and surgeon Donald R. Laub, who headed Stanford's Gender Dysphoria Program along with psychotherapist Norman Fisk.[6]

The SOC was approved in 1979 at the Sixth International Gender Dysphoria Symposium, where the Harry Benjamin International Gender Dysphoria Association (HBIGDA) was also officially founded and named after the man whose work inspired the field. Today, HBIGDA is known as the World Professional Association for Transgender Health (WPATH), and the organization continues to publish (and revise) the SOC to provide guidance to health professionals to assist trans people in achieving optimal health as their "gendered selves."[7]

On the whole, HBIGDA members from university-affiliated gender programs tended to be more conservative in their diagnosis and treatment than their counterparts in private practice, and in the early years of the association these members made up the majority. But in time HBIGDA's Standards of Care would bring about a transition in who was diagnosing and treating transsexuality and how they were doing so. Ratification of the SOC helped decentralize transsexual medical services by providing a protocol that private practitioners could follow in their own diagnosis and treatment of transsexuality.[8]

The SOC was adopted as the industry standard, but it was hard to enforce and subject to interpretation. Programs like the one at Stanford added their own diagnostic criteria to determine whom they would allow into their program for treatment. Stanford did not include sexual orientation as grounds for rejection from their program in any of their official documents or publications about their program in peer-reviewed medical journals, which Lou had read prior to applying there.[9]

Lou called the Center for Special Problems to get a requisite referral for the Stanford program. Lou did not see his previous psychotherapist, who likely did not submit a referral to Stanford the first time Lou asked in 1976, but found the new therapist no more receptive to his request. The note in Lou's file stating he had previously considered transitioning but changed his mind gave the new therapist pause. But more importantly, Lou saw himself as a gay man, and an effeminate one at that. Despite Georgia's caution, Lou was candid in disclosing this information. And the therapist declined to write a referral for Lou in favor of ongoing therapy.[10] While the therapist did not explain why, it is likely he hoped therapy would help Lou live as a straight woman.

CALLING IN THE REINFORCEMENTS

Lou despaired at the thought that transitioning was foreclosed to him because he identified as gay and refused to pretend otherwise. He knew who he was but lacked the validation of a therapist to assist him in embodying his identity. Lou was lying in bed one day, tears welling up over what he presumed to be a hopeless situation, when psychotherapist Lin Fraser called him.[11]

Lou had initially met Fraser at a GGG/G meeting back in January 1979. Fraser, who was not trans herself, was given honorary membership in the organization for her work with and on behalf of trans people. As an honorary member, she shared information and support with other members but never assumed a leadership role. Fraser differed markedly from the therapist Lou had seen at the Center. First and foremost, she unquestionably validated Lou's identity as a gay man. Also, Fraser had a private practice and her treatment of gender dysphoria was patient-oriented. She credited her patients with teaching her much of what she knew about diagnosing and treating transsexuality.[12] Fraser not only learned from her patients but from other trans people as well. Her interactions with trans people outside of the therapist office set Fraser apart from her colleagues.

Aware of his plight, Fraser had consulted with Steve Dain on Lou's behalf, and now called Lou to share that Dain wanted to meet with him.[13] After the media furor over his transition, Dain had been unable to secure another teaching position and began working as a trans counselor, both independently and for the National Sex Forum. By connecting Lou with Dain rather than having him see her in a professional capacity, Fraser was granting both men the power of self-determination and unequivocal validation.

Lou was initially nervous about meeting Dain, for he had never met another FTM in the flesh before. However, Dain's friendliness quickly put Lou at ease, and made him feel "like for the 1st time I was talking with someone who understood what I meant."[14] Dain asked Lou the same questions as the therapist at the Center, but Lou's experience meeting with Dain differed remarkably. For one thing, after eliciting Lou's transsexual narrative, he asked Lou if he had any questions *for him*. Lou asked him practical questions, primarily about the effects of taking hormones.[15] When Lou told Dain that he did not feel like a "man trapped in a woman's body," Dain laughed and said that no one did—that was just a catchy phrase coined by the medical profession.[16]

Dain also told Lou that being transsexual does not dictate anything other than one's feelings about oneself, and that Lou had a perfect right to be a gay man if that was what he wanted. Dain shared with Lou that he was counseling another female who felt like a gay man and cruised gay men in the Castro. It angered Dain that the (non-trans) medical professionals specializing in the diagnosis and treatment of transsexuality felt that transsexuals had to "fit a prescribed mold," and a decidedly heteronormative one. Dain told Lou he was behind him all the way, and that he should call Lin Fraser for a referral to an endocrinologist. Lou no longer had to get a referral from the Center or go through Stanford for hormonal therapy.[17] Lou sincerely thanked Dain for his support and encouragement:

I really needed for someone <u>who</u> <u>knows</u> to acknowledge the importance of the feelings I have had for so long.… I can see the pieces of my life falling into place and am extremely optimistic about my future. You've helped me more than you may know.[18]

The day after meeting with Dain, Lou called Fraser and she gave him a referral to an endocrinologist named Dr. George Fulmer. With the implementation of the Standards of Care, HBIGDA-affiliated psychotherapists like Fraser could recommend an individual for hormonal therapy, supplementing "an elite cadre of clinical specialists" as gate-keepers for transsexual treatment.[19] Displaying her patient-oriented slant, Fraser said she trusted Dain's and Lou's judgment in diagnosing Lou's transsexuality better than her own.[20]

The liberalization of trans health care services created by the SOC enabled Lou, through personal relationships and community contacts, to secure a referral for an endocrinologist and set up an appointment right away—regardless of his sexual orientation.[21] However, Dain recommended that Lou still apply to Stanford.[22] The changes to trans people's medical services access were only recently underway, and Stanford's program was established and had been in operation longer than the SOC. More importantly, Stanford's Dr. Laub was a world-renowned surgeon, so Lou felt confident placing his body in Laub's skilled hands.

Upon the recommendation of Dain, who had gone through Stanford's program himself, Lou sent a letter to Stanford asking to be admitted to their program. He listed Dain and Fraser as referrals.[23] Lou knew that the existence of gay FTMs was denied by gender professionals, but he also knew there were others like him who identified as gay. His identification was validated by Dain, and he had an appointment to meet with an endocrinologist to begin taking hormones. In Lou's mind he had done everything he could to live happily without transitioning. But in order to actualize his identity and live as a gay man, Lou had to physically transition and believed Stanford's program was the best place for surgery. "I keep thinking what a relief it will be to be in the gay men's world, finally, as a man," Lou reflected in his journal. "[M]y outward appearance & my mind will be together—for the first time!"[24]

STYMIED BY STANFORD

The Stanford University Gender Dysphoria Program was arguably the most reputable program in existence. Psychotherapist Dr. Norman Fisk and surgeon Dr. Donald Laub headed Stanford's program. Laub was on the board of directors for HBIGDA and helped draft its Standards of Care. Laub and Fisk had a much more conservative approach to diagnosis and treatment than Lin Fraser, whose faith in trans people's self-identification exemplified the more progressive strain of HBIGDA membership. University-affiliated members were highly critical of treating trans people based on self-diagnosis.[25] They conceded to referring to trans people as "consumers," but still felt authorized to determine who was eligible to utilize their services—who was or was not transsexual.

Programs like the one at Stanford were inundated with applications. Demand exceeded supply and the reputations of both the gender professionals and their universities were on the line. As a result, programs would only accept those who best reflected their ideas of who was (or should be) transsexual.[26] Lou's experiences with Stanford reveal underlying homophobic bias because sexuality became a deciding factor in diagnosing and treating his transsexuality.

At Stanford, applicants' transsexual life narratives—elicited through a lengthy, open-ended application—were weighted heavily in the admissions process.[27] For transsexuals, narrative serves as the means to the end of embodiment, because in order to access the medical technology for physical transition, transsexuals first have to convince clinicians that they are in fact transsexuals.[28] In large part, to be admitted to the Stanford program—or nearly any other gender program—applicants' narratives had to read like the archetypal transsexual narrative.[29] For all intents and purposes, Lou's transsexual narrative fit the archetypal story of transsexuality that the gender professional sought. He had experienced discomfort with being female since his youth. Lou had a strong desire to live as a man and had succeeded in being read as one for several years. He did not suffer from any mental disorders or neurotic symptoms, but rather was healthy and well-adjusted with the exception of his identifying as a man. However, there was one exception to him fulfilling the archetype: Lou identified as gay.

In the past three years Lou had recounted his transsexual biography many times over, including to Stanford, therapists at the Center for Special Problems, Steve Dain, Liz Fraser, members of GGG/G, numerous correspondents, family, friends and lovers. As with other transsexuals, he had become an "arch storyteller," consistently structuring a narrative filtered through the lens of gender dysphoria—and consistently claiming he wanted to be a gay man.[30]

In his application Lou candidly portrayed himself as well-adjusted, confident and comfortable in his gay identity. In response to what made him a "particularly good candidate," Lou wrote: "I am incredibly stable, logical, and responsible. I know myself, am self-analytical and reflective (I have kept a diary since I was 11 years old). I have been participating in the gay men's world for over 6 years and know I belong." The only thing Lou lacked was male embodiment to actualize his gay identity.[31]

Five months went by before Lou received a rejection letter from Stanford. Unlike the first time he applied, Lou followed up on his application this go-round. In January 1980, three months after submitting his application, Lou sent a letter of inquiry and an update informing them that he had been receiving testosterone injections since November and that his family and employer were "wholly supportive in [his] plans."[32] Two months later Stanford wrote back informing him that: "We have carefully reviewed your patient summary sheet and based on the information you provided, we have decided that we cannot be of assistance to you."

Stanford would not explicitly state that they rejected Lou because of his sexual orientation. Instead, they vaguely claimed that "[t]he history which [Lou] presented was not typical for the majority of persons who, in our program, have made successful adjustments with gender reorientation and who have been helped, not harmed, by sex reassignment."[33] Lou contacted Stanford in response and called them out on their homophobia, challenging their ability to identify transsexuals:

> It is unfortunate that your Program cannot see the merit of each individual, regardless of their sexual orientation. The general human populace is made up of many sexual persuasions—it is incredible that your Program requires all transsexuals to be of one fabric. I had even considered lying to you about my sexual preference of men, as I knew this would surely keep me out of your Program, but I felt it important to be straightforward, possibly paving the way for other female-to-males with homosexual orientations— and we do exist.[34]

T Time

While the transition in trans health care brought on by the Standards of Care granted transsexuals greater agency over their identification, it was far from fool-proof. At Lou's first appointment with his endocrinologist, Dr. Fulmer asked him "all the same questions about my life and feelings" as Stanford had, and told Lou that he hesitated to give him hormones because Lou was not interested in women. For a second opinion Fulmer sent Lou to see clinical psychologist Dr. Wardell Pomeroy.[35]

Pomeroy was dean of the Institute for Advanced Study of Human Sexuality and director of its parent organization, the National Sex Forum, which was housed in San Francisco's Tenderloin. Pomeroy was a colleague of Dr. Alfred Kinsey's and co-authored the revolutionary *Sexual Behavior in the Human Male* and *Sexual Behavior in the Human Female,* a.k.a. the Kinsey Reports. During the 1950s, Pomeroy collected data on transvestites and transsexuals for the Kinsey Institute. In the mid-1960s Pomeroy worked with Harry Benjamin, and in 1975 he published an article titled "The Diagnosis and Treatment of Transvestites and Transsexuals."[36]

To Lou's delight, Steve Dain sat in on his meeting with Dr. Pomeroy. Pomeroy went through a stream of questions that were very similar to those on the Stanford application. As always, Lou was honest and thorough in his responses, and was excited to have Pomeroy exclaim, "it's fine to be a gay man!!!!!!" In a matter of minutes Pomeroy agreed with Dain that Lou was fit for hormone replacement therapy. Lou was elated: "I'm actually going to live as a man. I can't believe it. Something I've wanted to do since I can remember—be a boy! God, it's too good to be true."[37] Unfortunately it *was* too good to be true as Dr. Fulmer proceeded to give Lou the run-around for a month and a half due to his lingering concerns about Lou identifying as gay. However, Pomeroy interceded and on November 16, 1979, Lou got his first shot of testosterone "in the ass," which he found amusingly appropriate.[38]

When Lou told his family and friends that he was beginning the process of transitioning, he received overwhelming support. Lou's siblings recounted childhood memories of Lou's acting like a boy and told him they felt like he already interacted with his nephews like he was their uncle.[39] Flame and the Sullivan sisters' boyfriends invited him to "boys' nights out," treating Lou "like one of their own."[40] Lou's mother said if that was what he wanted and what made him happy, and if he and the doctors agreed that was what was best for him, who was she to try and stop him?[41] His father Jack told Lou he was glad he was doing something to make himself feel better, and offered to help Lou in any way he could. Jack also said he felt very close to Lou after their conversation.[42] Lou's female co-workers were also very supportive (including those who had taken an interest in his feminizing attempts), as was his boss, who offered to give Lou glowing recommendations in his male name. Lou found that the "usual reaction" when he told people was that his transitioning was "neat" and "exciting," and also that others in turn "spill[ed] out their hidden secrets" to him.[43]

Lou marveled at the physical transformations brought on by injecting testosterone into his body. He examined himself in the mirror with anticipation and recorded each change he noticed in his journal. He noticed an increase in his sex drive almost immediately, followed shortly by a change in his voice. As his voice changed, Lou found himself wanting to talk more and liking what he had to say. He imagined that he could feel a tingling sensation as hairs grew on his upper lip. The thought of his having a mustache when kissing a man made him "crazy." To Lou, it seemed hairs appeared overnight on his legs and stomach. Lou noticed his clitoris enlarging, and decided to start wearing a jock strap stuffed with socks formed into the shape of a penis and testicles because he felt better with a bulge in his pants. "So this isn't all an illusion," he thought. "I am going to be a man. I can't describe how good I feel about myself."[44]

The most noticeable change in Lou during the first months of testosterone injections was his relationship to his body and how he perceived himself. Lou now felt confident about actively participating in San Francisco's gay sexual subculture. He began one evening in January 1980 by going to see a gay porn movie. Lou took a seat in the theater, and partway through the movie a man sat down next to him. Lou became slightly nervous that his "sock-penis & balls might not pass" as the two began fondling each other, and indicated through his actions that "I would do him but he couldn't do me." Eventually the man left and Lou headed to the drag bars, where he noticed how his perspectives had changed since beginning hormone therapy: "Instead of just watching the show & feeling self-conscious & worried I'd be read [as female], I was aware of who I liked & who was looking at me. Now when someone's looking, I think they're cruising me instead of reading me."

Lou caught the eye of a drag queen, and they left the bar together. On their way to Lou's apartment, he informed her that he was taking male hormones when she admitted that he was a bit feminine for her tastes. Once at his apartment Lou was embarrassed to disrobe, "but she was really free & open & told me not to be that way, that we are all okay no matter what we are." The drag queen made Lou feel relaxed and good about himself, and after they had engaged in anal sex, she told Lou that he "was going to make a really great gay boy!" Lou was ecstatic to have "finally… succeeded in getting a drag queen!"—fulfilling a dream born almost ten years ago when he first read John Rechy's *City of Night.*[45]

Unfortunately the excitement and confidence that Lou felt at the outset of transitioning soon began to wane. Lou worried that the changes made to his body by testosterone were insufficient for sexual liaisons with gay men. Furthermore, he assumed gay men would know nothing about transsexuality, and that he would be unable to "fool" them into believing he was cisgender like them.

So Lou tried pursuing relationships with an MTF, a feminine straight man and a lesbian, but these attempts did nothing to strengthen his confidence in or comfort with being transsexual. When Lou "put the heavy move" on an MTF he met at a drag bar, she said, "No! You're doing the same thing I'm doing except… No!!!" Another night Lou met a "small cute guy" at a "punk rock place" with whom he talked all night and "got along famously." The man was shocked when Lou invited him over to his place and disclosed to him that he was gay. The man shocked Lou in return by asking Lou if he was transsexual. He was familiar with Steve Dain and had seen a letter from him on Lou's desk, beside a book on transsexuality. When Lou expressed interest in him, the man said that he "couldn't get it on with me 'because as far as I'm concerned,' he said, 'you're a man',", and he was not attracted to men. Though the man had validated Lou's masculinity, Lou still felt rejected by his not wanting to have sex with him.[46] Two weeks later, hanging out at his favorite Polk Street gay men's bar, Lou approached a lesbian he found attractive, and "Hoping it would attract her to me, I told her I was a F-M TS. It didn't work." For the first time in a long time Lou "cried bitterly" and, against his better judgment, decided to try avoiding initial disclosure in the future.[47]

A month later, after dancing in the gay bars all night, Lou "was drunk & so damn starved for physical contact" that he positioned himself against a building on Polk Street "like all the other young hustlers." Lou was approached by a man who he described as being "a very 'screaming faggot' type, about 45 years old, but with a lean enough body." Lou told him that he lived close by, and they got into the man's car. Once they got to Lou's apartment he told the man his "conditions" were "that I don't take off my clothes, that I have a birth defect I don't want him to see, but that I'll do him." After awhile Lou decided to "risk it," and disrobed from the waist down. Lou was shocked that the man "couldn't really tell." When Lou eventually "told him what my scene was," the man worried that "this must mean he's really not a queer after all, etc.," but Lou assured him "I'm a boy." By the end of the night the man told Lou "that I'd put a lot of boys to shame," a compliment that elated Lou.[48]

Lou's confidence increased with the support of the trans community, his family and his ability to "pass" in social situations. Members of GGG/G regularly complimented Lou on how good he looked and how natural he was as a man.[49] When Lou met with Dain he was also complimentary of Lou's appearance.[50] Lou visited Milwaukee and was surprised when family members regularly referred to him by male pronouns. During the course of his visit, several people, including his mother, father and Patrick's girlfriend, pointed out how eerily he resembled his deceased brother. The purpose of the trip was to drive Flame's old car out to San Francisco. The car gave Lou and Flame's girlfriend Kathy terrific problems the entire way, and they ended up getting in an accident in Wyoming. Whether dealing with mechanics, truckers, or police, Lou noted that he "passed without any question on every occasion."[51]

TAKE IT FROM THE TOP

Despite the noticeable changes accrued from hormone replacement therapy, Lou believed that with chest reconstruction he would not "feel so awkward being a man," especially sexually.[52] Steve Dain recommended that Lou contact Dr. Edward Falces for top surgery. Falces was a plastic surgeon who ran a private practice in San Francisco and cofounded the Reconstructive Surgery Foundation (now part of RSF-Earthspeak), which provided free reconstructive surgery in developing countries.[53]

When Lou made an appointment with Falces, the receptionist followed the Standards of Care protocol and told him to bring in letters from Dr. Fulmer regarding his hormone therapy and from Dr. Pomeroy regarding his initial diagnosis.[54] While awaiting his appointment with Falces, Lou assured himself that he deserved a male chest. "This torture has gone on long enough," he wrote in his journal.

> I want to look in the mirror while lifting my weights & see
> a strong healthy body, not the hodge-podge of flesh I see
> now. I deserve to press a man against my solid hard chest,

feel his against mine, and have him feel mine against his. That's what my heart feels, that's what I want to express to him…. I deserve to have that pleasure, that freedom, that relief.

During his appointment, Falces set a date for Lou's surgery: July 15, 1980. Like Pomeroy, Falces saw no reason why Lou should not be able to undergo surgery and told him that he was "a very good candidate," leaving Lou to remark that he "loved dealing with these professionals." Drs. Falces and Pomeroy did not exhibit any signs of homophobia and acknowledged Lou's autonomy. Falces was also respectful in his choice of words (i.e., using "chest" instead of "breasts"), which was exemplary bedside manner for the time and greatly appreciated by Lou. After meeting with Falces, Lou felt like he could do anything, be anything that he wanted, that he could "challenge the wind…."[55]

Now Lou again marveled at the transformations he was undergoing, both physically and psychologically. "I love the sound of my voice, I laugh a lot, join in a lot, feel intelligent, worthy of attention, open to new ideas, new experiences. I can be silly, or wrong, or stupid, & not feel ashamed," he reflected. He also noticed a sudden interest in all men's bodies, wanting "to examine their shapes, their tastes, their smells, their textures," as he mentally explored all of the sexual possibilities available to him as a man.[56]

Two weeks after his appointment with Falces, Lou "finally had the nerve" to go into the backroom of a gay porn theater. The backroom enabled Lou to see all types of male bodies and to realize that if he underwent the same genital reconstructive surgery as Dain, he could "pass off as good as these guys did!" Lou did not have to undress in the backroom and he participated without hesitation. What "surprised & truly delighted" Lou about his experience in the backroom was "the display of affections & feelings going on in these reputed dens of anonymous sex." He had not expected such moments of tenderness to transpire among strangers engaging in anonymous "public sex," and in his journal this is how Lou summed up his experience: "Somehow those brief displays of tenderness between two men mean more to me than I can say…"[57]

As the date of his surgery approached, Lou began feeling distant from those to whom he was closest. Lou put a lot of weight into the significance of his surgery, imagining that he would wake up a different person, which made him wonder how his loved ones could act as if nothing out of the ordinary was occurring.[58] In Lou's mind, this surgery would not merely transform his body but turn him into a man. The protocol for "sex reassignment" and the medical literature on transsexuality contributed to this way of thinking. In medical parlance, transsexuality was a psychological disorder treated through physical means. Because the effects of hormone replacement therapy were deemed largely reversible, great emphasis was placed upon determining good surgical candidates. Case studies of "post-operative transsexuals" were used to justify or rework the criteria used by medical professionals to determine optimal candidates for surgery. In the Standards of Care and information Lou had received from Stanford, "cross-living" and hormone therapy were necessary proof that an individual would benefit from surgery; surgical candidates had to go through a "trial period" proving they could live as men in order to become men.[59]

By medical standards, sex was—is—changed with surgery. Due to the nature of the relationship between transsexual individuals and the medical establishment, transsexuals understandably placed great importance on surgery as well. In fact, the climax of the transsexual narrative—a narrative employed by gender professionals but adopted by transsexuals even outside the context of accessing medical services—was sex reassignment surgery. Little wonder, then, that in the weeks following his surgery Lou was surprised to notice that "since my surgery, I feel I should be changed, I should somehow be 'different' now. But I don't really FEEL different.... I'm not more 'male' than I was before."[60]

Lou was, however, more confident. He experienced a surge in confidence after his surgery, just as he had after beginning testosterone injections. Lou committed himself to remaining single, taking the time to adjust to his bodily transformations.[61] He viewed this time as important for "building this solid good person who deserves someone's love and who has something to offer to someone who deserves my love."[62] But for Lou, being single did not entail celibacy. On the contrary, he soon found himself commenting upon the fact that he had more sexual partners in the year since he began transitioning than he had had in the previous ten years.

To illustrate, one evening Lou met "a goddamn angel" at the gay discos on Polk Street—an unabashedly gay sailor who was docked in San Francisco for the weekend.[63] Lou marveled at this man who "appear[ed] very straight" but was "completely uninhibited in his sexual desire for a man"—who in this case happened to be Lou. Lou undressed completely when they got to his apartment. The white sailor seemed aware of Lou's anatomy but never asked any questions and treated Lou just like any other gay man he had spent the night with. He asked Lou about the Club Baths, leading Lou to declare "this guy is a real life homosexual," and Lou watched him closely "trying to learn from him."[64]

Two weeks later Lou "had another date with an angel," this time a white California highway patrolman who was "very affectionate." Lou did not completely disrobe, and the patrolman never questioned that Lou was a gay man.[65] The following month Lou had "another fling," this time with a white bisexual MTF transsexual.

> It was pretty fun & I was turned on all right—my first time with a female, tho I don't know how much her being a TS helped. I think a lot, as I wouldn't have pursued her had she been a genetic female. (I should think that over & reorganize my prejudices.) Though fun, being with her could in no way compare to the passion I've felt with other men.[66]

For Lou, nothing validated his gay identity more than having sex with gay men. Conversely, nothing triggered his self-doubt more than gay men sexually rejecting him.

Shortly after his "fling" with the MTF, Lou had three sexual interactions in less than a month that left him feeling rejected and insecure about his transsexual embodiment. The first was with an extremely feminine Latino. When Lou stripped down to his jockey shorts, the man quickly gathered up his things and left.[67] The second involved an older white man who refused to honor Lou's wishes to not be touched, and Lou felt forced to inform him that he was "deformed" and "[had] no cock."[68] And the third incident involved a feminine black man. "All fine until he discovered I had no cock," according to Lou. "Then at the same time he claimed it made no difference, he couldn't get a hard-on thereafter & kept asking 'What ARE you?!!!' though I explained in minute detail over & over. Then he remembered he had to leave."[69] Lou suddenly found himself having recurring dreams about "having to go back to being a girl," and even briefly considered getting back together with Mark, despite his discomfort with Lou's transsexuality.[70]

Lou also experienced moments of social validation that enabled him to forget his transsexual embodiment and feel like he was accepted unequivocally as a gay man. In early 1981 he reflected on this at length:

[I]t's been happening more & more often that I am walking along the street & am looking appreciatively at a man, and he looks at me, our eyes meet, I see a sparkle in his, and we smile and nod, acknowledging each other's appreciation. And when he's gone, I soar, I feel totally worthwhile, so satisfied with my life, so filled with loving feelings, that the isolation caused by my incomplete body is not all that important. I have more true love in my life now than I ever did—isn't that hard to understand? I can barely understand it myself. But it makes me know that what I've done, what I'm doing, is right, and that everything will turn out well.

But Lou still found it difficult to "allow myself the pleasure of finally being one of my group, [to] finally join the class of gay men, letting myself fit in the way I feel I do," because when it came to sex—which for Lou and others was the primary means of validating one's gay identity—he could not forget his transsexual embodiment.[71] When Lou looked in the mirror, he could "hardly believe how beautiful" he was. "I feel so desirable, yet I can't offer myself to a partner," he believed. "If I had a man's genitals I could be so much freer with potential lovers."[72]

Steve Dain encouraged Lou to find pleasure in his body as it was. He also showed him how it could be by sharing with Lou his metoidioplasty with testicular implants that he had undergone with Dr. Laub at Stanford. "His whole body looked beautifully male," Lou commented in his journal, "& I was really relieved" because Lou felt that type of surgery would enable him to engage in sex with gay men without batting an eye.[74] But whereas it was relatively easy for Lou to find an endocrinologist to administer testosterone and a surgeon to perform top surgery, he would find it quite difficult to access genital reconstructive surgery.

FTM FOREFATHER

As Lou struggled through the elaborate and multi-faceted process of transitioning, he was compelled to map out and help others navigate the process as Dain had for him. While Lou simply may have been in the right place at the right time, it is undeniable that as Lou physically transitioned and grew as an FTM leader, the number of individuals identifying as FTM grew dramatically.

Dain helped Lou to physically transition and to become a forefather of the FTM community. Dain modeled mentorship for Lou and encouraged him to become an FTM spokesman. One day when Dain had a prior engagement, he asked Lou to fill in for him as a speaker at the Institute for Advanced Study of Human Sexuality. The Institute's instructors and students enjoyed Lou's compelling and informative presentations so much that he began speaking to classes on a regular basis. Lou liked to inform the audience not to rely too much on their textbooks because according to them, he—a gay FTM—did not exist.[75] Lou so valued the opportunity to speak to these professionals, many of whom would take on trans patients, that only severe illness could keep him away.

Lou would become a regular speaker at the Institute for the next ten years, but over the next couple of years Lou's work on behalf of the trans community largely took shape in written form. Publications and letters did the essential work of fostering identity and creating a sense of community at a time when so little information was available to FTMs—that physical communities were as yet unable to exist. Lou continued to publish articles in *GPU News*, and he edited and largely wrote GGG/G's newsletter *The Gateway* until the fall of 1980. At that time Lou quit publishing *The Gateway* and reduced his participation in GGG/G to focus more on FTM matters. [76]

Lou decided to devote all of his activist time to working with psycho-therapist Dr. Paul Walker at the Janus Information Facility. Walker was one of the six gender professionals selected to draft the Standards of Care and served as HBIGDA's first chairperson.[77] He had, in his words, "pretty much [run] the gender clinic" at Johns Hopkins University from 1969-1976, then directed the gender program at the University of Texas Medical Branch before moving to San Francisco and opening a private practice.[78] Walker became a spokesperson for transsexuality in the Bay Area and collaborated with trans people in his outreach.

Volunteering with Janus provided Lou with a venue in which to incorporate his trans and gay identities. Lou frequently disclosed in his correspondences that he was gay, and in Paul Walker Lou had another gay man with whom he could speak about his transsexuality.[79] Although from time to time Lou and Walker would teasingly flirt with one another, their relationship remained platonic.

Lou's volunteer work consisted primarily of answering letters sent by FTMs to the Janus Information Facility. Letters came from individuals across the U.S. and around the world. The volume of letters they received was so immense that at one point they received approximately 500 letters in the space of two days. The trauma that some of these FTMs endured, especially those hailing from "tiny rural Southern towns," made Lou feel like his struggles paled in comparison.[80]

Lou's correspondents wrote to Janus for more information about accessing transsexual services, and Lou responded by not only sharing information about services but also about his personal experiences. Many continued corresponding with Lou because he was knowledgeable, sympathetic, nonjudgmental, caring, and oftentimes the only other FTM they knew.[81] Lou was fulfilling his teenage desire to help "wayward boys" and becoming the FTM mentor, friend and confidant he himself had yearned for for many years.

In October 1980 Lou began work on what many trans men would later refer to as their bible: an informational booklet titled *Information for the Female-to-Male Crossdresser and Transsexual*, which was published and distributed by Janus.[82] The first edition was so well received that Lou published a second edition in 1986 and a third one in 1990, both with updated and expanded information. Although Lou's primary audience was other FTMs, his booklet was also widely read by gender professionals and loved ones of FTMs.

Information for the Female-to-Male Crossdresser and Transsexual was unique in its attention to FTMs and its discussion of medical topics from a trans perspective. One of the biggest sections, "How to Look 30 When You <u>Are</u> 30," provided practical tips on how to be read as a man. "The biggest problem when going female-to-male," Lou wrote, "is that a 30-year-old female, when crossdressed as a man, can end up looking like a 14-year-old boy."[83] In the second biggest section, "Sex Reassignment," Lou outlined the process of acquiring and administering hormone replacement therapy, and described the surgical processes of top surgery (which he acknowledged most FTM transsexuals were "especially interested in") and bottom surgery (warning that there was "still no successful surgical technique" that would enable one to urinate and ejaculate through the penis and have an erection for penetrative sex).[84]

Lou's booklet not only filled a void in publications by and about FTMs, it also established two important expectations about being FTM. First, he matter-of-factly identified the sexual partners of FTMs in his booklet as being either female or male.[85] Lou now knew several FTMs who identified as gay men (primarily through correspondence) and simultaneously assumed and normalized his readers' awareness that FTMs were not inherently attracted to women. Second, Lou included both transvestites/crossdressers and transsexuals in the definition of FTM. Though Lou stopped identifying as an FTM transvestite, he considered it a viable identity category and argued for its existence for the rest of his life. This inclusiveness was reminiscent of Milwaukee's Gay People's Union and laid the foundation for an FTM community comprised of all individuals across the transmasculine spectrum.

Lou's booklet became indispensable reading by and about FTMs. He had written what he himself had spent years searching for: a thorough, factual and accessible source of information that identified and validated his feelings and provided practical steps for actualizing his identity. Lou's booklet and other work at Janus garnered him a certain celebrity among other FTMs. For many, Lou was the first FTM they knew or knew of. Individuals began making cross-country trips to see Lou, to meet another FTM in person. The first time that this happened, Lou wrote in his journal that the FTM from Denver "was as thrilled about meeting me (possibly more) than I was when I met Dain."[86] And by the spring of 1981 there were enough FTMs in the Bay Area to hold an informal gathering in San Jose.[87]

Many of these Bay Area FTMs had gone through Stanford's program, including Jude Patton, who attended the San Jose gathering. Patton was another FTM pioneer who started a publication for transsexuals called *Renaissance Newsletter*, gave lectures to medical professionals and college students, and from 1979-1981 served as the first and only transsexual member of the HBIGDA board. Eventually Patton's organization J2CP, which he started with Sister Mary Elizabeth (then Joanna) Clark, would inherit the educational work of Janus when it ceased operations.[88]

The gathering enabled activists like Lou and Patton to "talk shop," but its primary purpose was fellowship. The majority of those in attendance, including Lou, had never been around more than one or two FTMs at a time. Those in attendance shared their experiences, challenges and surgical alterations with one another, but the greatest benefit to the gathering was being surrounded by others who *understood*—without need of explanation or justification. The gathering allowed them to simply be and to be in community with one another. Lou attended several of these informal gatherings over the next few years, joining other FTMs from around the state to spend a couple of hours hanging out together.

Transitioning Jobs and Homes

Lou's employer was very supportive of him transitioning on the job at Wilson Sporting Goods. His boss did everything in his power to make the process easy for Lou, but Lou's fellow employees either struggled or refused to use the correct name and pronouns.[89] So Lou decided to look for another job where he would only be known as a man and no one knew his past. While he wanted an interesting job with growth potential, Lou was more interested in simply working to pay the rent—which allowed him to devote more time and energy to his activist work—rather than to build a career.[90]

Lou found it difficult to get hired as a male secretary. Eventually, at the end of August 1980, he was hired as an "administrative aid" at ARCO Engineering, Inc., a position that Lou (correctly) interpreted as being a male secretary.[91] His former employers at Wilson Sporting Goods and University of Wisconsin-Milwaukee gave him glowing references that provided no indication Lou had transitioned or ever lived or worked as anything other than a man. At ARCO Lou was "just another youngman working," and he felt very masculine and professional working at his new job. An added benefit to the job was that it was located downtown, where there were "amazingly beautiful men all over," and "not too infrequently one will look at me as intently as I at him," which made Lou "want to melt with passion."[92]

Working as a man at ARCO, Lou benefited from white male privilege. He was smart and a hard worker, and as usual became bored with his secretarial work. When he put in his two weeks' notice at ARCO in hopes of finding a job that felt more interesting and meaningful, his boss responded by offering him a raise and stating that he was "overqualified for the job"—something Lou had never been told as a female secretary.[93] Word of Lou's putting in his notice quickly spread amongst the managers at ARCO and he was soon approached by a manager from the Engineering Department about working for him. He told Lou "That he doesn't need a 'secretary' but someone to organize him," and that Lou had leadership potential.[94] The new job resulted in a promotion, and he received another promotion the following year.

When Lou was promoted to Associate Engineering Technician in the summer of 1982, he was put in the position of hiring his own secretary. Lou chose a white woman working for the company who he felt had gotten "the shaft" from her former boss for being a lesbian. Her former boss warned

Lou that she had an "attitude problem," which Lou interpreted as being her disinterest in her male superiors' sexual harassment. When Lou offered her the job, she told him "I always wanted to work for a faggot," and he thought, "she'll work out fine."[95]

Lou was comfortable with being out as gay at work, but not with being out as trans. The gay liberation movement and widespread visibility and acceptance of gays in San Francisco emboldened Lou to be out as gay. Though no legal protection existed, Lou did not fear for his safety or fear losing his job because he had a certain level of social protection as a gay man in San Francisco during the early 1980s. Trans people, on the other hand, were at best treated as tabloid fodder by the mainstream, were largely excluded from the gay and women's liberation movements and did not yet have a movement of their own.

Lou panicked the day that one of his co-workers approached, informing him that there was a "rumor" at work that he had appeared on a talk show about transsexuality. Lou "denied the whole thing," and wrote in his journal that "[his co-worker] was very freaked out by it & said she knew it couldn't possibly have been me, because she knows I'm not that weird, etc. I assured her it wasn't, but could feel sweat forming on my forehead." In truth, Lou *had* appeared on a San Jose talk show about transsexuality, and agreed to do so because he was under the impression that no one in San Francisco would be able to view the show.[96]

At the outset, early tabloid talk shows sensationalized trans people to draw in their viewership, but their guests were transsexual activists and public figures who upended sensationalistic assumptions. When the shows' producers went looking for guests, those known to be trans were people who chose to out themselves for educational purposes. They were publicly trans so other transsexuals could privately go about their lives simply being men and women. These activists and public figures were experienced in thinking and talking about transsexuality and capitalized upon the television talk show medium, which gave them the opportunity to speak to the public about their lives and to do so in their own voices. More often than not, the audience tuned in to jeer—only to find themselves moved to tears.

Lou had agreed to do the talk show out of a desire to help educate the public about trans people, and he was additionally excited by the fact that he was able to use the show as an opportunity to raise awareness of the existence of gay FTMs.[97] But suddenly Lou's (public) trans activist self seemed to be threatening the (private) gay businessman self he was trying to construct. Too little was known about trans people, which made Lou fear that coming out at work would result in devastating repercussions. Lou had spent years struggling to incorporate his whole self only to discover a sense of self-preservation that demanded he compartmentalize his gay and trans identities, and his activist work and ARCO job. Lou spent a great deal of time and energy wanting to tell his co-workers he was transsexual yet working to ensure no one knew that he was.

At work, Lou stuck up for transsexuals when his lesbian secretary disapprovingly accused them of "fooling with nature," but hesitated to disclose that he himself was trans.[98] When another secretary told Lou that he never would have been promoted from administrative aid had he been female, Lou "felt like saying, 'Hey, I KNOW that!'" but did not for fear that she might suspect he was trans.[99] And when a woman at work asked Lou if being gay meant that he wanted to be a woman, saying that stories she had read about transsexuals "brought tears to her eyes," Lou decided to handle the situation by explaining to her the difference between sexual orientation and gender identity, consciously trying "to educate as much as possible without identifying too much with the sentiments." Lou often thought to himself, "If they only knew!" that he was transsexual and had lived as a woman.[100]

Lou not only opted for a new job after going on testosterone and undergoing top surgery, but a new home as well. By moving from the Tenderloin, where many people had known him before he began transitioning, Lou felt like he was "getting out there and being the gay man I've always wanted to be," and chose not to tell anyone in his new neighborhood that he was trans.[101] He briefly considered moving to the Castro but decided upon the neighboring Mission District instead, which was reflective of Lou's present belief that as an FTM he could be close to gay men but not at home among them.

When Lou moved in the spring of 1981, the Valencia Street corridor in "The Mission" was central to the punk scene, but still a predominantly Latino neighborhood. Initially, Lou described the neighborhood as "more questionable" than the Tenderloin because he experienced frequent verbal harassment for looking gay, "usually by teenaged Latino guys going by in cars."[102] Later, he would be shocked by all of the "action" he was getting in the Mission from "these macho Latinos [who] are supposed to be beating me up…"[103] Lou also had a brief relationship with a "good-looking black man" who he met at a neighborhood garage sale while looking for furniture for his new apartment. The man was very understanding and empathetic when Lou told him that he had a birth defect, but Lou found himself unable to fully disclose that he was transsexual and (therefore perhaps not surprisingly) unable to commit to a lasting relationship with him.[104] Lou loved the new life that he was making for himself as a gay man, and the more settled he became in his body and life, the more he wanted to share these things with someone special.

"MY WHOLE SEX CHANGE WAS WORTH IT!"

Gay Pride in June 1981 was like a dream come true for Lou, as he got the chance to join the ranks of gay men marching in the parade. Five years earlier the parade had made Lou cry with desperation and desire—a soul tormented within as he looked without. Now Lou wrote in almost magical terms of "Feeling lean and alive and beautiful—Saying I am a man—Saying I love men." He was enchanted by all of the "beautiful lusty men in this city" among whom he now walked.[105] But Lou's heart only yearned for one.

Earlier that week Lou had met a white, twenty-year-old "gorgeous boy" named Keith.[106] Uncharacteristically and to his astonishment, Lou fell in love with him immediately. Lou's initial impression of Keith led him to think, "It's supposed to work. One day I'll find someone who likes me so much [that being transsexual] won't matter."[107] Within a week of meeting Keith, Lou confessed his love for him, but Keith did not immediately return the sentiment. Lou was introduced to Keith by a heterosexual couple living in his building, and they insisted that Keith was "100% straight."[108] Keith himself repeatedly mentioned that Lou was gay and he was heterosexual, almost as if by doing so he could negate the obvious attraction that they felt toward one another.[109] Days stretched into weeks, which stretched into months.

In moments when he was not with Keith or thinking about Keith, Lou unquestioningly embraced his body and his gay identity. However, Lou's desire to have a serious and meaningful relationship with Keith caused him to feel ambivalence about being transsexual. For one thing, Lou viewed his present embodiment as an asset because Keith identified as heterosexual. When Keith told Lou "he just wanted an older woman to love him," Lou thought, "little does he know how close he's come."[110] But at the same time, Lou desperately wished to fully embody maleness, which in his mind would unequivocally make him the gay man Keith believed he was.

Furthermore, Lou felt that "All the interesting things I've done & am doing are [trans]-related," but he feared being rejected by cisgender people like Keith and his new friends in the Mission District if he told them about his activist work and trans embodiment.[111]

After seeing each other nearly every day for two months, Lou finally came out as trans, seemingly at Keith's urging. Keith told Lou that he had once slept with a man and that he found MTF transvestites attractive, which encouraged Lou to think they might have a chance at a relationship.[112] When Keith asked Lou why he always put tape on his chest when his shirt was off (a recommendation from Lou's surgeon to minimize scarring from his top surgery due to sun exposure) and passed on the tip that he had received that injecting testosterone could help Lou grow more facial hair and lower his voice more (not realizing that, unlike men like Keith, Lou already did so because he had been assigned female at birth), Lou decided to tell Keith that he was transsexual. Lou "tried to act as normal & un-freaked-out as I could" when he told Keith. Keith honored Lou's request not to tell others after Lou explained that he did not like how people acted differently toward him once they knew he was trans.[113] Lou wished to be treated as a man. A gay man. But not a *trans* gay man because he found that cisgender people had a harder time seeing him as a man when they knew that he had once lived as a woman. When it came to Keith, however, Lou cared more about Keith seeing all of him than about what exactly it was that he was seeing.

For better and worse, Keith did not treat Lou much differently for the first several days after Lou told him that he was trans. But then the emotional intimacy of their relationship began to manifest itself in physical form and Keith struggled to understand his attraction to Lou given that Lou was trans. According to Lou, "[Keith] said But I don't even know what you <u>are</u>! I said yes you do, I've been very honest with you." Lou told him "What I want is to be able to function as a gay man. But I can't. So I do whatever I can," and then "He said 'But what ARE you? You're not a man & you're not a woman!' I said well I guess I'm just ME then." When Keith asked him to take off his clothes, Lou "didn't feel self-conscious. I just stripped myself & thought: this is it, and I love you so goddamned much I'm laying myself at your feet. I can't be hurt. You can't hurt me, because I believe you love me too."[114] And Lou was "overwhelmed how good sex is with someone I love so much."[115] He marveled at how, with Keith, "<u>I am there</u> when I have sex."

I am not fantasizing about men together, or of some other sex scene—I am feeling my body against his—I am feeling his hands touching me—I am excited as I look at him as he looks at me. Such feelings I've never known. He always refers to me in the masculine & there is no doubt we are two men who love each other.[116]

Keith gave Lou a "sense of being part of the world" that he had "never experienced before." Keith made Lou "feel strong & good & as though I am important."[117] When Keith told Lou that he wanted to publish a magazine, Lou told him about *The Gateway*, and Keith wanted to revive it with him. But Lou was hesitant about "getting involved in being a 'TS,'" and about their friends finding out that he was transsexual. Keith supported and reassured Lou.

He made me feel it's OK to be what I am—I should not feel like I have to hide or suppress myself or be guilty or feel like a weird-o anymore. That I can keep my anonymity as much as I want while still being an authority on the subject I know best & can address better than anyone else. I have all the sources & connections I need to make it go.

Ultimately Lou told Keith that the "unhappiness of being female was still too fresh & it still hurt me," and that he did not want "to get back into doing a TV/TS publication because I'm tired of the subject & of identifying as a TS all the time."[118] But at the same time, Lou wanted to write about "how my [sex] change has opened up a new world of love & happiness for me.… I have never felt stronger about anyone… I feel safe & sure with Keith. I feel strong & steady. I feel only good things can happen."

After only two months, Lou and Keith decided to move in together. Keith expressed some concern regarding what others might think about him "living with a sex change," but Lou assured him that "no one needs to know" that they were sleeping together or that Lou was trans. Both assumed they would continue sleeping with other people, and Keith was relieved when Lou said he would not mind if Keith brought "his girlfriends" home, that they would be living together as roommates rather than as lovers.[119] In time, Keith told Lou that he no longer cared if people knew they were in a relationship. Lou interpreted this as meaning Keith was "willing to be open about being my homosexual lover," and wrote: "Slowly the blinders are falling from my eyes. I am breathing so easy. I feel like a whole and worthy, fine, and important person. He loves me.—I am learning to love in the way I always wanted to love someone."[120]

Before transitioning, Lou had been saddened at the thought "that if I got together with a gay man, I would have to turn him heterosexual in order to have a relationship with me." But Lou felt "so proud, and isn't it wonderful, that Keith had to turn <u>homosexual</u> in order to have a relationship with me! That he had to present himself as a gay man to our friends and neighbors. Just for that fact, my whole sex change was worth it!"[121]

ENDNOTES: CHAPTER 4

1. Sullivan Journal, 10 September 1979, box 1 folder 11, LGS Papers.

2. Sullivan Journal, 11 September 1979, box 1 folder 11, LGS Papers.

3. Ibid.

4. Susan Stryker, "Portrait of a Transfag Drag Hag as a Young Man: The Activist Career of Louis G. Sullivan," in *Reclaiming Genders: Transsexual Grammars at the Fin deSiècle,* ed. Kate More and Stephen Whittle (London: Cassell, 1999), 69.

5. Stryker, "Portrait," 70; Meyerowitz, 255.

6. Standards of Care, ca 1980, box 6 folder 208, LGS Papers.

7. "The Standards of Care," WPATH site accessed 17 October 2015, http://www.wpath.org/site_page.cfm?pk_association_webpage_menu=1351&pk_association_webpage=4655

8. Stryker, "Portrait," 70-71; Meyerowitz, 273.

9. For example, see Norman M. Fisk, "Gender Dysphoria Syndrome— The Conceptualization that Liberalizes Indications for Total Gender Reorientation and Implies a broadly Based Multi-Dimensional Rehabilitative Regimen," *The Western Journal of Medicine* 120.5 (May 1974): 389.

10. Sullivan Journal, 27 September 1979, box 1 folder 11, LGS Papers.

11. Ibid.

12. In May 2009 this information was accessed from Dr. Lin Fraser's website at http://linfraser.com/transgender-subspecialty/. However, she has since updated her website, and this information is no longer included.

13. Sullivan Journal, 27 September 1979, box 1 folder 11, LGS Papers.

14. Ibid.

15. Sullivan Journal, 28 September 1979, box 1 folder 11, LGS Papers.

16. Sullivan Journal, 3 October 1979, box 1 folder 11, LGS Papers.

17. Sullivan Journal, 28 September 1979, box 1 folder 11, LGS Papers.

18. Sullivan Journal, 30 September 1979, box 1 folder 11, LGS Papers.

19. Stryker, "Portrait," 70-71.

20. Sullivan Journal, 28 September 1979, box 1 folder 11, LGS Papers.

21. Stryker, "Portrait," 68.

22. Sullivan Journal, 28 September 1979, box 1 folder 11, LGS Papers.

23. Sheila/Lou Sullivan, Application to Stanford University Gender Dysphoria Program, 17 October 1979, box 1 folder 1, LGS Papers.

24. Sullivan Journal, 27 September 1979, box 1 folder 11, LGS Papers.

25. For example, see Donald R. Laub and Norman Fisk, "A Rehabilitation Program for Gender Dysphoria Syndrome by Surgical Sex Change," *Plastic and Reconstructive* Surgery 53, no. 4 (April 1974): 388.

26. Stanford's Laub and Fisk stated that the qualifications for admittance at Stanford were similar to those used by the University of Minnesota, the University of Virginia, Northwestern University, the Clarke Institute, the Gender Identity Association, and Dr. William McRoberts' group. See Laub and Fisk, 392.

27. Laub and Fisk, 391. In the letter sent with the application and description of the program, they noted: "In some cases, additional information will be requested before we make a decision." Judy Van Maasdam to Lou Sullivan, 2 October 1979, box 2 folder 45, LGS Papers.

28. Prosser, 9.

29. On clinicians and archetypal transsexual narrative see Prosser, 104.

30. According to Jay Prosser, "*to be* transsexual, transsexuals must be arch storytellers—or if they are not, must learn to become passable ones." See Prosser, 113.

31. Sheila/Lou Sullivan, Application to Stanford University Gender Dysphoria Program, 17 October 1979, box 1 folder 1, LGS Papers.

32. Lou (Sheila) Sullivan to Judy Van Maasdam, 24 January 1980, box 2 folder 45, LGS Papers.

33. Judy Van Maasdam to Sheila Sullivan, 12 March 1980, box 2 folder 45, LGS Papers.

34. Lou Sullivan to Judy Van Maasdam, 22 March 1980, box 2 folder 45, LGS Papers.

35. Sullivan Journal, 5 October 1979, box 1 folder 11, LGS Papers.

36. Meyerowitz, 213-214; Wardell Pomeroy, "The Diagnosis and Treatment of Transvestites and Transsexuals," *Journal of Sex and Marital Therapy* 1.3 (Spring 1975): 215-225.

37. Sullivan Journal, 10 October 1979, box 1 folder 11, LGS Papers.

38. Sullivan Journal, 30 November 1979, box 1 folder 11, LGS Papers.

39.	Sullivan Journal, 16 October 1979, box 1 folder 11, LGS Papers.

40.	Sullivan Journal, 25 October 1979, box 1 folder 11, LGS Papers.

41.	Sullivan Journal, 2 January 1980, box 1 folder 12, LGS Papers.

42.	Sullivan Journal, 12 October 1979, box 1 folder 11, LGS Papers.

43.	Sullivan Journal, 5 November 1979, 16 November 1979, box 1 folder 11, LGS Papers.

44.	Sullivan Journal, 19 December 1979, box 1 folder 11; 7 January 1980, 31 January 1980, 19 February 1980, box 1 folder 12, LGS Papers. Occasionally Lou taped facial hair clippings into his journal.

45.	Sullivan Journal, 14 January 1980, box 1 folder 12, LGS Papers.

46.	Sullivan Journal, 1 March 1980, box 1 folder 12, LGS Papers.

47.	Sullivan Journal, 12 March 1980, box 1 folder 12, LGS Papers.

48.	Sullivan Journal, 18 April 1980, box 1 folder 12, LGS Papers.

49.	Sullivan Journal, 14 January 1980, 12 March 1980, box 1 folder 12, LGS Papers.

50.	Sullivan Journal, 17 February 1980, box 1 folder 12, LGS Papers.

51.	Sullivan Journal, 25 March 1980, box 1 folder 12, LGS Papers.

52.	Sullivan Journal, 12 March 1980, box 1 folder 12, LGS Papers.

53.	Michael Taylor, "Edward Falces—Surgeon Dedicated to Pro Bono Medicine," *San Francisco Chronicle* (2 January 2005): A-23.

54.	Sullivan Journal, 29 March 1980, box 1 folder 12, LGS Papers.

55.	Sullivan Journal, 5 May 1980, box 1 folder 12, LGS Papers.

56.	Sullivan Journal, 8 May 1980, box 1 folder 12, LGS Papers.

57.	Sullivan Journal, 19 May 1980, box 1 folder 12, LGS Papers.

58.	Sullivan Journal, 12 July 1980, box 1 folder 12, LGS Papers.

59.	Standards of Care, ca 1980, box 6 folder 208, LGS Papers; Marti Norberg to Sheila Sullivan, 28 September 1976, and Judy Van Maasdam to Lou Sullivan, 2 October 1979, box 2 folder 45, LGS Papers.

60.	Sullivan Journal, 24 July 1980, box 1 folder 12, LGS Papers.

61.	Sullivan Journal, 5 August 1980, box 1 folder 12, LGS Papers.

62.	Sullivan Journal, 12 July 1980, box 1 folder 12, LGS Papers.

63.	Sullivan attributed his use of "angel" to John Rechy.

64.	Sullivan Journal, 31 August 1980, box 1 folder 12, LGS Papers.

65.   Sullivan Journal, 15 September 1980, box 1 folder 12, LGS Papers.

66.   Sullivan Journal, 7 October 1980, box 1 folder 12, LGS Papers.

67.   Sullivan Journal, 20 October 1980, box 1 folder 12, LGS Papers.

68.   Sullivan Journal, 10 November 1980, box 1 folder 12, LGS Papers.

69.   Sullivan Journal, 18 November 1980, box 1 folder 12, LGS Papers.

70.   Sullivan Journal, 12 October 1980, 16 October 1980, 6 November 1980, 18 November 1980, box 1 folder 12, LGS Papers.

71.   Sullivan Journal, 10 February 1981, box 1 folder 12, LGS Papers.

72.   Sullivan Journal, 23 March 1981, box 1 folder 12, LGS Papers.

73.   Sullivan Journal, 17 February 1980, box 1 folder 12, LGS Papers.

74.   Sullivan Journal, 31 July 1980, 28 August 1980, box 1 folder 12, LGS Papers.

75.   Sullivan Journal, 7 October 1980, box 1 folder 12, LGS Papers.

76.   Meyerowitz, 254; Standards of Care, ca 1980, box 6 folder 208, LGS Papers.

77.   Lou Sullivan, "Dr. Paul Walker Returns to Address the TV/TS Community," *FTM* 12 (June 1990) in Rawlings-Fein, 65. See also Meyerowitz, 257-258.

78.   Walker came out to Sullivan as gay soon after Sullivan began volunteering at the Janus Information Facility. See Sullivan Journal, 15 September 1980, box 1 folder 12, LGS Papers.

79.   Sullivan Journal, 10 February 1981, box 1 folder 12, LGS Papers.

80.   See box 2 folders 48-80, LGS Papers.

81.   Sullivan Journal, 7 October 1980, box 1 folder 12, LGS Papers.

82.   Louis Sullivan, *Information for the Female-to-Male Crossdresser and Transsexual*, 2d ed (San Francisco: Zamot Graphic Productions, 1986), 22. I was unable to access a copy of the first edition of *Information for the Female-to-Male Crossdresser and Transsexual*, so all information included here comes from the second edition. I found information about the first edition's contents in an advertisement/review published in Rupert Raj, "Information for the Female-To-Male," *Metamorphosis* 3.5 (October 1984): 7. I have not cited anything that I know Lou changed from the first edition to the second.

83.   Sullivan, *Information for the Female-to-Male*, 29-36.

84.   Sullivan, *Information for the Female-to-Male*, 38.

85. Sullivan Journal, 17 February 1981, box 1 folder 12, LGS Papers.

86. Sullivan Journal, 7 April 1981, box 1 folder 12, LGS Papers.

87. Meyerowitz, 275; Jude Patton, "Jude Patton, FTM Advocate and Licensed Therapist," *FTM Informational Network*, http://www.ftminfo. net/jude.html.

88. Sullivan Journal, 31 January 1980, 31 July 1980, box 1 folder 12, LGS Papers.

89. Sullivan Journal, 19 August 1980, box 1 folder 12, LGS Papers.

90. Sullivan Journal, 28 August 1980, box 1 folder 12, LGS Papers.

91. Sullivan Journal, 29 August 1980, box 1 folder 12, LGS Papers.

92. Sullivan Journal, 23 February 1981, 28 February 1981, box 1 folder 12, LGS Papers.

93. Sullivan Journal, 28 February 1981, box 1 folder 12, LGS Papers.

94. Sullivan Journal, 16 July 1982, box 1 folder 13, LGS Papers.

95. Sullivan Journal, 8 October 1981, box 1 folder 13, LGS Papers.

96. Sullivan Journal, 29 September 1981, box 1 folder 13, LGS Papers.

97. Ibid.

98. Sullivan Journal, 8 October 1982, box 1 folder 13, LGS Papers.

99. Sullivan Journal, 7 May 1982, box 1 folder 13, LGS Papers.

100. Sullivan Journal, 24 August 1982, box 1 folder 13, LGS Papers.

101. Sullivan Journal, 10 February 1981, 1 May 1981, box 1 folder 12, LGS Papers.

102. Sullivan Journal, 26 May 1981, box 1 folder 12, LGS Papers.

103. Sullivan Journal, 7 September 1981, box 1 folder 13, LGS Papers.

104. Sullivan Journal, 26 May 1981, box 1 folder 12, LGS Papers.

105. Sullivan Journal, 28 June 1981, box 1 folder 12, LGS Papers.

106. Keith is a pseudonym.

107. Sullivan Journal, 26 June 1981, box 1 folder 12, LGS Papers.

108. Sullivan Journal, 26 June 1981, 27 June 1981, box 1 folder 12, LGS Papers.

109. Sullivan Journal, 5 July 1981, box 1 folder 12, LGS Papers.

110. Ibid.

111. Sullivan Journal, 17 July 1981, box 1 folder 12, LGS Papers.

112. Sullivan Journal, 8 August 1981, box 1 folder 12, LGS Papers.

113.   Sullivan Journal, 15 August 1981, box 1 folder 12, LGS Papers.

114.   Sullivan Journal, 22 August 1981, box 1 folder 12, LGS Papers.

115.   Sullivan Journal, 27 August 1981, box 1 folder 12, LGS Papers.

116.   Sullivan Journal, 1 October 1981, box 1 folder 13, LGS Papers.

117.   Sullivan Journal, 28 August 1981, box 1 folder 13, LGS Papers.

118.   Sullivan Journal, 27 August 1981, box 1 folder 12; 4 September 1981, box 1 folder 13, LGS Papers.

119.   Sullivan Journal, 30 August 1981, box 1 folder 13, LGS Papers.

120.   Sullivan Journal, 24 September 1981, box 1 folder 13, LGS Papers.

121.   Sullivan Journal, 27 July 1987, box 1 folder 15, LGS Papers.

Chapter

Public and Privates

A s far as transition stories go, it seemed that Lou's was complete. Not only did he now move, live and work in the world as a (gay) man—he had also gotten the guy. But Lou's story was far from over and, sadly, it was not to have a fairy tale ending.

From 1982-1986, Lou struggled with his relationship with Keith, with his trans identity and with accessing bottom surgery. However, he also found community amongst those experiencing the emerging AIDS crisis and those building a new trans community, and amongst those who founded the GLBT Historical Society. During these years Lou struggled to reconcile his trans and gay identities but also found and forged new communities that reshaped the LGBT community in San Francisco and beyond for years to come.

Domestic Bliss

In January 1982, beginning what Lou would later describe as the best year of his life, he and Keith moved to the Haight-Ashbury neighborhood.[1] Rent was cheap and they moved into a three-bedroom flat with a backyard and a gay couple living next door.[2] As they left, the Mission was becoming an enclave for lesbian feminists as women-oriented businesses emerged along the Valencia Street corridor.[3] If someone had told Lou back in 1969 when he was an eighteen-year-old working at the Garde and steeped in the counterculture that he would be moving to "the Haight," the center of the hippie movement—when he was thirty—Lou would have laughed.[4]

Lou and Keith easily slipped into domestic bliss, and Lou felt like his dreams had come true. "This is what I've wanted all my life," Lou wrote in his journal.[5] Lou and Keith made meals together, discussed their days, watched TV together in bed, cleaned house on the weekend, babysat Lou's nieces and nephews, and in the final months of winter curled up together in front of the fireplace. In the spring and summer they worked on their backyard, went on bike rides, and took picnics in Golden Gate Park.[6] At the end of June, Lou watched the Gay Pride parade with Keith, "Remembering how I'd watched all the other parades alone, wondering where amongst them all I'd ever find someone to love me, feeling so alone and sorry for myself. And here he is, smiling at me, loving me."[7]

However, their relationship was not without its challenges. Keith continuously struggled with his identity in light of Lou's being trans, and the difference between how Keith related to Lou in private versus in public began to wear on Lou. In private, Keith was very understanding, affectionate and loving. In public, Lou described them as appearing like "just two friends," and said Keith had "a habit of commenting on nearly every female in the right age range he sees."[8] This aggravated Lou, especially since he believed that with Keith he could at last have the gay relationship he had always dreamed of. Lou worried that "one day I'll lose his attentions to some girl."

> I want to be his "partner" in some way anyhow & must learn to be satisfied with his company as a roommate or whatever. I know I'm extremely lucky to have him even in that sense. But there's no doubt the jealousy is there & I wish the social taboo of loving someone like me wasn't there to sway him away. I know that's a big part of it.—How easy it must be! How simple to be either male or female, to have a place among humankind that needs no explanation, no compromise, no excuses.[9]

Keith continued having sexual relationships with cisgender women while in a committed relationship with Lou, and decided that his feelings for Lou meant he was bisexual.[10] But the reason that Keith acted so differently toward Lou when they were in public was because he worried what others thought about their relationship—especially those who knew that Lou was trans. According to Lou, every once in a while Keith would say things like "it's too weird for him to be with me & he thinks he should see a psychiatrist," then later apologize, saying "he just freaks out sometimes and that if I were a girl everything would be different."[11]

Keith loved Lou very much, but the only romantic future that he could imagine for himself involved marrying a woman. In the early 1980s gay marriage was an impossibility. Gay and straight people alike conflated marriage with heterosexuality, and while many gays and lesbians enjoyed the freedom of embracing alternate romantic arrangements, lacking the option of marriage could also make it difficult to imagine how long-term love and commitment between gay people would be manifested—or if it could be at all. Keith's solution to this uncertainty was that Lou should cease hormones and go back to living as a woman so that they could marry and live happily ever after.[12] Keith loved and wanted to be with Lou—it did not matter to him what Lou's body looked like, whether he was male, female or a combination of the two. Vaginal penetration was Keith's preferred method of sexual contact, but he consistently validated Lou's gender identity and always used masculine pronouns in reference to him, even referring to "his pussy," which Lou found amusing.[13] Keith's love transcended Lou's embodiment, but it was constrained by societal expectations.

Lou's love transcended societal expectations but was constrained by his embodiment. He was committed to loving Keith however worked best for both of them and for as long as they were both happy—not because something like marriage dictated how they act and that they remain together.[14] Paradoxically, being transsexual meant that Lou transcended his embodiment inasmuch as he identified as a (gay) man with or without hormones and surgeries that modified his female body. But he was also terribly constrained by his embodiment because those very modifications were necessary for him to be able to live in the world as the (gay) man that he knew himself to be. In effect, he was constrained by societal expectations about gendered embodiment. And Lou had to modify his body not only to be able to feel connection with others, but within himself as well.

It seemed that history was destined to repeat itself but, unlike with Mark, Lou informed Keith that he would rather lose him than give up his testosterone shots and go back to living as a woman. He tried to explain to Keith how much it meant to him to live as a man and how unhappy he had been before transitioning:

> …[I] relish these moments of living easy, of responding to everyday occurrences in a correct manner, without thought, without reflection (as simple as not knowing what to do with my hands when I stood there, as complicated as not feeling I was inside my body when having sex with

someone) and the constant realization that my thoughts are of my responses as a youngman.[15]

Keith could not understand what it felt like to be trans but he could understand that it was very important to Lou to be a man. And Lou could understand Keith's concern about others finding out he was trans. In fact, Lou felt concerned himself about people finding out he was trans. He tried to keep neighbors, friends and co-workers from finding out while remaining very open about being gay.

TIRED OF BEING A SEX CHANGE

For several years Lou greatly curtailed his activism. For one thing, he had gone to great lengths to construct a new life for himself as a gay man living with his partner in the Haight and working at ARCO, and Lou feared losing this new life that he loved if people found out he was trans. Also, as Lou told one of his fellow FTM activists, he was "tired of being a sex change."[16] For nearly a decade Lou had been consumed with a myriad of trans-related struggles, and now he was free to direct his energies anywhere he wished. As he told Keith, "It's the first time in my life I've been able to kick back & enjoy the world around me & not be preoccupied with myself..."[17] In his correspondence with other FTMs, Lou wrote about his relationship with Keith and the joys of day-to-day living made possible by his consistently being read as a man.

Lou stopped volunteering with Janus, withdrew from organizing, and stopped going to trans-related gatherings. But as Lou settled into his life as a man and inhabited his gay identity, the knowledge that many gay FTMs were still denied recognition and the ability to transition kept him from withdrawing from activism altogether. Lou still spoke about his trans and gay identities to classes at the Institute for Advanced Study of Human Sexuality and at San Francisco State University, where he was assured of confidentiality. He also continued his correspondence with other FTMs, making sure they all knew that he was gay and that there were other gay FTMs out there.

For Lou, it was exceptionally important that trans people know about and embrace the diversity of trans experiences. He believed trans people were the authorities on trans identity—not gender professionals—and encouraged his fellow trans people to resist subscribing to and reiterating the existing medical definitions of transsexuality and transvestism, which denied the diversity of trans experiences. Lou believed trans people should be collaborators on the information distributed about them and medical services offered to them by gender professionals—rather than being passive recipients. His extensive (and continuously growing) network of correspondents provided Lou with the means to both collect and disseminate information about the diversity of trans experiences to fellow trans people.

One of Lou's most fruitful correspondences was with Rupert Raj. Raj was a Canadian and self-identified FTM who described himself as being "blessed with a multicultural heritage—Eurasian ancestry: a Polish mother and an East Indian father—and, as such, entertains no racial, ethnic, social or sexual prejudice, and, is proof positive that East and West do meet—to mutual benefit."[18] He and Lou began corresponding in 1979. At that time, Lou was involved in GGG/G and editing its newsletter *The Gateway*, and Raj was involved with Foundation for the Advancement of Canadian Transsexuals (FACT) and editing its *Gender Review*. In their correspondence they bemoaned the lack of FTM-specific resources, and in 1980 both ceased their work on behalf of their respective co-gender trans organizations and publications. Doing so enabled them to devote all of their energy and skills to FTM matters. Lou incorporated information shared by Raj in his booklet *Information for the Female-to-Male Crossdresser and Transsexual*, and shared Raj's referrals for "counselors & doctors sympathetic to gender dysphorics" in Canada with the Canadians who wrote to Janus seeking information.[19]

In 1982, Raj established Metamorphosis Gender Counseling and Educational Services and started *Metamorphosis*, the first FTM-specific publication. At the outset Raj recruited Lou to assist with both, but Lou declined saying he was "too consumed by daily life to invest time" and also that he did not want to be a "renowned transsexual."[20] Lou did, however, find it difficult to resist publishing occasional pieces in *Metamorphosis*. His first *Metamorphosis* publication was a letter to the editor in which Lou took issue with the "classic textbook definition" of FTM transsexuality:

> I truly doubt that all (or even most) of us have had exactly the kind of experiences/background/feelings outlined in [this] definition. I know it took me a long time just to determine that I was in fact TS [transsexual] because my experiences/background/feelings were not textbook. Not all of us were rough-and-tumble tomboys who bitterly resented female pubescence & were turned off by boys.

> Not all normally born men are that way & I see no reason
> to deny a F-M TS his true identity as a man because he
> does not fit the mold. [It's] now OK to be quiet, sensitive,
> warm & non-hetero and still "be a man."… The blending
> of male & female in us can only be resolved by each of us
> in our own way, while we always look toward the ultimate
> goal of the masculine.[21]

Lou's initial compulsion to publish on the diversity of trans experiences in *Metamorphosis* inspired many of his subsequent publications, which included more letters to the editor, an article titled "Are There Really Female-to-Male Transvestites? Why?" and book and film reviews.

Lou also tried to bring the existence of gay FTMs to the attention of the local gay community through a letter to the editor that he published in the *Bay Area Reporter*. He was no longer able to address the gay community on a national scale through *GPU News* because it had ceased operations in 1981. The AIDS crisis would later launch the *Bay Area Reporter* onto the national stage, but at the time of Lou's publication, the aptly nicknamed *B.A.R.* was a free weekly newspaper distributed in local gay bars. Lou titled his *B.A.R.* letter to the editor "Another Sexual Minority," and published it under the pseudonym L.G.S. Reed (L.G.S. stood for Louis Graydon Sullivan, his legal name, and Reed was after his namesake Lou Reed). In his letter, Lou addressed the disproportionate media coverage of heterosexual MTF transsexuals, explaining that there were also FTMs such as himself and that "There are those of us who make the most serious decision of our lives (Should I change my sex? Really go through with it?) Because we want more than anything to be Gay!" Lou described himself as exhibiting true gay pride: "I am glad that I cannot complain that 'I can't help' being Gay, but can proudly say that I chose to live as a Gay man, knowing it as the only honest love for me." He also tried to connect with the gay community by discussing how hard it is for trans people to come out when they think they are the only ones, and wrote that he specifically hoped his letter would help other guys like him—assigned female at birth—know that they could become gay men.[22]

Lou's letter to the editor in the *B.A.R.* reflected his present thinking that his transsexuality was the means to the end of being a gay man. He was not simply privileging his gay identity over his trans identity, but rather treating his being trans as a condition rather than as an identity. Lou wanted to be known solely as a gay man and even pulled away from Keith, not wanting to have sex with him and wishing Keith did not know about his transsexuality. Keith tried to help, encouraging Lou to act "like a gay man" during sex. He made references to Lou's "little dick" and attempted to engage it as such, but Lou became very frustrated by what he referred to as his "little dick problem."[23] Lou wanted to be able to penetrate during sex and worried that he would never know what it was like to be a man unless he could; his sense of being anatomically inadequate translated into a more general sense of inadequacy as a man. Under tragic circumstances, it was his father who helped Lou to address this issue and his struggle with identifying as trans.

In the years after Lou began transitioning he grew closer to his father Jack, who quickly came to see Lou as his son. For his part, Lou came to know Jack as an individual during that time, not just as his father. Jack went through a major life transition himself. After years of suffering through an unhappy marriage, followed by an ugly divorce, Jack found happiness and remarried—against the rules of the Catholic Church. He told Lou that "he would live how he had to," and that "he was going to live the best way he could."[24] Given that Jack was happier than Lou could ever remember him being, Lou was especially saddened by the news that his father had suffered an aneurysm rupture. To Lou it seemed that Jack had "just waited 'til the last minute" to do what he wanted to do with his life.[25]

Lou and his siblings reunited around their father's bedside at the Milwaukee VA Medical Center. Jack seemed to rebound with all of his children together in Milwaukee, and the hospital staff was amazed by his "miraculous recovery." With Jack seemingly in recovery, the Sullivan siblings began to depart. However, when Lou and Maryellen told their father that they would be returning to San Francisco, "the eager bright face that shone at us fell and his eyes drifted away from us, his heart visibly sunk as he nodded in understanding."[26] They promised to stay a few more days, but blamed themselves when Jack's aneurysm burst again the next morning. To Lou it appeared that his father was in the same state in Intensive Care as his brother Patrick had been, and "I said into his ear as he lay there, hoping he could still hear, knowing he knew, I said, 'Dad, if it seems right, if you think it's time, then go…'"[27] Jack died shortly thereafter.

Jack's death had a profound impact on Lou in several ways. For one thing, Lou learned from his father how to die. Lou thought of Jack and death every day for over a year. Lou could not stop thinking about Jack "lying there, probably knowing he was dying," and yet looking "so loving and alive with happiness."[28] Sooner than he expected, Lou would find himself in a similar situation and striving to behave in a similar manner. Lou processed Jack's aneurysm and subsequent death through the lens of his personal experiences with embodiment as a trans person. In the hospital Lou saw his father as a "bright shining spirit stricken with a fallen body" and exclaimed "How we are encumbered by our bodies! How burdensome our bodies are!" Lou was left believing that everyone would be better off without bodies, which was a gift offered by death.[29]

In addition to learning from his father how to die, Lou also learned from him how to live. Jack's "last real words of advice" to Lou were to "Do what you want to do and don't give a fuck! what anyone else says, just do what you want to do!"[30] These words not only validated the decisions that Lou had made to move to San Francisco, transition and live as a gay man. They also inspired Lou to overcome his own internalized transphobia. Embracing his trans identity was arguably the most profound way in which Jack's death impacted Lou's life. Lou reasoned that his fear of others learning that he was transsexual was nothing compared to the fear of death, and watching Jack die had made Lou no longer fear death. He began coming out to co-workers at ARCO and resumed his activist work with a new sense of purpose. Lou decided that the meaning of life was to "live in the kind of world WE want for ourselves and for those we love" and set out bringing it about.[31]

Lastly, when Jack died in the summer of 1983, Lou inherited enough money from Jack's estate to be able to pursue genital reconstructive surgery. Once Jack's estate was settled Lou had the financial means to attain the full embodiment that he desperately desired. Lou believed that genital reconstructive surgery would enable him to have uninhibited, unquestionable gay sex, but unfortunately it would take several years for Lou to find a surgeon who was willing to make this happen.

Sexual Healing

Keith was very compassionate and supportive of Lou while he dealt with the grief of losing his father. As Lou contemplated the meaning of life, he realized there was no place that he would rather be—"here on earth or elsewhere"—than with Keith.[32] But when Lou learned that he was inheriting enough money from his father's estate to undergo genital reconstructive surgery, he became increasingly uncomfortable with vaginal penetration during sex. Keith insisted that he saw Lou as a man and loved him as a man, but Lou questioned this because of the nature of their sexual relationship.[33] So Lou refused to have what he called "girlsex" with Keith anymore, and as they reached a sexual impasse, Lou committed to undergoing bottom surgery while Keith committed to a cisgender girlfriend.[34] Despite their sexual and corresponding romantic troubles, Lou and Keith continued to live together and even established a printing business with money Lou received when he was laid off by ARCO after their San Francisco-based project concluded.

To undergo genital reconstructive surgery Lou applied to the same gender program for a third time. Technically the Gender Dysphoria Program was no longer affiliated with Stanford as universities like Stanford had disassociated themselves from gender programs in the early 1980s following the release of a report published by Jon Meyer and Donna Reter in *Archives of General Psychiatry* that stated there was "no objective improvement" for individuals who had undergone sex reassignment. The report "was eventually revealed to be contrived and possibly fraudulent," and several programs continued as private for-profit centers, including Gender Dysphoria Program, Inc., which was run by the same three individuals who had run Stanford's gender program: Donald Laub, Norman Fisk and Judy Van Maasdam, the program's coordinator.[35]

A gay FTM friend of Lou's told him that Van Maasdam knew Lou by name and had said that Lou had the "wrong impression of their attitude toward female-to-male gay men."[36] So Lou sent a letter, informing Van Maasdam that he had "finally become financially able to seriously pursue completion of my female-to-male transition," and that he was interested in undergoing the same procedure as Steve Dain: a metoidioplasty. Lou wanted the best surgery that money could buy, and Dr. Laub had received great acclaim for his version of the metoidioplasty.[37]

Lou heard nothing from the gender program for more than three months, and in the meantime sought the sexual affirmation of his body that he did not receive from Keith. Lou wanted a partner who would "treat [him] like a man" and thought, "only a M-F will know how to do it" given his present embodiment.[38] He placed a personals ad in the *Bay Area Reporter* that read:

Bisexual TVs

Handsome, masculine female-to-male transsexual in SF seeks pretty, slim male-to-female crossdresser under 35 for mutual pleasuring at your place. It's not easy for us to find

> understanding partners, here's someone who knows what it
> is. Let's indulge our fantasies… the possibilities are endless.

Lou also began frequenting a "drag queen bar" called the Black Rose in hopes of finding a sexual partner, and let people at the bar know that he was FTM because he believed MTFs could be the type of "understanding [sex] partners" that he sought.[39]

Lou rang in 1985 at the Black Rose, and that night he experienced first-hand the stark contrast between his economic conditions as a white middle-class FTM and those of poor MTFs of color. After midnight Lou left the bar with "a cute tall drag queen," who Lou noted was not taking hormones and was black.[40] When they arrived at her building, Lou had to pay the desk clerk $5, and seemed to resent having to do so as it implied his paying for sex. Three days earlier Lou left the Black Rose alone after another MTF, with whom he was flirting, informed him that she was "charging."[41] To Lou, who was already feeling insecure, this was an affront to his sexual attractiveness. However, then as now, it was not uncommon for MTFs to engage in sex work. Due to social ostracism and relentless employment discrimination, trans women often did whatever they could to get money in order to meet their basic survival needs.[42] Despite feeling resentful about doing so, Lou paid the desk clerk $5, and he and the black drag queen "fucked and fooled around in the hallway bathroom and the stairwell" until she told Lou that he had to leave. Adding insult to injury, Lou later remembered having had a joint in his wallet and more money than what remained, and felt it was "Real shitty to be ripped off by someone you were kissing and liking 2 seconds before."[43]

Two weeks after his New Year's tryst, Lou went on a date with an MTF named Monica who answered his personals ad. Upon meeting, Monica quickly suggested that they go to her place, which made Lou glad since he "wanted to mess around more than I want to 'date.'" Lou found it "nice to jump right in bed with someone without worrying about how they'll react to my body." The fact that he still "felt very [physically] inept," even with an understanding sexual partner, made Lou realize again how important it was to him to have his genitals reconstructed. However, despite his sense of physical ineptitude, Lou "had no trouble feeling masculine" with Monica, and easily satisfied her—which no one else had done before. For Lou, "this kind of contact [with MTFs] is good for me insofar as stroking my male ego and making me think what kind of sex am I capable." But at the same time Lou found sex with MTFs—even MTFs who derived sexual pleasure from their penises—less erotic than sex with a man, and as a result could not see "any permanent or serious kind of attachment" with Monica or another MTF.[44]

Just as Lou's sex life seemed to be taking off he had to take a one-month hiatus. The evening after his liaison with Monica, Lou came down with a 102 degree fever that lasted more than a week. Lou could neither eat nor sleep, and experienced swelling of the lymph nodes in his neck.[45] After exhibiting these symptoms for nearly two weeks, Lou was misdiagnosed as having mononucleosis.[46] In actuality, he was experiencing symptoms of seroconversion that can occur when someone is newly infected with HIV.

The first time that Lou mentioned AIDS in any of his writings was nine months later, in October 1985. The nonchalant way in which Lou noted the epidemic revealed his familiarity with it: "They've closed the back rooms of the theatres because of this AIDS disease—a venereal disease spreading through the gay community that kills you in about 2 years. No cure, no treatment, they're not even sure how you get it, etc., etc."[47] Lou lived in the west coast epicenter of the epidemic and had undoubtedly known about AIDS since its emergence in 1983, but he did not consider it an immediate threat to him. Despite identifying as a gay man, Lou still used language suggesting ambivalence over whether or not he *was* a gay man—such as his oft-used statement "I have been living in the gay men's world"—and AIDS had been portrayed as a decidedly gay disease.[48] AIDS had also been associated with promiscuity, and Lou could "count on one hand" the number of sexual partners he had had since moving in with Keith in 1981—a far cry from promiscuity for a gay man living in San Francisco in the early 1980s.[49]

Nearly a year lapsed from the time Lou began seroconverting until "safe sex" entered his consciousness and practices, as well as his peers'.[50] Meanwhile, Lou and Monica continued to sleep together until she moved away. Lou also had sex with Keith on occasion despite how intensely dissatisfying it was for him.[51] And Lou acquired a third sexual partner in the spring of 1985 named Joseph. Joseph was a cisgender gay man who responded to Lou's personals ad, informing him that he had dated a gay FTM in New York. Joseph was an actor and singer currently performing in cabarets, and according to Lou, "very cute."[52] Lou was delighted to have found another sexual partner who was not only very "understanding," but also found him extremely sexy.[53] Lou and Joseph slept together several times over the course of a year but did not develop anything more serious as Lou remained emotionally committed to Keith.

DIS-ORIENTATION

In the midst of suffering the physical effects of seroconversion, Lou learned that Dr. Laub refused to perform genital reconstructive surgery on him because he was gay.[54] To her credit, Judy Van Maasdam, the program coordinator who worked with Laub, began trying to help Lou find another surgeon.[55] Lou also contacted Dain, who had a professional relationship with Laub, and both he and Van Maasdam offered to speak with Laub on Lou's behalf.

Lou tried to enlist Paul Walker, who served on the Board of Directors for Laub's Gender Dysphoria Program. Because Walker was gay, Lou "[couldn't] see him letting them reject me because I am, too."[56] From Walker, Lou learned that Laub's longtime professional partner, psychotherapist Dr. Norman Fisk, had once made a public announcement that he would never approve a gay FTM for surgery. Walker told Lou that even if they were unsuccessful in convincing Fisk and Laub, "we'll find SOMEONE to do the surgery" and recommended that Lou wait to see what happened at the Ninth International Symposium on Gender Dysphoria, which was being held in seven months' time.[57] Unfortunately, though Lou and Walker had developed a rich and meaningful relationship as therapist and peer counselor for Janus, their relationship became complicated after Lou turned to him for help in accessing bottom surgery and advocating for gay FTMs among his gender professional colleagues.

Lou contacted his fellow FTM activist Rupert Raj about his rejection from the Gender Dysphoria Program and declared: "It is apparent that even the so-called gender specialists don't understand the difference between gender orientation and sexual preference."[58] Lou did not mean that "gender specialists" literally could not differentiate between "gender orientation" and "sexual preference." He was expressing an emerging political consciousness surrounding gender identity and sexual orientation in the wake of gay liberation that was invested in clearly delineating the two.

The gay community of the 1970s that had emerged in the wake of gay liberation had transformed significantly. In places like San Francisco that had a large number of gay, lesbian, bisexual and trans individuals, the gay community had fissured into more distinct gay, lesbian and transvestite/transsexual communities that had coalesced in the 1980s. Even Lou, who identified as both gay *and* FTM, saw gender identity and sexual orientation as the basis for separate communities prioritizing either sexual orientation or gender identity. This perception was crucial to the formation of an FTM community and to the later transgender community. It allowed individuals to focus on and unite around experiences as people navigating the world with non-normative gender identities—experiences that the vast majority of people with non-normative sexual orientations would never have or fully understand.

Lou's choice of words in stating that "even the so-called gender specialists don't understand" reveals an underlying frustration with prevailing notions of gender identity (not just among gender professionals) that was necessary for forging a transgender movement, which would emerge in the early 1990s. While the early 1990s is considered the time when the word *transgender* became popularized, Lou used it in his writings in February 1985 while he was contending with this latest round of rejection from transsexual medical services for being gay.[59] At the heart of this emerging transgender consciousness lay the seeming paradox that there were transvestites and transsexuals who identified as gay, lesbian and bisexual. In fact, someone like Lou had to identify as transsexual in order to embody his identity as a gay man, yet access to transsexual services was a transsexual issue, not a gay issue. All transsexuals sought these services regardless of what Lou referred to as their sexual preferences. What Lou was arguing was that sexual orientation should play no role in the diagnosis and treatment of transsexuality; individuals identifying as transsexual should not be discriminated against on the basis of their sexual orientation. Luckily, in the early 1980s the medical establishment seemed to realize this and stopped denying feminizing hormones and surgeries to MTFs who identified as lesbians.

At the 1981 Seventh International Gender Dysphoria Symposium held in Lake Tahoe, Nevada, a psychiatrist presented a case study of a lesbian-identified MTF. This presentation served as a springboard for other gender professionals to acknowledge that MTFs could be lesbians. Within three to four years, gender professionals estimated that approximately 30% of male-to-female transsexuals identified as lesbians.[60]

Once those specializing in the diagnosis and treatment of transsexuality accepted the viability of MTF lesbianism, more MTFs were willing to openly identify themselves as lesbians to them. While a seemingly new phenomenon to gender professionals, this was not the case for transsexuals. Transsexuals with connections to other transsexuals were especially aware that there were transsexuals of all sexual orientations. When sexual preference for women no longer served as a barrier to accessing transsexual services, lesbian MTFs came out in droves. However, no respected medical professional had undertaken a case study of a gay FTM, and gender professionals continued to deny services to FTMs who identified as gay.

Lou knew "at least ten other female-to-males who feel they are homosexual men and are afraid to be honest with counselors and clinics, fearing the same discrimination I have experienced."[61] Unfortunately Lou and every other trans person was prevented from giving presentations at the HBIGDA biennial symposia, and there were no leadership positions available for trans people in this preeminent gender dysphoria association.[62] Lou found himself wholly dependent upon Walker to make the case for his and other gay FTMs' access to genital reconstructive surgery at the upcoming symposium in September 1985.

Tragically, one of these ten gay FTMs died by suicide in the midst of Lou's struggles to access surgery, and the news of his death shook Lou deeply. The man's mother had been very loving and accepting of her son, and when she wrote Lou to inform him of her son's death, she thanked Lou for reaching out to him and told him that her son had admired his courage.[63] In his letters, as in so many other letters Lou received from FTMs, the deceased had repeatedly commented on how grateful he was to have someone understanding with whom to correspond. Though "not the crying type," Lou "broke down and cried."[64]

FINDING JACK B. GARLAND, FOUNDING THE GLBT HISTORICAL SOCIETY

Two of Lou's FTM correspondents died by suicide in less than a year, and he was very frustrated by the influence that misinformed gender professionals could have on the well-being of FTMs. For the most part Lou was unable to directly address the gender professionals, so he did everything that he could to reach out to his fellow FTMs and provide them with accurate information. In 1985 Lou purchased his own personal computer with a word processing program, making his home one of less than 15% of American homes to own a computer at the time. He described the PC as "a writer's dream" and used it to compose a second edition of his *Information for the Female-to-Male Crossdresser and Transsexual* booklet.[65] He sent copies to his correspondents, advertised the booklet in transvestite/transsexual, gay, and lesbian publications and succeeded in having it sold in several local stores, including the sex-positive woman-centered bookstore Good Vibrations.[66]

By publishing the booklet through the printing company that he co-owned with Keith, Lou was able to act as both author and publisher, and had free reign over the design and content of the booklet. The most noticeable difference between Lou's first and second editions was his enhanced discussion of transsexuality and historical figures he identified as FTMs. Lou added seven sections pertaining to transsexuality, transforming his booklet from a how-to guide to a treatise on FTM transsexuality that systematically highlighted and corrected all pertinent information on the topic. Lou also inserted twenty-eight biographical vignettes of historical figures who had been assigned female at birth but lived as men. He had researched historical figures for over a decade and discovered that the inclinations of modern-day FTMs had existed for centuries.

One of the historical figures Lou included in the booklet, and the one with whom he most closely identified, was Jack B. Garland. Lou first learned of Garland, or "Babe Bean," in 1979 when he attended a benefit for the newly-formed San Francisco Gay and Lesbian History Project. The benefit was a lecture with slides presented by gay historian Allan Bérubé titled "Lesbian Masquerade: Some Lesbians in Early San Francisco Who Passed as Men." Lou reported on the presentation in the GGG/G's newsletter *The Gateway* and identified Garland as "by far the most lovable character presented." At the time, Lou was serving as editor of *The Gateway* and treasurer of GGG/G and identified as a female transvestite. In reference to Garland, he wrote:

> It is unfortunate that Babe was lumped under the title of 'Lesbian Masquerade.' Her sentiments were with the young men she met: she was truly a heterosexual female transvestite lost in the stereotypes. Babe was pursued by many women, but she took a policy of never receiving "any visitors in petticoats."[67]

Lou later claimed (after he had transitioned) that his "gay sensibility told me Bean was a man-loving man, and I craved to know everything about him."[68]

In the fall of 1984 Lou saw the recorded slideshow version of Bérubé's work, making it the sixth time he had seen the presentation. This time Lou attended the presentation "mostly to get dates so I can research the info myself." Before the show Lou recognized Bérubé in the audience, and afterwards they talked. Lou explained his identification with Garland and showed Bérubé the research he had done.[69] Bérubé said that Lou made him feel "that those long hours alone in the libraries squinting to read the microfilms of old newspapers was worth it all!" and encouraged Lou to write Garland's biography.[70] For his part, Bérubé had been working over the past five years "to uncover and make public" the "hidden stories" of lesbian and gay GIs in World War II, which would eventually culminate in the publication of *Coming Out Under Fire: The History of Gay Men and Women in World War Two*.[71] Lou had entertained the idea of writing Garland's biography for some time, and receiving this validation from a gay historian whom he deeply respected convinced him to do so.

After getting laid off from ARCO, Lou spent several months working full time on Garland's biography.[72] Lou's journal entries suggest that Garland became a part of his everyday thoughts and actions during this time. For example, while on a road trip, Lou uncharacteristically gave a young "bum" $20 and shared a joint with him, thinking about Garland's giving his money and a place to stay to "homeless runaway boys."[73] When Lou felt he was "the only one with this problem—a gay man in a woman's body—and so alone, so left out," he drew comfort from comparing his life to Garland's.[74] He wondered if he would have had "the strength" to live full time as a man, like Garland, without "the luxury" of hormones and surgery, and decided "I want to have all the surgery—to go all the way in memory of Jack Garland."[75]

Without the aid of indices, let alone search engines, Lou did the tedious and time-consuming work of sifting through microfilms of old newspapers for articles by or about Garland. He searched at the San Francisco Public Library, the California Historical Society, and Berkeley's Bancroft Library where he also accessed the personal letters of Garland's parents, José Marcos Mugarrieta, the first Mexican consul in San Francisco, and Eliza Alice Denny Mugarrieta (née Garland), daughter of a U.S. Congressman from Louisiana. "I gather each tidbit, each lead I pursue as if I am finding someone with whom I am in love," Lou confessed.[76] Unfortunately, after three months of intensive research, Lou seemed to run out of sources, and he was unable to find any leads to the last thirty years of Garland's life.[77]

Lou's research on Garland stalled for two years, but in the meantime he stayed busy helping the GLBT Historical Society get off the ground. He attended the first meeting of what was then the San Francisco Bay Area Gay and Lesbian Historical Society on March 15, 1985. Lou became a founding member at that meeting and immediately assumed responsibility for the publication of the Historical Society's newsletter, utilizing the old *GPU News* typesetter that he purchased from Eldon Murray for his printing business with Keith.[78]

The GLBT Historical Society grew out of the San Francisco Gay and Lesbian History Project, and the driving force behind its formation was Bill (a.k.a. Willie) Walker. Walker had moved to San Francisco in 1981, and his work as a nurse on the AIDS ward at San Francisco General Hospital impressed upon him the need to collect and preserve gay history before it was too late.[79] In 1982 he joined the San Francisco Gay and Lesbian History Project, along with Allan Bérubé, Jeffrey Escoffier, Estelle Freedman, Eric Garber, Amber Hollibaugh, Gayle Rubin, and other academics, community activists and grassroots historians.[80] The History Project had formed in the late 1970s and was a working group geared toward historical research. In 1983, Walker proposed that the History Project also engage in the preservation of historical materials. Over the next two years, Walker, Greg Pennington, and others decided to establish an historical society—an entity separate from but affiliated with the History Project—that would engage in collecting, archiving, researching and creating an understanding of the history of gays and lesbians.[81]

In June 1985, Lou proudly marched with the GLBT Historical Society in the Gay Pride Parade and helped distribute its first newsletter there, visibly establishing the organization within the community.[82] Eric Garber, "one of the big shots" at the Historical Society who had long been an associate of Allan Bérubé's and was familiar with Lou's research interest in Garland, encouraged Lou to write an article about Garland for the newsletter. Lou felt motivated by Garber's encouragement and seeing Garber's presentation on gays and lesbians during the Harlem Renaissance, which would form the basis for later publications.[83] However, neither Garber nor Lou's other associates at the Historical Society had any "concrete suggestions" as to how Lou might locate information about the last thirty years of Garland's life.[84] Lou met with Bérubé one afternoon, lamenting his inability to locate more information, only to have Bérubé point out that Lou had a tremendous amount of information given that Garland was not a famous person. He pointed out that Lou was ready to begin writing.[85] Shortly thereafter Lou published an article on Garland in the Historical Society newsletter.[86] In addition to publishing the newsletter, Lou also volunteered his time to the Archives Committee by cataloging the GLBT Historical Society's impressive periodicals collection that included over 600 individual titles.[87]

Although some members of the Historical Society were aware of Lou's research interests and of the fact that he had written *Information for the*

Female-to-Male Crossdresser and Transsexual, Lou left no record of telling anyone at the Historical Society that he was FTM nor of experiencing any anxiety about their knowing that he was trans. It is likely that because of his scholarship and the fact that Bérubé knew he was a gay FTM, Lou viewed his being trans as an open secret. What is undeniable is that Lou's involvement with the Historical Society and the research he contributed ensured a trans presence in the organization from its inception.

SURGERY SAGA

The Harry Benjamin International Gender Dysphoria Association's symposium came and went and Lou was no closer to accessing bottom surgery. He had placed all of his hopes in Dr. Paul Walker, one of the world's most respected and best connected gender professionals, and someone whom Lou viewed as a colleague and friend. Walker had known Lou for more than five years, dating back to when Lou volunteered as a Janus Information Facility FTM peer counselor. Walker still sought his expertise and regularly referred FTMs to Lou—gay and straight alike—for information and companionship. However, whereas Walker initially seemed willing to advocate on Lou's behalf for bottom surgery—and for the treatment of gay FTMs in general—Lou was painfully disappointed by Walker's change of course after the symposium.

Walker still felt that the homophobia of his fellow gender professionals needed to be challenged, but claimed that what they needed was a "squeaky clean" test case—and that Lou would not do because of his sexual history. Lou argued that he had "felt and acted consistently as a gay man," regardless of those with whom he had had relations. But Walker wanted a gold star fag, or an FTM who had only ever had sex with cisgender men, and preferably no vaginal sex. Adding insult to injury, Walker charged Lou an appointment fee for telling him all of this and then nonchalantly asked to advertise the second edition of Lou's booklet through his Janus mailings.[88]

Frustrated and disgusted, Lou made an appointment with Dr. Wardell Pomeroy. As in 1979, Lou felt that Pomeroy "was immediately on my side and very helpful."[89] At Pomeroy's suggestion, Lou submitted an application to Dr. Stanley Biber. Since the 1970s, Biber's practice in Trinidad, Colorado had served as an alternative to the paternalistic gender programs. Biber taught himself how to perform gender confirmation surgeries and operated on patients at their request. It was estimated that in the 1980s

Biber's practice was responsible for approximately two-thirds of the nation's gender confirmation surgeries, and Trinidad became known as the "Sex Change Capital of the World."[90] Ultimately, Biber declined to operate on Lou not because he was gay but because Biber did not perform metoidioplasty surgeries as "We find that it makes a very small penis."[91] Pomeroy did not charge Lou for his appointment but happily accepted Lou's gift of his booklet *Information for the Female-to-Male Crossdresser and Transsexual*.[92]

Despite Pomeroy's suggestion to stay away from the Gender Dysphoria Program, Lou still arranged a meeting with Judy Van Maasdam. Lou was surprised to find her "very nice and not defensive or curt like she had been to me before." Van Maasdam acknowledged that surgeons would operate on lesbian MTFs "as a matter of routine," but that no one wanted to "stick their necks out" and be the first to operate on gay FTMs. She encouraged Lou not to give up hope, explaining that he was "just a little ahead of the doctors." Van Maasdam claimed to know three gay FTMs and suspected the numbers would increase once gender professionals had given *gay FTM* their stamp of approval. She wondered aloud if Paul Walker or Dr. Ira Pauly might do a presentation on gay FTMs at the next HBIGDA symposium and suggested Lou contact Pauly.[93]

Dr. Ira Pauly was the current president of HBIGDA and professor and chairman of the Department of Psychiatry and Behavioral Sciences at the University of Nevada School of Medicine in Reno. Most importantly, Pauly was considered the (medical profession's) expert on FTM transsexuality. Lou did not contact Pauly at this time because he was unsure as to whether or not Pauly would be receptive to his identity. Lou was also concerned that going the route of working with Pauly, having him give a presentation at the 1987 HBIGDA symposium, then waiting to see how surgeons responded could result in having to wait several more years to undergo genital reconstructive surgery.[94] Lou did, however, send Pauly and every other member of the Harry Benjamin International Gender Dysphoria Association a combination announcement/order form for his booklet.[95]

Meanwhile, Lou was impatient and discontented. He felt "so goddamned tired of being a freak," and like "Life is passing me by and everyone else finds their slot, but I'm always on the outside looking in." Lou thought "I'm never going to have a good relationship with someone when I am so ashamed of my body," and that genital reconstructive surgery would enable him to not feel ashamed of his body anymore. That line of thought was now extending beyond intimate sexual relationships. For example, when Lou visited the Eagle Tavern, "headquarters for the gay motorcycle clubs," Lou commented upon how comfortable he felt there, yet still noted: "I know I'll be able to be among them and things will be OK after I get the rest of my body done."[96]

Aware of Lou's struggles, mutual MTF friend Kim Stuart reconnected him with Lin Fraser. Six-and-a-half years earlier Fraser had helped Lou begin his transition by connecting him with Steve Dain and providing him with a referral for an endocrinologist.[97] Now, Fraser was "furious" that Lou "would be denied surgery on the basis of [his] sexual preference."[98] She told Lou that there was "NOTHING" in the Standards of Care on sexual orientation.[99] Fraser recommended a local surgeon, Dr. Michael Brownstein, who had performed metoidioplasty on one of her clients.[100] Lou and Brownstein already had a working relationship—he had done revision surgery on Lou's chest in the fall of 1984—and Lou was pleased to learn that Brownstein could perform the type of bottom surgery he sought.[101]

Dr. Brownstein, a native Chicagoan, opened his own plastic surgery practice in San Francisco after completing his specialty training at the University of California, San Francisco (UCSF) Medical Center. Three years later, in 1978, an FTM named John L. contacted Brownstein and asked him if he would be willing to perform chest reconstructive surgery on him. Brownstein thought nothing of it—he thought he could do it, and he did.[102] Word quickly spread, and soon FTMs were "flocking to him," including some who had not had any so-called gender counseling.[103] Brownstein knew nothing of the Standards of Care—he was simply providing plastic surgery at the request of his patients—until Paul Walker contacted him. Walker "scared the hell out of [Brownstein] for not following protocol," and thereafter Brownstein started requesting referrals from his trans patients.[104] Brownstein's FTM patients described him as being "very picky," but this surgical perfectionism generated "outstanding results."[105] At Brownstein's suggestion Lou contacted one of his metoidioplasty patients. The FTM "raved about [his surgery] and said it's fantastic and his sex life is better!" and only had good things to say about Brownstein.[106]

Paul Walker and Judy Van Maasdam knew Brownstein, but had not recommended him to Lou. Their decision may have stemmed from their discomfort with the way medical transition services for transsexuals were becoming decentralized. One of the motivations behind implementing the Standards of Care was to help protect transsexual patients from becoming victims of irreversible hack jobs by surgeons with no institutional affiliations. Its authors (including Walker, who chaired the draft committee) had established protocol akin to that used by gender programs in the hopes that those operating outside of gender programs would abide by the same procedures and standards. Brownstein followed the Standards of Care and demonstrated himself as a skilled surgeon who cared about the well being of his patients.[107] Yet Brownstein was not affiliated with an institution like the Gender Dysphoria Program but rather the HBIGDA, and the success and popularity of professionals like Brownstein threatened the pre-existing HBIGDA hierarchy that favored universities and gender programs. In the end, Walker came through for Lou—despite his potential reservations about Brownstein and the changing landscape of accessing care—by submitting a referral to Brownstein on Lou's behalf.

Lou had an appointment for surgery with Dr. Brownstein a month after learning he could perform it. Brownstein knew Lou was gay, practiced in San Francisco, and he charged half of what gender programs charged for the same procedure. Anticipating the surgery, Lou wrote:

> It's like before it would never happen, and now suddenly it's happening NOW. I suddenly feel ALIVE and awakened to myself, imagining I have a cock and balls! and how will I be different?? I feel cocky, and what an appropriate word with my true feelings all in one…. It's going to be such an exciting existence just having an intact body like everyone else and I can stop feeling ashamed and unworthy and gross.[108]

Brownstein had only performed this particular type of surgery once or twice before, but he felt confident in his abilities and was excited at the challenge. Both he and Lou were excited about the upcoming surgery.[109]

On April 22, 1986, Lou underwent genital reconstructive surgery, specifically a metoidioplasty with urethral extension and testicular implants.[110] When Lou arrived at the hospital, he found Brownstein looking very handsome in 1930s style gangster clothes. Lou eagerly consented to Brownstein's taking photos of the surgical process as he hoped it would benefit others. Also, Lou had sent the surgeon a copy of his booklet along with his check for surgery, and he was pleased that Brownstein had not only read his booklet but thought it was excellent. As Lou was wheeled into the operating room, he thanked his deceased father for making this surgery possible because of the money he willed to Lou.

Afterwards Brownstein enthusiastically told Lou that all went well and said he would make house calls because he did not want Lou to travel while he healed. His sister Maryellen took Lou home from the hospital, and she and Bridget cared for him as he recovered. Steve Dain called to check up on Lou and provided post-surgical advice over the next several days. Lou felt like surgery had "free[d]" him from a "mental prison."[111]

Lou also felt very sexy after his surgery. He looked forward to being able to masturbate and to beginning an avid sex life that summer. Several days after surgery, Keith told Lou that he was glad Lou had had it and hoped he would be able to find a boyfriend.[112] In addition to finding another boyfriend, Lou also hoped to have sex with Keith once he had fully recovered. But almost immediately Lou began having problems with his testicles and had to put his sex life on hold.

Less than two weeks after undergoing surgery, Lou's left testicular implant burst. He was devastated: "I was ready to ride that big wave of loving my body and wanting others to love it, and to loving and wanting theirs. But the humiliation of my incomplete body continues to plague me." When Brownstein removed the implant, Lou "felt like I'd been amputated." Lou mourned the loss of his testicle, but Brownstein remained optimistic. Eventually, Lou "[felt] pretty macho and butch, having endured this pain. Really proves how much I want this, how much better I feel as a man." He also "[felt] fortunate I even have one ball and am glad I found a doctor to even work with me."[113]

Two months after his initial surgery, Dr. Brownstein inserted another testicular implant in Lou's scrotum.[114] Unfortunately, a week later Brownstein "was very upset by the state of affairs." Lou did all he could to stay immobile, "nursing my precarious left ball."[115] Bedridden, Lou spent the 4th of July in deep reflection. He remembered meeting "some cute sailor boy in a gay bar" during the bicentennial ten years earlier and thought about his relationships with Mark, Keith and himself.

> I'm really feeling I need to fall in love with myself before involving myself in another intimate relationship. That was why I wanted to change my sex in the first place... so that I could love myself, sleep with myself, know myself and enjoy everyday living. It's as though I'm playing my favorite game all day, and now it's just become so easy and natural and fun that I don't want anything else. I want to learn to love my body and feel all its sensations, to be with other guys who look at my body and they want to "dick off"

too. It sure is hard when my body won't cooperate with my quickly changing psyche.[116]

Lou was determined to "hang tough and try to save this implant," but the skin at the incision site refused to heal and a second hole developed in his recently constructed scrotum.[117] Brownstein removed the implant and told Lou he would have to wait at least six months before trying again. Immediately Lou felt much better—physically, at least. "Of course I feel sorry for myself. But I am happy I have <u>something</u>," Lou wrote, "and now I am a deformed <u>male</u> instead of a female. I'd much rather be any kind of male than be a female!"[118]

Lou joined a therapy group for gay men with disabilities to help him come to terms with his body. When signing up for the group, Lou "simply did not mention I was female when I told [the coordinator] honestly about my past," and described his disability in terms of his having a "non-functional micropenis with only one testicle."[119] Little did Lou know that although he joined the group because of his trans embodiment, it would prove vital to him as a PWA (person with AIDS).

CULTIVATING COMMUNITY

In the summer and early fall of 1986, Lou experienced a sudden burst in social activity. He had experienced bursts in *sexual* activity after beginning hormones and undergoing top surgery, but this transitioning milestone—his bottom surgery—was not yet complete. As with hormones and top surgery, Lou felt excited and more confident. But while his body healed in preparation for surgical completion, Lou channeled his energies into social interactions rather than sexual encounters and found many new socializing opportunities in San Francisco both as a gay man and as an FTM.

In addition to joining the group for gay men with disabilities, Lou also joined the Fraternal Order of Gays (FOG), which was one of a number of new social outlets that emerged during the AIDS crisis as alternatives to the bars and bathhouses. FOG functions included lectures, language classes, dinners, theater, parties, outings, trips and game nights.[120] Lou became a member of FOG primarily because of their game nights, which entailed large groups of gay men gathering to play games like Scrabble.[121]

The landscape of gay San Francisco was changing in the face of the AIDS crisis. In the summer of 1986, Lou recorded in his journal that "over 1,000 gay men in San Francisco have died so far." Lou began attending workshops to learn more about AIDS, never thinking that the information could apply to him one day.[122] He also volunteered with the "NO on 64" public advocacy group.[123] Ultimately, the group played an integral role in the sound defeat of Proposition 64, which was, in Lou's words, "a super vicious anti-gay measure perpetrated by right-winger Holy Rollers" who organized under the Prevent AIDS Now Initiative Committee (PANIC). The initiative identified AIDS as an "infectious, contagious and communicable disease," required that all known cases be reported (and thus made public), and provided health officials with the power to quarantine persons with HIV/AIDS "to preserve the public health from AIDS."[124]

Coincidentally, at the same time that the landscape of San Francisco was changing in the face of the AIDS crisis, it was also changing with an increasing presence of FTMs. Lou's life mirrored the changing landscape of his city, for the number of FTMs in his life increased dramatically during the summer of 1986, unrelatedly coinciding with his participating in organizations responding to the AIDS crisis.

During the first week in August, Lou met with Steve, a white "22-year-old female who feels she is a gay man." Steve's psychologist in Berkeley called Paul Walker, who referred Steve to Lou.

> How wonderful it was for me to be there for her—telling her she's NOT the only one and she HASN'T invented a brand new perversion that's never been heard of before. She's been prowling the libraries as I had, trying to find a single mention of such feelings.... We talked for several hours and she said I don't know how great it was to meet me, but then quickly added, "well, maybe you do."[125]

Lou told Walker that the thank you letter he received from Steve "almost made [him] cry." He thanked Walker for the referral, saying, "It made me feel so good to be there for someone with those feelings, because it was horrible for me when I found no one who knew what I was saying."[126]

Later that same week Lou met with two other FTMs. Brice was a white 39-year-old "old-timer" who had begun taking hormones twelve years prior. Lou had met John L., another white FTM, five years ago at another FTM's home, and he was Brownstein's first FTM patient.

> We spent several hours talking, of course they wanted to see my [surgical results]. It was fantastic talking to these

"more experienced" guys instead of me being the one further along the way. I know they both really liked me and somehow treated me with more respect and acceptance as a gay man than I sometimes feel from my hetero peers. I gave them both a copy of [*Information for the Female-to-Male Crossdresser and Transsexual*].

Immediately after writing about John and Brice, Lou noted in his journal that a week before he had run into two other FTMs coming out of the theater after seeing *The Mystery of Alexina*, a movie based on the book *Herculine Barbin: Being the Recently Discovered Memoirs of a 19th Century French Hermaphrodite*, which Lou had reviewed for the February 1984 issue of *Metamorphosis*. Lou wrote: "A black FTM gay man, Chad (who I met last year at the FTM picnic as 'John') was with his white FTM lover (who says he likes girls better) and recognized me. We all went out to a gay men's bar on Polk St. and talked a long time…. All of a sudden I have a million FTM contacts."[127]

Lou had been thinking about starting an FTM group in San Francisco for some time, and the growing number of FTMs he knew in the area suggested the time had come. A boost of encouragement set things in motion. In early October, John G., a "well-known" FTM who had appeared in the HBO-aired documentary *What Sex Am I?* phoned Lou and encouraged him to start a group.[128] Before he began transitioning himself, John had heard Lou speak at the Pacific Center for Human Growth about being an FTM, and he had since heard rumblings about Lou's desire to start a group.[129] After getting off the phone with John, Lou wrote in his journal:

> I'm very excited by the idea of calling a gathering of F→M's just to talk to each other, exchange information, and just "be there" for new F→M's coming out, and in steering them away from Judy [Van Maasdam] and Laub, and toward Brownstein, who I really talked up. I'm very excited… oh, I already said that… but I <u>am</u>, about maybe even getting a small newsletter going and I'm sure it's possible if we can get other F→M's to "sign up." And you know how I LOVE to put little newsletters together![130]

A month later Lou sent out invitations for an FTM get-together. Steve Dain was the first to RSVP, "commenting that not only were these gatherings good for new people, but 'it's also good for us old-timers to get together once in a while.'" Being called an "old-timer" made Lou feel "so proud—makes me feel that I really have experienced/accomplished something."[131]

In addition to sending out invitations for an FTM get-together, Lou also became a member of ETVC. ETVC (Educational Transvestite Channel) had formed in 1982 as a social group and initially met in the homes and backyards of its members. When Lou joined, he described it as being *the* S.F. Bay Area TV/TS group now and very active and together."[132] Within days of receiving Dain's phone call, Lou attended the ETVC Dinner Social and found it fortunate that the coordinator of the Social Committee sat across from him and "talked non-stop about the group." Not only was Lou able to glean useful information about hosting get-togethers, he was also able to impart his own knowledge and told the coordinator he would like to be involved in the group's FTM aspects.[133] Lou hosted the first FTM Get-Together on December 6, 1986. The event was "well attended and brought many new and old friends together."[134]

Today Is the First Day of the Rest of Your Life

After entertaining the idea for a year-and-a-half, Lou decided to move out of the home he shared with Keith. To the rest of the world they looked like a gay couple—but not to Lou. On one hand Lou felt "like a gay guy in love with my straight roommate," and on the other, like Keith did not treat him like a man. Lou realized that if he stayed with Keith he would not be able to grow.[135]

Several months prior Lou and Keith dissolved their printing business. The two had different ideas about what it meant to be partners and different approaches to the work. Lou had trouble separating their business partnership from their romantic partnership, and it seemed to Lou that being Keith's partner—in any capacity—meant doing things his way. In Lou's mind, joint proprietorship had been as close to marriage as they could get, and when he and Keith dissolved the business it felt like a divorce.[136] To support himself financially Lou drew from his savings and took on more freelance word processing jobs.

On November 28, 1986 Lou decided it was time to move out, and the following day he and his new roommate Jim rented a place in the Mission, only blocks away from where Lou lived previously. Lou had known Jim for a number of years, having met him at Wilson Sporting Goods before Lou began transitioning. After signing the lease, Lou felt "excellent and

[had] no hesitation about leaving" Keith and their home in the Haight.[137] Lou could not believe that he had lived with Keith for five years when the last two had been "so sad." But now Lou was optimistic: "I've gotten past sadness now and I think things are going to get better."[138]

Sitting in his new apartment, Lou felt "so light and free"—that "this freedom is going to nurture me." And he embraced the motto: "Today is the first day of the rest of your life."[139] Lou had no idea how brief the rest of his life would be.

ENDNOTES: CHAPTER 5

1.   Sullivan Journal, 28 December 1982, box 1 folder 13, LGS Papers.

2.   Sullivan Journal, 2 February 1982, box 1 folder 13, LGS Papers.

3.   Susan Stryker and Jim Van Buskirk, *Gay by the Bay: A History of Queer Culture in the San Francisco Bay Area* (San Francisco: Chronicle, 1996), 99.

4.   Sullivan Journal, 29 January 1982, box 1 folder 13, LGS Papers.

5.   Sullivan Journal, 5 February 1982, box 1 folder 13, LGS Papers.

6.   Sullivan Journal, 11 December 1981, 2 February 1982, 7 June 1982, box 1 folder 13, LGS Papers.

7.   Sullivan Journal, 28 June 1982, box 1 folder 13, LGS Papers.

8.   Sullivan Journal, 20 October 1981, 26 October 1981, box 1 folder 13, LGS Papers.

9.   Sullivan Journal, 30 November 1981, box 1 folder 13, LGS Papers.

10. Sullivan Journal, 3 June 1982, box 1 folder 13, LGS Papers.

11. Sullivan Journal, 22 November 1982, box 1 folder 13, LGS Papers.

12. Sullivan Journal, 26 April 1982, box 1 folder 13, LGS Papers.

13. Sullivan Journal, 24 November 1981, box 1 folder 13, LGS Papers.

14. Sullivan Journal, 26 April 1982, box 1 folder 13, LGS Papers.

15. Sullivan Journal, 22 November 1982, box 1 folder 13, LGS Papers.

16. Lou Sullivan to Nick Ghosh, 30 December 1981, box 2 folder 92, LGS Papers.

17. Sullivan Journal, 16 August 1982, box 1 folder 13, LGS Papers.

18. "Introducing Rupert Raj," 1982, box 2 folder 92, LGS Papers.

19. Lou Sullivan to Nick Ghosh, 6 November 1980, box 2 folder 92, LGS Papers. Please note that Raj went by the name Nick Ghosh until 1982. All correspondence between Lou and Raj from 1979-1981 is found in box 2 folder 92, while correspondence from 1982-1990 is found in box 2 folder 116, LGS Papers.

20. Lou Sullivan to Rupert Raj, 8 December 1982 and Rupert Raj to Lou Sullivan, 18 October 1982, box 2 folder 92, LGS Papers.

21. Sullivan Journal, 27 May 1983, box 1 folder 13, LGS Papers; Lou Sullivan, "Letter to the Editor," *Metamorphosis* 2.3 (June 1983): 8.

22. L.G.S. Reed "Letter to the Editor," *Bay Area Reporter* (26 May 1983): page unknown, in Sullivan Journal, box 1 folder 13, LGS Papers.

23. Sullivan Journal, 3 January 1983, 7 January 1983, box 1 folder 13, LGS Papers.

24. Sullivan Journal, 29 July 1983, box 1 folder 13, LGS Papers.

25. Sullivan Journal, 5 August 1983, box 1 folder 13, LGS Papers.

26. Sullivan Journal, 29 July 1983, box 1 folder 13, LGS Papers.

27. Sullivan Journal, 30 July 1983, box 1 folder 13, LGS Papers.

28. For examples see Sullivan Journal, 15 August 1983, 19 August 1983, 16 September 1983, box 1 folder 13, LGS Papers.

29. Sullivan Journal, 22 July 1983, box 1 folder 13, LGS Papers.

30. Sullivan Journal, 22 July 1983, 5 August 1983, box 1 folder 13, LGS Papers.

31. Sullivan Journal, 15 September 1983, box 1 folder 13, LGS Papers.

32. Sullivan Journal, 10 August 1983, box 1 folder 13, LGS Papers.

33. Sullivan Journal, 12 October 1984, box 1 folder 14, LGS Papers.

34. Sullivan Journal, 14 September 1984, 26 September 1984, box 1 folder 13, LGS Papers.

35. Dallas Denny, "Transgender Communities of the United States in the Late Twentieth Century," in *Transgender Rights*, ed. Paisley Currah, Richard M. Juang and Shannon Price Minter (Minneapolis: University of Minnesota, 2006), 176.

36. Sullivan Journal, 30 September 1984, box 1 folder 13, LGS Papers.

37. Louis G. Sullivan to Judy Van Maasdam, 29 September 1984, box 2 folder 45, LGS Papers.

38. Sullivan Journal, 10 December 1984, box 1 folder 14, LGS Papers.

39. Sullivan Journal, 29 December 1984, box 1 folder 14, LGS Papers.

40. Sullivan Journal, 31 December 1984, box 1 folder 14, LGS Papers.

41. Sullivan Journal, 29 December 1984, box 1 folder 14, LGS Papers.

42. Stryker, *Transgender History*, 67.

43. Sullivan Journal, 31 December 1984, box 1 folder 14, LGS Papers.

44. Sullivan Journal, 13 January 1985, box 1 folder 14, LGS Papers.

45. Sullivan Journal, 20 January 1985, box 1 folder 14, LGS Papers.

46. Sullivan Journal, 26 January 1985, box 1 folder 14, LGS Papers.

47. Sullivan Journal, 27 October 1985, box 1 folder 14, LGS Papers.

48. For example see Lou Sullivan to Jude Patton, 26 June 1985, box 3 folder 113, LGS Papers.

49. Sullivan Journal, 7 January 1987, box 1 folder 14, LGS Papers.

50. Sullivan Journal, 31 January 1986, box 1 folder 14, LGS Papers.

51. Sullivan Journal, 24 February 1985, box 1 folder 14, LGS Papers.

52. Sullivan Journal, 6 March 1985, box 1 folder 14, LGS Papers.

53. Sullivan Journal, 31 March 1985, box 1 folder 14, LGS Papers.

54. Sullivan Journal, 26 January 1985, box 1 folder 14, LGS Papers; Judy Van Maasdam to Louis G. Sullivan, 9 January 1985, box 2 folder 45, LGS Papers.

55. Sullivan Journal, 26 January 1985, box 1 folder 14, LGS Papers.

56. Sullivan Journal, 8 February 1985, box 1 folder 14, LGS Papers.

57. Sullivan Journal, 11 February 1985, box 1 folder 14, LGS Papers.

58. Lou Sullivan to Rupert Raj, 6 February 1985, box 3 folder 116, LGS Papers.

59. Sullivan Journal, 16 February 1985, box 1 folder 14, LGS Papers.

60. Ira B. Pauly, *Female to Gay Male Transsexualism: Part III* (Reno: Department of Psychiatry & Behavioral Sciences, University of Nevada School of Medicine, [1989]).

61. Lou Sullivan to Jude Patton, 26 June 1985, box 3 folder 113, LGS Papers.

62. Program Committee Chairman Dr. Aaron T. Billowitz qtd in Rupert Raj-Gauthier, "Eleventh International Symposium on Gender Dysphoria: An Insider's Report," *FTM* 11 (March 1990) in Rawlings-Fein, 60.

63. FTM's mother to Lou Sullivan, 10 February 1985, box 2 folder 67, LGS Papers.

64. Lou Sullivan to FTM's mother, 15 February 1985, box 2 folder 67, LGS Papers; Sullivan Journal, 16 February 1985, box 1 folder 14, LGS Papers.

65. Sullivan Journal, 15 April 1985, box 1 folder 14, LGS Papers.

66. Sullivan Journal, 21 November 1985, box 1 folder 14, LGS Papers.

67. Lou Sullivan, "Lesbian Masquerade: some lesbians in early san francisco who passed as men," *The Gateway* (July 1979): no pages given.

68. Louis G. Sullivan, "A Biography of Jack Bee Garland (a.k.a. Babe Bean)," *Metamorphosis* 6.4 (July-August 1987): 18.

69. Sullivan Journal, 28 August 1984, box 1 folder 13, LGS Papers.

70. Allan Bérubé to Lou Sullivan, 3 September 1979, box 2 folder 84, and Sullivan Journal, 6 October 1984, box 1 folder 14, LGS Papers.

71. Allan Bérubé, *Coming Out Under Fire: The History of Gay Men and Women in World War Two* (New York: The Free Press, 1990), ix.

72. Sullivan Journal, 17 September 1984, box 1 folder 13, LGS Papers.

73. Sullivan Journal, 27 October 1984, box 1 folder 14, LGS Papers.

74. Sullivan Journal, 11 October 1984, box 1 folder 14, LGS Papers.

75. Sullivan Journal, 30 November 1984, box 1 folder 14, LGS Papers.

76. Ibid.

77. Sullivan Journal, 10 December 1984, box 1 folder 14, LGS Papers.

78. Sullivan Journal, 4 March 1985 and 15 April 1985, box 1 folder 14, LGS Papers; Bill [Willie] Walker to Lou Sullivan, undated, box 4 folder 162, LGS Papers.

79. "Obituary—Willie Walker," *Bozeman Daily Chronicle* (9 October 2004), http://bozemandailychronicle.com/articles/2004/10/10/obituaries/walker.txt; Stryker and Van Buskirk, 101.

80. "Obituary—Willie Walker"; Bérubé, x, xii.

81. Martin Meeker, "Archives Review: The Gay and Lesbian Historical Society of Northern California," *Journal of Gay, Lesbian, and Bisexual Identity* 4.2 (April 1999): 197-198.

82. Sullivan Journal, 30 June 1985, box 1 folder 14, LGS Papers.

83. Sullivan Journal, 14 June 1986, box 1 folder 14, LGS Papers. Garber later published on this research, and his article laid the foundation for further research endeavors by other scholars. See Eric Garber, "A Spectacle in Color: The Lesbian and Gay Subculture of Jazz Age Harlem," in *Hidden from History: Reclaiming the Gay and Lesbian Past*, ed. Martin Bauml Duberman, Martha Vicinus and George Chauncey Jr. (New York: New American Library, 1989), 318-331.

84. Sullivan Journal, 19 October 1986, box 1 folder 14, LGS Papers.

85. Sullivan Journal, 7 November 1986, box 1 folder 14, LGS Papers.

86. See Louis G. Sullivan, "Members' Work in Progress: A Biography of Jack Bee Garland AKA Babe Bean," *San Francisco Bay Area Gay & Lesbian Historical Society Newsletter* 2.3 (March 1987): 1, 4-5.

87. Sullivan Journal, 19 October 1986, box 1 folder 14, LGS Papers; "'You Can Help Preserve Lesbian and Gay History!': A Brief History of the GLBT Historical Society," *San Francisco Bay Area Gay and Lesbian Historical Society Newsletter* 1.3 (March 1986): 5.

88. Sullivan Journal, 17 January 1986, box 1 folder 14, LGS Papers.

89. Sullivan Journal, 22 January 1986, box 1 folder 14, LGS Papers.

90. Margalit Fox, "Stanley H. Biber, 82, Surgeon Among First to Do Sex Changes, Dies," *New York Times* (21 January 2006), http://www.nytimes.com/2006/01/21/national/21biber.html; Meyerowitz, 272.

91. Stanley H. Biber to L.G. Sullivan, 31 March 1986, box 2 folder 39, LGS Papers.

92. Sullivan Journal, 22 January 1986, box 1 folder 14, LGS Papers.

93. Sullivan Journal, 10 February 1986, box 1 folder 14, LGS Papers.

94. Sullivan Journal, 26 March 1986, box 1 folder 14, LGS Papers.

95. Lou Sullivan to Kim Stuart, 16 March 1986, box 3 folder 118, LGS Papers.

96. Sullivan Journal, 25 February 1986, box 1 folder 14, LGS Papers.

97. Sullivan Journal, 11 September 1979, 27 September 1979, 28 September 1979, box 1 folder 12, LGS Papers.

98. Kim Stuart to Lou Sullivan, 20 March 1986, box 3 folder 118, LGS Papers.

99. Sullivan Journal, 22 March 1986, box 1 folder 14, LGS Papers.

100. Kim Stuart to Lou Sullivan, 20 March 1986, box 3 folder 118, LGS Papers.

101. Sullivan Journal, 11 October 1984, box 1 folder 14, LGS Papers.

102. Michael L. Brownstein, interview by author, 31 March 2007, Milwaukee.

103. Kim Stuart to Lou Sullivan, 20 March 1986, box 3 folder 118, LGS Papers.

104. Michael L. Brownstein interview.

105. Kim Stuart to Lou Sullivan, 20 March 1986, box 3 folder 118, LGS Papers; Michael L. Brownstein interview.

106. Sullivan Journal, 3 April 1986, 13 April 1986, box 1 folder 14, LGS Papers.

107. Michael L. Brownstein interview.

108. Sullivan Journal, 13 April 1986, box 1 folder 14, LGS Papers.

109. Michael L. Brownstein interview; Sullivan Journal, 13 April 1986, 19 April 1986, box 1 folder 14, LGS Papers.

110. One of the effects of testosterone therapy is clitoral enlargement. A metoidioplasty entails releasing the clitoral tissue from its position and moving it forward to better approximate the position of a penis. The urethral extension allows urination through the neopenis. Testicular implants are inserted into the labia majora and then the labia majora are sewn together to form a scrotal sac.

111. Sullivan Journal, 24 April 1986, box 1 folder 14, LGS Papers.

112. Sullivan Journal, 28 April 1986, box 1 folder 14, LGS Papers.

113. Sullivan Journal, 5 May 1986, box 1 folder 14, LGS Papers.

114. Sullivan Journal, 25 June 1986, box 1 folder 14, LGS Papers.

115. Sullivan Journal, 2 July 1986, box 1 folder 14, LGS Papers.

116. Sullivan Journal, 5 July 1986, box 1 folder 14, LGS Papers.

117. Sullivan Journal, 5 July 1986, 10 July 1986, box 1 folder 14, LGS Papers.

118. Sullivan Journal, 15 July 1986, box 1 folder 14, LGS Papers.

119. Sullivan Journal, 11 September 1986, box 1 folder 14, LGS Papers.

120. Nicholas Sempeti to Lou Sullivan, 15 September 1986, box 4 folder 157, LGS Papers.

121. Sullivan Journal, 5 May 1986, box 1 folder 14, LGS Papers.

122. Sullivan Journal, 14 June 1986, box 1 folder 14, LGS Papers.

123. Sullivan Journal, 8 September 1986, box 1 folder 14, LGS Papers.

124. March Fong Eu to All County Clerks/Registrars of Voters, 25 June 1986, Proposition 64, University of California Hastings College of the Law Library, http://holmes.uchastings.edu/initiatives.pdf/373.pdf; Kevin Roderick, "Questions on Prop 64: Clearing the Confusion," *Los Angeles Times* (29 October 1986), http://www.aegis.org/news/Lt/1986/LT861002.html.

125. Sullivan Journal, 3 August 1986, box 1 folder 14, LGS Papers.

126. Lou Sullivan to Paul Walker, 8 August 1986, box 3 folder 121, LGS Papers.

127. Sullivan Journal, 7 August 1986, box 1 folder 14, LGS Papers.

128. See *What Sex Am I?* VHS, dir. Lee Grant (USA: Joseph Feury Productions, 2005).

129. Sullivan Journal, 4 October 1986, 5 October 1986, box 1 folder 14, LGS Papers.

130. Sullivan Journal, 4 October 1986, box 1 folder 14, LGS Papers.

131. Sullivan Journal, 7 November 1986, box 1 folder 14, LGS Papers.

132. Sullivan Journal, 9 November 1986, box 1 folder 14, LGS Papers. ETVC is now TransGender San Francisco, "one of the most respected transgender organizations in the country." TransGender San Francisco, "TGSF History," *TransGender San Francisco*, http://www.tgsf.org/who/history.html.

133. Sullivan Journal, 9 November 1986, box 1 folder 14, LGS Papers.

134. "Female-to-Male Get-Together #3," *FTM* 1 (September 1987) in Rawlings-Fein, 1.

135. Sullivan Journal, 12 June 1985, box 1 folder 14, LGS Papers.

136. Sullivan Journal, 5 January 1985, box 1 folder 14, LGS Papers.

137. Sullivan Journal, 29 November 1986, box 1 folder 14, LGS Papers.

138. Sullivan Journal, 30 November 1986, box 1 folder 14, LGS Papers.

139. Sullivan Journal, 4 December 1986, box 1 folder 14, LGS Papers.

CHAPTER

6

PWA

L ou was in the hospital for a week before he picked up a pen to record his thoughts and feelings in his journal. He began the entry like he was writing a letter to an old friend: "Well, diary, I didn't think I'd be writing the Last Chapter so soon. My penmanship is pretty bad because I have an intravenous needle in my right wrist and I'm in the hospital. I have AIDS."[1] Lou's diagnosis was shocking and devastating. But in time it became transforming and inspiring.

Lou was not afraid of death. He rose to the challenge instead. He made his AIDS diagnosis a catalyst for becoming one of the most prolific and accomplished FTM activists in history. What Lou feared was dying an outcast; more specifically a sexual outcast, never knowing the joy of sharing with others the body that he had gone to great lengths to remake—the body that finally felt like his own.

DIAGNOSED

Three weeks after leaving Keith and moving into his new home in the Mission, Lou noticed that he was having difficulty breathing. At first he attributed it to the stress of moving, working and preparing for Christmas.[2] When Lou and Maryellen went to eat at the German Cook, one of his favorite restaurants, Lou told her: "You know, something is wrong, and I don't know what it is. I don't feel good. I feel like something is just really wrong with me."[3] Maryellen suggested he take yoga classes to help with his breathing, and Lou tried to blow off his sense of dis-ease. To help his breathing Lou tried taking decongestants, figuring the trouble was with his sinuses, which had always given him problems.[4]

When Lou went to the December 28, 1986 GLBT Historical Society meeting and explained what he was experiencing with his health, one of his gay colleagues said it sounded like walking pneumonia and that he should see a doctor right away. Lou made an appointment for a few days later to see Dr. Fulmer, who served as both his endocrinologist and primary care physician. But by noon the day before his appointment, while working on a freelance word processing job downtown, Lou found that his heart was pounding and he was gasping for air. With great effort, Lou rode his motorcycle to a free walk-in clinic where he had an X-ray taken of his chest. After looking at the X-ray, a doctor told Lou that he needed to go to the hospital immediately. Lou went to Maryellen's, and as she drove him to the UCSF Medical Center, Lou began to fear that he might have pneumocystis carinii pneumonia (PCP) and AIDS.[5]

Lou and Maryellen were sitting in the UCSF treatment room, sharing a soda as they waited for the results of his blood tests, when a doctor came in and confirmed Lou's fears. In a very matter of fact manner, the doctor told Lou he had PCP (the most frequent opportunistic infection seen with AIDS), that tests indicated Lou had an advanced case of AIDS, and that he should put his affairs in order because he did not have long to live. According to Maryellen, she and Lou "just looked at each other like, 'Holy crap! Did you hear what I just heard? I don't believe this.'"[6] Lou was immediately admitted to the hospital and put on oxygen. Later, all Lou remembered of his first days in the hospital was having fitful dreams wherein the Boogie Man was after him, and Maryellen—his sister and best friend—sleeping in the extra hospital room bed. Three days into his hospital stay, Keith was visiting Lou when his doctors came in to confirm that he had AIDS.

Lou wrote about the reactions of his loved ones to his diagnosis like a detached observer. According to Lou, Maryellen was "falling apart," so he offered to pay her airfare to fly to Pennsylvania and pick up their sister Bridget "so [she] didn't have to face this alone." "Of course the whole family is stricken with grief," he wrote. "The misfortune in the Sullivan family has just been too much." Patrick died after a motorcycle accident, Kathleen had recently been diagnosed with multiple sclerosis, and now with Lou's AIDS diagnosis the Sullivan siblings began thinking their family was cursed. Lou also recorded his observations of Keith: "The last time Keith visited I could see the terrible sadness lined into his face. He said he lit a candle for me and that the flame burned high and strong for a long time so he was sure it was a good sign…. He tries to project optimism, but I know he's hurting inside." During that first week, the only time that his AIDS diagnosis "really hit" and "saddened" Lou was when Maryellen brought his niece and nephew to visit him in the hospital: "I realized that they are going to have to see their Uncle Lou die and how really sad that is… they love me so much."

Lou admitted to being in "a state of shock and disbelief" about his diagnosis, primarily because AIDS was then associated with promiscuity while Lou considered himself as being "a sexual recluse for so long."[7] After meeting Keith in the summer of 1981, Lou remained sexually monogamous until January 1985, after which time he had five additional sexual partners—three cisgender gay men and two MTFs. Many of Lou's contemporaries had that many sexual partners in one week. Some in one day.

One of the gay men with whom Lou had sex during this time was his old friend Charles. Lou and Charles had taken a trip to the Southwest at the end of March 1986, staying with Charles's family in Farmington, New Mexico.[8] Charles tested negative for HIV. The second was a man who did not orgasm when Sullivan performed oral sex upon him in January 1986. Singer/actor Joseph was the third gay man, and Lou began a sexual relationship with him in March 1985. Joseph would eventually die from AIDS, but Lou never mentioned him having the disease.[9]

The fate of the two MTFs—Monica from Sweden and the unnamed "queen" whom Lou met on New Year's Eve at the Black Rose—may never be known. Even if Lou had left a record of their full women's names, death records contain legal names. In the 1980s few trans people had access to the knowledge and resources to legally change their names, and given that Monica was a foreigner and the "queen" was likely a sex worker, the chances of their legally changing their birth (male) names seems a remote possibility at best. While it is impossible to know exactly how Lou contracted AIDS, the timing of his seroconverting in January 1985 meant that Lou was infected either by Keith or one of these two MTFs. Keith tested negative.

Poor trans women of color, like the individual with whom Lou had had sexual relations two years prior, comprised one of the populations most at risk for contracting and spreading the AIDS virus. The same remains true to this day. Then as now, a disproportionate number of trans women of color found themselves on the street, relying upon sex work for survival due to overt and systemic racism and transphobia. Risk increased by sharing needles for injecting hormones and participating in the gay male sexual subculture, where the virus was more concentrated.[10]

But how he had contracted HIV/AIDS would prove irrelevant to

Lou—what mattered to him was that he was dying from what was still largely seen as a gay men's disease.

> It really hasn't hit me that I am about to die. I see the grief around me, but inside I feel serene and a certain kind of peace. My whole life I've wanted to be a gay man and it's kind of an honor to die from the gay men's disease.... [The gender programs] decided that I couldn't live as a gay man, but I am going to die like one.[11]

In his correspondence, publications in the gay and trans presses, lectures, interviews, conversations with other FTMs—any time he spoke about his identity after being diagnosed with AIDS—Lou would repeat derivations of that final sentence: The gender programs decided that I couldn't live as a gay man, but I am going to die like one.

Lou would remain selective about whom he informed that he was trans but was open about having AIDS. On one hand, Lou found it quite upsetting to tell those who cared about him that he had AIDS. On the other, he found that having AIDS seemed to validate his identity as a gay man more than anything else had (or possibly could)—particularly for gender professionals, such as Paul Walker.

A month after his diagnosis, Lou penned a letter to Walker, who had alternately confirmed and questioned the validity of Lou's being a gay FTM. "Strange how things turn out," he wrote. "There may have been doubts that I could live as a gay man—there seems no doubt that I'm going to die like one."[12] Walker responded very compassionately to Lou's diagnosis, and the complications that had arisen in their relationship when Lou sought Walker's help in accessing bottom surgery disappeared. "So many of my friends have been diagnosed," Walker wrote. "The rest of us are probably right behind."[13] In fact, Walker's lover would be diagnosed as having AIDS the following year, and shortly thereafter Walker himself would be diagnosed as having AIDS.[14]

Lou worried that contracting the virus would "prevent me from ever completing my surgery," which devastated him. Lou promptly contacted Dr. Brownstein upon receiving his diagnosis, informing Brownstein that he had AIDS. When Brownstein heard the news, he "was very upset and said he felt awful."[15] Through all of the frustrating and painful surgical complications, Lou had remained very encouraging and supportive of Brownstein, and the two had a warm relationship.[16] Brownstein was understandably concerned about the possible risk of infection from operating on Lou, but told him he would conduct research and consult with colleagues before ruling out the possibility of completing Lou's surgery.[17] Lou got the go-ahead from the director of the UCSF AIDS Clinic, provided he wait at least a month to fully recover from his pneumonia so his body would be strong enough.[18] In fact, it is likely that Lou's ongoing surgical complications led to him developing full-blown AIDS, because his immune system had been compromised for an extended period of time. But completing surgery was very important to Lou, and every day began to feel like torture because of his discomfort with his "deformed body."[19]

Years after Lou's death, Dr. Brownstein humbly revealed that he completed Lou's surgery despite the potential risks to himself because he considered Lou "a special guy" and wanted to finish what he started.[20] At the time, Brownstein courageously and empathetically told Lou that he himself could just as easily be HIV positive as the next person, and implied that having AIDS should not prevent someone from embodying their identity. In response, Lou "urged [Brownstein] to continue perfecting his technique and [told him] that he definitely must continue" performing surgeries for FTMs.[21] Over the next twenty-five years, Brownstein would perform surgeries on more than 3,000 FTMs.[22] A remarkable number, but perhaps not surprising given Lou's early, glowing, widespread referrals, which spread like wildfire once patients experienced Brownstein's talents and concern for trans patients.

On March 2, 1987, under local anesthesia, Dr. Brownstein inserted another testicular implant in Lou's scrotum. The second FTM Get-Together was held a couple of weeks later on March 14, but Lou did not attend. Determined not to lose his third implant, wisely Lou stayed home and allowed his body to heal.[23]

Lou's brother Flame cared for him as Lou's testicle slowly but successfully healed.[24] Shortly after learning of Lou's AIDS diagnosis, Flame had come from Milwaukee to stay with him. Flame studied all of the AIDS literature available at the time and dreamed up ways of fighting the disease to save his brother.[25] With Kathleen incapacitated because of multiple sclerosis, Bridget in Pennsylvania, and Maryellen caring for her three small children in Oakland, Flame assumed the role of Lou's primary caretaker for several weeks. Flame was a "good influence" on Lou, encouraging him to eat three meals a day and "take it easy."[26]

While Lou had successfully completed surgery, he still worried that

AIDS would make him unlovable to others and unworthy of physical affection. "The thing that hurts me most," he wrote in his journal shortly after receiving his diagnosis, "[is thinking] that I will never know a man's loving touch on my whole completed body."

> That even though I may still be able to undergo the surgery to get my left testicle, that because of my disease I will never find a lover who will suck me, lick me, kiss me there. The enormous injustice of that possibility almost overwhelms me with despair. How close I was! How good it feels to have even one ball! A miniscule cock! And now I feel like a leper, something diseased and fearsome and unlovable. This is what is haunting me. Not the imminence of death. We all know from the moment we are born that we are destined to die. That's OK. I just dread having to spend these last precious years as an outcast AGAIN.[27]

Lou used to have "a shred of hope" that he might find a gay man who would not care that he was born female or had "a 1-inch dick that was nonfunctional." "But now that I also have a sexually transmitted fatal disease, I don't think I'll ever find anyone who'll look twice at me."[28] However, Lou was determined not to succumb to negative thinking because he knew that it would "simply breed more ill health."[29]

First Known FTM PWA

AIDS was a puzzling disease to medical professionals back then. When Lou was discharged from the hospital on January 12, 1987, after receiving his AIDS diagnosis, he was at a loss. "I feel like, hey, I got this deadly disease and no one can give me any guidance as to how to manage it or what I should do differently—other than eat well, get lots of rest, wear gloves when I change the newspaper in the bottom of the bird cage," he wrote in his journal.[30] But San Francisco was the best place in the world to receive care.

In 1981, at the beginning of the onslaught of the virus, UCSF's Dr. Marcus Conant, a gay physician, established a functional clinic for those afflicted with AIDS with the backing of the UCSF Medical Center.[31] The world-renowned UCSF Medical Center AIDS Clinic opened at San Francisco General Hospital, its teaching hospital, in 1983.[32] Four years later, Lou signed up at this AIDS outpatient clinic, where as a PWA (person with AIDS) he was treated with compassion and given access to proven and experimental treatments for the remainder of his life.

Initially Lou was assumed under the care of Dr. Harry Hollander, who was then serving as director of the AIDS Clinic. Lou later realized it was because, as an FTM, he was a "special case."[33] In fact, Lou is the first known FTM AIDS case ever.

Lou was also fairly unique in that he did not fear disclosing his trans status to these medical providers. When filling out his intake questionnaire at the clinic, Lou was given the options "homosexual, heterosexual, bisexual," and wrote in "F→M transsexual with male sex partners."[34] As a white middle-class FTM who was consistently read as a man, Lou's privilege bestowed him with confidence that disclosing his trans status would not result in being denied access to these life-and-death medical services. For Lou, access to healthcare was a right, not a privilege. He had not known the same social and economic vulnerabilities that either barred other trans people from accessing healthcare services or at the very least kept them at bay. Additionally, well-meaning medical professionals in the field of AIDS treatment and research may have been aware that AIDS affected people of all sexual orientations, but they were largely ill-versed in gender dysphoria. Luckily Lou put his privilege to good use, educating all of the providers with whom he interacted at the AIDS Clinic about what it meant to be trans and about challenges trans people faced.

Trans PWAs were even more reticent about accessing support services than healthcare services. Shortly after receiving his diagnosis, Lou learned of a new "Transsexual/Transvestite Support Group for People with AIDS." "That should be interesting," he wrote, "Talk about minority groups."[35] When he arrived at the meeting location, he found himself alone—not even the group organizers had shown up. Eventually one MTF showed up who did not have AIDS, apparently seeking a venue for socializing.[36] Lou tried the meeting a second time the following month, but again he was the only trans person with AIDS who attended. This time two cisgender counselors attended, both of whom had, incidentally, seen Lou speak at the Institute for Advanced Study of Human Sexuality. Frustrated that he was the only trans person with AIDS to show up, Lou never attended again.[37] Instead, he found—and founded—other support groups. This early attempt at AIDS community outreach to trans people failed due to lack of awareness. The group's organizers failed to realize that support groups are largely organized by white middle-class people and are seen as being for white middle-class people, while the vast majority of the Bay Area's trans PWAs were not white or middle-class.

Lou's privilege not only ensured his access to support groups and healthcare. When he sought healthcare and was diagnosed as having AIDS, Lou immediately qualified for disability benefits and for having all of his medical bills covered by the state of California.[38] Unaware of his privilege, Lou initially felt resentful about this: "It's like if you got AIDS you instantly get total disability and the State pays all the bills and all you need to do is wait around to die. Thanks a lot."[39]

At this point, Lou was by no means ready to die, and he continually found the stipulations for receiving disability benefits to be restricting. Disability did not provide enough money to live on. But if Lou felt well enough to work and did so to supplement his income, he chanced losing his eligibility for disability benefits altogether. Lou quickly informed the office manager of the downtown investment firm for which he did freelance work that he had AIDS. When she asked Lou what to tell the bosses when they wondered why he could no longer work, Lou encouraged her to be honest: "I think it's good that people see those with AIDS so it's not just another newspaper story."[40]

After learning he had AIDS, Lou seemed to suddenly notice the constant reports of people dying from AIDS in the newspaper or on televison.[41] He began to regularly note AIDS statistics in his journals—how many people had been reported as having AIDS and how many had died. A month after his diagnosis, Lou reported that in San Francisco more than two people a day were dying from AIDS.[42]

Lou may have been the first known FTM PWA but he knew that he would not be the last and he was determined that his impending death not be in vain. Lou contacted gay professional photographer Jim Wigler, who was working on a project called "Faces of AIDS," which later toured the world with the Names Project AIDS Memorial Quilt. When Lou initially contacted him, Wigler said that he already had enough people, "but when I told him I was a female-to-male transsexual, he suddenly wanted me BAD," and photographed Lou for the project.[43]

On June 16, 1987, Lou's 36th birthday, he rode his motorcycle to see the "Faces of AIDS" exhibit at the San Mateo Hall of Justice in Redwood City, California.

I wanted to stand and stare at my photo and read the words over and over, but it seemed like everyone else there (and the place was mobbed) wanted to do the same thing. For sure people lingered at my photo, I'm sure because it was the first time they had ever seen a female-to-male, and my quote. There was a big close-up of my face, and beside it my name and age and "I am a female-to-male transsexual living as a gay man. AIDS was the last thing I expected—I haven't had that many contacts. They told me at the gender clinic that I could not live as a gay man, but it looks like I will die as one." I got the feeling several people "recognized" me, so I didn't want to stand and stare at my own photograph. But my face was so masculine and my eyes truly looked sad.[44]

In a review of the exhibit in the *Bay Area Reporter*, Lou's quotation was characterized as ironic. When Lou briefly became concerned about how many people would come to know he was transsexual through this exhibit and its ensuing publicity, he reminded himself that he had chosen to participate in this project as a way to "document that a female-to-male CAN live as a gay man."[45] When viewing the exhibit, Lou noted that five of the sixty photographs had black ribbons on them, and it took him awhile to realize that the ribbons signified that the subjects had died. He wondered how many more would be added before the exhibit ended the following month.[46]

A reporter named Jim Dickey from the *San Jose Mercury News* tracked down Lou's contact information after seeing the "Faces with AIDS" exhibit and phoned him for an interview. "Of course I agreed, in the interest of spreading the facts on the female-to-male, but my main blockage is whether or not to use my real name and/or let him publish my photograph." Lou engaged in complete disclosure in certain educational contexts, but he feared that mainstream coverage would transform his experiences into tabloid fodder.[47] To his surprise, Lou found Dickey quite understanding and attributed his comfort with Dickey to the fact that Dickey was gay. Lou and Dickey agreed to use a pseudonym and chose the name that Lou used in childhood while "playing boys."[48] It took more than two months for Dickey to convince his editor to print the article, and it made Lou laugh to think: "My life is too weird for the general reading public."[49] But on May 7, 1988, the *San Jose Mercury News* printed Dickey's article, "The Transformation of Bobby Cordale: How a Midwestern Girl Who Felt Trapped as a Female Became a Man—and a Victim of the AIDS Epidemic."[50]

BEST PLACE IN THE WORLD

Lou was acutely aware that San Francisco was the best place in the world to live as a person with AIDS, even if he was the first known FTM PWA. In San Francisco, years of political organizing, decades of visibility and the sheer number of gays and lesbians wrought a unique collaboration between community activists, government and the medical profession in response to AIDS.

One month after receiving his AIDS diagnosis, Lou's doctor at the AIDS clinic suggested he take AZT, which he was told "may possibly retard the spreading of the AIDS virus in my body and brain."[51] To research this new "experimental drug," Lou attended a discussion on AZT held by the Alice B. Toklas Gay Democratic Society. At the discussion Lou learned that those like himself who had PCP and took AZT experienced longer periods of wellness before contracting pneumocystis again.[52] Lou also attended a lecture at Project Inform. Founded in 1985, Project Inform sought to empower PWAs with information about their conditions and available treatment options, thus making doctors and patients "co-conspirators" in their fight against AIDS.[53] Interestingly, with all of the information and sources of support regarding AIDS that were available to Lou, it was his gay men with disabilities support group—which he began attending to help him feel more comfortable with his trans body—that convinced Lou to begin taking AZT.

Lou took his first dose of AZT the same day that he read a front-page article in the *San Francisco Chronicle* titled "FDA APPROVES FIRST AIDS DRUG, AZT attacks virus, slowed progress of diseases in 5,000."[54] If—as the article said—there were 20,000 AIDS patients, the UCSF Medical Center played a key role in administering this experimental drug to twenty-five percent of all AIDS patients. After reading the article, Lou wrote in his journal that "The worst part of the article says, 'Pneumocystis carinii patients,' that's what I had, 'usually live an average of 40 weeks from the time an infection first appears.'… 40 weeks—less than a year. This is just too brutal to be real." Lou's doctor cautioned that he might be "too far gone"—his disease too advanced—to hope for much longevity.[55] Plus, the side effects of AZT caused Lou to experience headaches, decreased energy levels, nausea and loss of appetite. However, luckily he continued taking the drug, for it would prove to extend his life (and the lives of countless others.)

Three weeks after he began taking AZT—which ostensibly doubled the chances of survival after six weeks of treatment—Lou noted that now four San Franciscans died from AIDS-related illnesses each day, the number of daily deaths doubling in the space of two months.[56] Among the dead was the partner of Lou's fellow historian, Allan Bérubé. When Lou read in the *Bay Area Reporter* that Bérubé's partner died in his arms from AIDS complications, Lou broke down and cried. This was the first time that Lou cried since receiving his AIDS diagnosis. Lou had been living with AIDS for four months, and his physical outpouring of empathy for Bérubé brought forth a watershed of feelings that Lou had about his own diagnosis. Caring for another had enabled Lou to care about himself, and he was overcome with a sense of injustice.

> I feel so hopeless and like all I can do is wait to croak. Any therapy or treatment I take is in vain. I feel pretty good right now, but statistics say I should be dead by November.... I guess I just feel that my body has been one big burden throughout my life, and getting this fatal disease… one that can be transmitted to anyone who loves my body… is just the last straw. Just knowing that this is the way I will be until I die is so hard to accept. I haven't been a very fortunate person in this life.

Lou decided it was time to admit that he had AIDS and that he would die in the near future. But he also decided to be proactive about his disease even if others thought he was "too far gone."[57]

Lou combined Eastern and Western medical practices. He began receiving weekly massages from a gay masseuse, which he found immensely therapeutic both physically and emotionally because the touch helped him to feel better about his body.[58] In addition to AZT, Lou also signed up to take the experimental drug aerosol pentamidine, which had been invented by a doctor at the UCSF Medical Center, and thus far had proven 100% effective in preventing the return of PCP.[59] Lou began receiving aerosol pentamidine treatment once a month and later signed up for an aerosol pentamidine-related study, willingly volunteering to be an experimental subject in order to help others seeking medical treatment in the future.[60] Ultimately pentamidine proved highly successful in preventing PCP, especially for those who had never had PCP. In Lou's case, he was able to ward off PCP recurrence for more than two years.

For emotional support in coping with his disease, Lou continued attending the gay men with disabilities support group and also signed up with the Shanti Project. The Shanti Project was largely a volunteer outreach organization that received funding from the San Francisco city government and quickly became a widely emulated model of AIDS services.[61] In addition to peer counselors, Shanti also provided "buddies" to help with practical matters like cooking, cleaning and shopping, and had contracted with the San Francisco Department of Public Health to provide housing for PWAs.[62] When Lou contacted Shanti, he was given an "emotional support counselor" named Bruce. Unfortunately, Lou struggled for eighteen months over disclosing to Bruce that he was trans, only to discover that Bruce had known for at least a year because one of his friends told him he had seen Lou give a presentation on being an FTM.[63]

It was with Bruce that Lou went to visit the Names Project AIDS Memorial Quilt. At the time that Lou visited the quilt, in December 1987, there were over 2,000 panels, each bearing the name of one individual who had died from AIDS.

> What did I feel as I wandered through the vast graveyard, looking at all those tombstones bearing the names of my gay brothers? I feel so sad for the gay liberation movement. All these years we've been fighting for our self-pride and our dignity, and now it seems like a giant battlefield covered with our dead. And it is so like gay men to devise such a gentle, loving, sweet symbol of our devastation: this pretty, warm, colorful blanket… when I want them to be angry and defiant and MAD![64]

The idea for the quilt was conceived by Cleve Jones, the same veteran activist who had helped channel the gay community's pain, sadness and anger over the assassination of Harvey Milk into a moving candlelight march. A quilt, Jones thought, was "such a warm, comforting, middle-class, middle-American symbol. Every family has a quilt; it makes them think of their grandmothers. That's what we need: We need all these American grandmothers to want us to live, to be willing to say that our lives are worth defending."[65]

The Names Project AIDS Memorial Quilt, Shanti, Project Inform, the

San Francisco AIDS Foundation and Project Open Hand (which delivered meals to PWAs) were all community-based responses to the epidemic ravaging San Francisco. Veteran activists were surprised to see thousands suddenly galvanized into action, and witnessed a shift among their fellow gays from individualized pleasure-seeking to communal caring.[66] AIDS politicized the gay community in ways that gay liberation had not. Politics was no longer a matter of gaining political clout. Gays were—as the phrase went—fighting for their lives. In the words of one journalist, "AIDS brought the gay community *as* a community out of the closet."[67] What is more, they came out as a gay and lesbian community. Lesbians concluded that the decade-long antagonisms between gays and lesbians (largely over sexism) were counterproductive and tragic; lesbians and gays had a shared history, and, in the face of AIDS, common homophobic enemies who did not differentiate by gender.[68] Worth noting, however, is this move toward (re)unified political consciousness largely omitted trans people.

In stark contrast to San Francisco, Milwaukee had dedicated community activists with years of organizing experience but who lacked the same level of systemic support. In the mid-1980s the GPU-founded BESTD (Brady East STD) Clinic formed the Milwaukee AIDS Project.[69] Lou's long-time friend Eldon Murray, who had been instrumental in founding the clinic, was also instrumental in securing initial grants for the Milwaukee AIDS Project. At the end of 1985, the Milwaukee AIDS Project formed a new corporate umbrella called the AIDS Resource Center of Wisconsin (ARCW) in order to attract more substantial resources, and the organization exists to this day.[70] Through his contact with Eldon, Lou learned that ARCW successfully secured tens of thousands of dollars from the city and state governments in its initial years, but as the sole provider of AIDS-related services for the entire state, these funds were woefully inadequate.

From Alyn Hess, another one of his old GPU friends, Lou also learned of the discrepancy in medical care between Milwaukee and San Francisco. Alyn had very compassionate doctors at the VA hospital who knew about AIDS but lacked the knowledge to properly diagnose and adequately treat the disease. In a letter to Lou in April 1987, Alyn explained that he had self-diagnosed himself as having AIDS-Related Complex (ARC) and had determined his own methods of treatment.[71] ARC had been identified as a precursor to full-blown AIDS, and having ARC meant displaying symptoms due to HIV infection. Alyn's doctors failed to diagnose him as having ARC, and only diagnosed him as having AIDS after he was hospitalized with PCP in July 1988.[72] Over the next nine months, Alyn suffered from two brain tumors and a number of other debilitating AIDS-related maladies. On the morning of April 1, 1989, Eldon phoned Lou to inform him Alyn had died. It would be several more months before AZT and aerosol pentamidine—the AIDS treatments Lou received from the UCSF Medical Center AIDS Clinic—were made available to AIDS patients in Milwaukee.[73]

San Francisco was the best place in the world to be a person with AIDS. But if Lou had not moved to San Francisco, would he have become a PWA? San Francisco was, after all, the epicenter of the epidemic. The high concentration of those infected put Lou at greater risk of contracting the disease in San Francisco than in Milwaukee. However, it is impossible to know whether or not Lou would have become a PWA had he stayed in Milwaukee, just as it is impossible to know whether or not Lou would have been able to transition and, if so, when. Perhaps Lou would still be alive today had he not moved to San Francisco, but who would he be? The fact is, Lou never gave a thought to what might have been had he not moved, instead only expressing gratitude for living in San Francisco as a gay FTM PWA.

DIFFERENT EXCUSE FOR THE SAME DILEMMA

Lou found that amidst the AIDS crisis, cisgender gay men experienced isolation, frustration and despair akin to what he experienced as an FTM. Lou had greatly curtailed his participation in San Francisco's bar scene since his AIDS diagnosis. Now when he went out, he attended PWA Night at Moby Dick's in the Castro. The local AIDS group advertising PWA Night encouraged PWAs to wear a red ribbon when they attended the event in an effort to generate compassion and a sense of solidarity within the community. Doing so brought visibility to the disease and also encouraged its wearers to confront their shame at being PWAs. Lou wrote in his journal that the first two times he attended PWA Night no one wore a ribbon, including him. The third time, Lou tied a red ribbon to his motorcycle jacket.

> I felt proud and tough in the bar—and I was THE only person with a red ribbon. Well, at least it got several guys talking to me, and I had a fun time flirting. But DAMN— everyone is so uptight, so on the defensive, so sad. I want to say to these guys, "Hey, we haven't the time to be embarrassed—let's kiss."[74]

When Lou returned nearly a month later, he was still the only one in the bar wearing a red ribbon.[75]

Unlike the other men at Moby Dick's, Lou had a long history of feeling shame about his body. Several days after Lou attended PWA Night sporting a red ribbon, he went to the "Male Express Strip Revue Show at the End-Up gay bar" with a man on kidney dialysis whom he had met in the gay men with disabilities support group.

> Getting dressed up to go out, for a moment I felt like a kid again—that same flood of energy and excitement I used to get in 1973, dressing to go dancing at the River Queen. But that abandon certainly wasn't there and I tried to identify why. I rationalized to myself that, hey, I'm <u>used</u> to going out to the bars with little or no hope of meeting a sexual partner. Before it was because I didn't want to be female with someone. Now it's because I'm infectious.

"Just a different excuse for the same dilemma," he wrote: the dilemma of being in his body and how it was received by others.[76]

In a few short years AIDS turned thousands of individuals into people with disabilities. However, most individuals thought in terms of dying from AIDS rather than living with a disability. Lou was surprised to find the gay men with disabilities group doubly useful in terms of living with AIDS and living with his trans embodiment, despite the fact that Lou never told the group "of my transsexual past."[77] When attending the disabilities group Lou felt he was addressing his issues as a gay man, not as a trans man—seeing the two as distinct. Group members may not have had AIDS themselves or known that Lou was transsexual, but they understood the challenges of living and being sexual with non-normative bodies. The gay men with disabilities group helped Lou conclude that "It doesn't matter HOW I got the body I have, it only matters that I DO have the body I have."[78]

AIDS threatened to end Lou's life, but he also desperately wanted to experience sex with (what he considered) his new body. Lou accepted "that I was never meant to experience the ease with which people all around me use their bodies," and endeavored to experience as much sexual pleasure as he could while he still had time.[79] Lou applied for membership in a club called "Small Guys & Fans" for men "hung like hamsters" and those like the club's founder who found small penises attractive.[80] He sent off a personal description to be included on their contact list, saying he had a "1[-inch] micropenis," "PWA ok," and safe sex only.[81]

Within a month of joining the club, Lou had three men respond to his ad, including the club organizer. Lou informed the first man he hooked up with that he had AIDS, but felt uncomfortable with and evaded the man's questions about the scars on his chest and genitals. "He was also trying to keep some truth from me," Lou wrote, "as he had a large scar on his stomach and said he had his spleen removed due to immune system problems (which can only mean AIDS in this day and age), and he has candida in his mouth (another symptom) but he never came right out and said he has AIDS"—instead offering that he *might* have AIDS-Related Complex (ARC).

> All in all, he was a rather depressing person and even told me he was very negative and thinks life is a tragedy and if he ever got K.S. (Karposi's sarcoma) or began losing a lot of weight because of "ARC," he would commit suicide. Well, needless to say, my upbeat love of life and humorous outlook that "life is just a big fuckin' joke" did not agree with him.

In addition, Lou found "all those non-stop questions about every tiny detail of my life" exhausting: "I am not particularly interested in 'getting to know' someone and even less interested in their 'getting to know' me!" However, Lou enjoyed receiving oral sex for the first time after his genital reconstruction, and assured himself that it was safe sex.[82]

The following month Lou hooked up with another man who answered his Small Guys & Fans ad, and the two quickly became "fuck buddies."[83] In his journals Lou wrote that he admired Cory's body, but on the whole did not find him handsome nor consider Cory his "type." However, "at this point in my life," Lou realized, "'my type' is any homosexual… who will have sex with me without questioning me. So he's definitely 'my type' by those standards."[84] Cory never asked about Lou's scars nor commented on his embodiment in any way that was less than complimentary, and Lou thoroughly enjoyed their sexual relationship. However, he found it difficult to negotiate safe sex with Cory.

Initially, Lou did not tell Cory that he had AIDS. However, he began to worry that he may have infected Cory because when they engaged in oral sex, Lou emitted bodily fluids.[85] Lou was somewhat reassured when he heard that cunnilingus was on the "possibly safe" list, for he considered it the most accurate description of oral sex with him. Yet, when he asked his doctor at the AIDS Clinic why cunnilingus was considered "possibly safe," "She said no way was it safe and no way is any kind of intercourse—oral, anal, vaginal—safe, not even with a condom... that I was putting Cory at grave risk... that 'masturbation and dildos' are some of the safe things I can do," but that "the few moments I've had enjoying my body and my finally-emerging sexuality are very bad." On the other hand, various AIDS groups were publicizing that it was safe to use condoms, and "The underground even says oral/genital sex is safe."[86] Lou was extremely frustrated by the lack of consensus because he wanted to enjoy his body as much as he could for the time he had left—but he also did not want to deliver someone else a death sentence.

Lou informed Cory that he had AIDS within days of their first encounter, but then felt frustrated when Cory was lax in his safe sex practices.[87] Lou repeatedly spoke with Cory about safe sex, only to have Cory nonchalantly brush it aside. After weeks of worrying, Lou made peace with the fact that he had been upfront with Cory and realized "he has to decide what he feels is safe for him, and I have to decide what I feel is right to do, for me and for him.... I just have to be very alert to what's what, cuz he's really into inhaling poppers (amyl nitrate) (YUCK!) and obviously doesn't care."[88] It was five months into their sexual relationship before Lou found out why Cory was so lax in his safe sex practices.

> [Cory] said he was so tired of burying his friends and so tired of the whole topic. Said he's never taken "the test" to find out if he's antibody positive (i.e., also infectious) but he just assumes he is. He's of the opinion that since we "both" have the virus, we needn't be so concerned about passing it onto each other.[89]

Lou conceded responsibility for Cory's HIV status and stopped feeling guilty about acquiescing to Cory's sexual practices.

Cory expressed interest in having a committed relationship, but Lou resisted and kept their relationship at the level of fuck buddies. He feared that his relationship with Keith, not his AIDS diagnosis, had changed his views on love, sex and the relationship between the two.

> No matter what [Keith and I] did—even sex acts I disliked—it was so much more erotic because I lusted after

his body and I cared about his life. I regret to say that I still think back daily of the good times we had and how much I loved him. I miss that feeling so very much. I guess I can't give up or think "I'll never fall in love again."… Yet somehow I find myself withdrawing from that possibility, and I wonder if it's because I don't want to have someone fall in love with me, only to have him watch me become sick and die soon.[90]

Lou never fell in love again.

The last time that Lou wrote of physically seeing Keith was one year before he died. But on several occasions Lou wrote of seeing Keith in his dreams. The last time that Lou saw Mark, the other great love in his life, was nearer the end of Lou's life when it seemed death was quickly approaching. When Mark visited Lou, they went for "a stroll through the Castro"— accompanied by Mark's wife and two children. After filling hundreds of pages in his journals about his thoughts and feelings regarding Mark over the years, Lou simply wrote of their parting: "I must admit I felt pretty choked up as we hugged each other."[91]

ANGELS

Though Lou never had another serious boyfriend, he still had a lot of love in his life. He was adored by his family and loved by his friends. In the final years of Lou's life, some of these friends seemed more like angels sent to Lou to help him overcome struggles and make peace with himself before he died.

One of these friends was a cisgender gay man named Jerry. They met in November 1988 when Lou presented on AIDS and transgender people at the Institute for Advanced Study of Human Sexuality. After the talk, Jerry approached Lou and gave him "a big bear hug."[92] Later that month, Jerry somehow spotted Lou amongst the 25,000 people in attendance at the tenth anniversary memorial candlelight march commemorating the assassinations of supervisor Harvey Milk and mayor George Moscone.[93] The two exchanged phone numbers and began hanging out regularly. Lou found that Jerry reminded him of his brother Flame and described him as "an aging hippie, [and] an 'anarchist' politically." While Lou and Jerry hung out smoking marijuana, Jerry "talked about helping people be comfortable with their bodies and their sensuality, learning to relax with sexuality—all things I need <u>badly</u>.... I can't think of a better person/situation for me to be in/with at this particular moment in my life." Jerry presented panels on "group sex" at the Institute for Advanced Study of Human Sexuality, and was one of the founders of the San Francisco Jacks, which Lou excitedly explained was "the gay men's jerk-off club!!"[94]

Jerk-off—or jack-off—clubs became popular in San Francisco amidst the AIDS crisis. They provided alternative spaces to the baths and porn theaters and allowed gay men to be with one another in a sexual manner that was considered safe because the men came together to masturbate—as opposed to engaging in anal and/or oral sex. It took Lou several months after receiving his AIDS diagnosis and completing bottom surgery to muster the courage to attend a jack-off club. Doing so made him exclaim in his journal: "Finally! I feel like a gay man!"[95]

Lou came to greater realizations after attending Jerry's "Pan International Global Jack Off" on Folsom Street with approximately thirty other men. Of the October 1989 event, he wrote in his journal:

> Somehow I felt very relaxed and confident about going to this event.... Of course my dick looks much different than everyone else's, but I figure all dicks look different and I'm confident no one will be mean to me there because I've got a small dick. I also realize that, as out of shape and pathetic as my body is, it will only get more out of shape and pathetic as days go by, and I probably look better today than I ever will, so I better seize the moment.... I am very proud of myself for feeling so confident about my status as a man and my realistic body image.

Lou had a great time even though he did not touch anyone and no one touched him.[96] Lou was finally comfortable in his own skin and seeing positive results coming from his years of frustration, determination and hard work understanding and realizing his embodiment.

In addition to enabling Lou to embrace his body, Jerry's friendship also encouraged Lou to engage in AIDS activism and gave him the gift of feeling like a man among men. Jerry brought Lou into the folds of ACT UP, which protested the treatment and media representation of PWAs—or lack thereof.[97] And in May 1989, Lou attended the eleventh annual California Men's Gathering held at Camp Swig, near San Jose, at Jerry's invitation. Lou viewed the gathering as a product of the short-lived men's liberation movement—the male (and also feminist) counterpart of women's liberation—and thought it funny that he had gone through both women's liberation in the 1960s and now men's liberation in the 1980s. In both movements Lou's embodiment assured his membership. Unfortunately, the transvestite liberation for which he had advocated in the 1970s had not come to pass.

Initially, Lou was amazed at how comfortable and at ease he felt among the group of strangers at the men's gathering. He remembered how withdrawn he had been throughout his youth and early adulthood, and now attributed this newfound sense of comfort to being accepted as a man among men. Of the welcoming ceremonies, Lou wrote:

> There was lots of intense and intoxicating male energy, and I became quite overwhelmed (one of the few times) and I just let the tears fall, thinking of my life, of the journey I've made, how sad and hopeless I was as a young person feeling I could never belong, never be one of the guys. And here I am, after so many years, so many struggles, here I am, a man among men, and not too bad of a one, either. I've found my place in this world, when before I felt so alienated, a creature from outer space. This "male bonding ritual" just seemed to bring me to the peak of my journey. I've made it! And then the irony, the brick wall, the downward spiral of this disease in my body. But I feel so proud to have really reached my male aspirations, my goals, that to be faced with an end to my life seems not so awful.[98]

At the gathering Lou was able to attend several AIDS-related workshops and enjoyed being around "all the male bods."[99]

Another angel sent to Lou came in the form of his old friend Liz from Milwaukee. In June 1987 Lou returned to Milwaukee to appear in a theater production titled "History of Sexuality," presented by Milwaukee's Broadway Theater Company. Incidentally, the Broadway Theater Company had moved into the same space once occupied by the gay bar the Factory. Flame was involved in set production and suggested his brother be included in the show, thus bringing Lou back to his old stomping grounds.

The play was unscripted and consisted of three- to five-minute segments in which an individual commented upon what sexuality was. According to those in attendance, the show was a tremendous success.[100] Lou noted that he "got a lot of positive strokes and feedback" from others afterwards, including the show's "interviewer" who told Lou he was the best inter-viewee. Lou likened his performance to "all the other interviews or talks I've given about myself," but while onstage wondered whether the audience thought he was an actor and not an actual gay FTM with AIDS.[101] To assure the audience he was "for-real," Lou announced he would be selling copies of his booklet after the show. Lou sold eight copies and was shocked when the purchasers asked him to autograph them—because he was by no means famous.[102] Weeks later the show's interviewer sent Lou a letter stating: "I still have people telling me how wrapped up they were in your narrative. Most people were really moved by your integrity—something that's clearly part of your tale, but above and beyond it, too."[103]

Eldon, Flame and Lou's mother attended the show, as did a local gay FTM named Joe with whom Lou corresponded. After the show Lou went with Joe to meet another FTM named Chris and Chris's MTF partner. Lou did not contact anyone else while visiting, choosing instead to spend his time in Milwaukee libraries with Flame doing historical research on FTMs.[104] Lou located "a lot of stuff" about Ralph Kerwinieo, an FTM who had lived in Milwaukee and whose picture Lou used for the cover of the second edition of *Information for the Female-to-Male.*

As he was leaving the Milwaukee Public Library on his final day of research, Lou suddenly ran into Liz, the first trans person he had ever personally known. Lou and Liz had not corresponded—let alone seen each other—in over five years. When last in touch, Lou was in love with Keith and Liz had decided to repress her trans identity and live as a man. Liz did not recognize Lou, and he was amazed by how much she had changed. To Lou, Liz now looked "so beautiful! so together!... the tranquility in her eyes was so wonderful to see—something [she] never had before." Lou learned that the previous November Liz had undergone genital reconstructive surgery with Dr. Biber in Colorado. They talked for hours.

> It made us both feel so good, I know, to finally be sitting there with each other, both of us finally through the whole change.... We've both finally made it over to where we struggled for so long. As we talked and eased back into our old familiarity, she made hand gestures and joking asides that were those of the old [Liz] I used to know, and it made me love her even more to recognize my old friend in this lovely lady.

Lou "felt I was falling in love," and suddenly found it very difficult to leave Milwaukee, wishing to remain with Liz.

> When we said goodbye, we held each other and again gazed long and silently and lovingly into each other's eyes, reading there the years we had gone thru with each other and the happiness of our accomplishments of our goals, our deep understanding of what has happened to us.

Lou believed running into Liz was "Fate, it was necessary that it happen."[105] Though initially he interpreted this encounter in romantic terms, "finding Liz" had actually served as a valuable means for Lou to find himself. Lou projected his own sense of evolution and inner peace upon Liz. And—as fate would have it—he carried this with him when he left Milwaukee for San Francisco.

For two and a half years, driven by his desire "to use my remaining life on earth to leave an impression on others—to help where I can," Lou defied the odds of his AIDS diagnosis by experiencing remarkably good health.[106] But during Gay Pride in June 1989 Lou was shocked to discover AIDS taking a visible toll on his body. As he recounted in his journal:

> I was in a poorly-lit public restroom the other day and happened to catch sight of myself in the mirror. To my horror, the shadowy lighting accentuated my sunken features and I was staring back at a gaunt, drawn, emaciated face. All I could think was "poor Lou." Something really is happening to me.[107]

Lou attended Gay Pride with his fellow gay FTM friend Denis, a third angel who appeared in Lou's final years. Lou had befriended Denis through correspondence, and that spring Denis had moved to San Francisco from Philadelphia.[108] At first Denis helped Lou as any friend would, giving him rides to and from the hospital and other appointments, and accompanying him to events like Gay Pride. But as Lou's health worsened, Denis came to split caregiving services with Lou's sister Maryellen, thinking nothing of attending to the bodily needs of a dying man whom he loved so much. Lou served as a mentor and an inspiration to Denis, and Denis returned the favor by becoming one of Lou's primary caretakers. Through his care for Lou, Denis embodied the gratitude of countless other FTMs who credited Lou with enabling them to become the men they were meant to be.

TERMINAL STAGE

After 1989 Gay Pride, Lou's health quickly declined over the space of a month. Lou discontinued AZT because he had become anemic. Also, his red blood cell and platelet counts were low, indicating internal bleeding. Lou's spleen and liver were "huge" from swelling, and the swelling moved into his upper abdomen, extending to his diaphragm. Now when Lou inhaled, his diaphragm pressed against a network of nerves that caused pain in his chest and left shoulder.[109] The internal swelling Lou experienced made it difficult to breathe and painful to walk. Lou had trouble sleeping because of night sweats.[110] And in the space of a week, Lou lost seven pounds, putting him at 5'7" and 109 pounds as he began experiencing wasting syndrome. One of Lou's concerns about his wasting syndrome was the difficulty he had locating muscle in his thigh to give himself his testosterone injections.[111]

Lou's doctors officially diagnosed him as having mycobacterium avium intracellulare (MAI), which Lou described as "some nebulous generalized infection," and informed him that he had reached the "terminal" stage of his disease. "They have no time parameters of how long this all takes, so I could be where I'm at for a while, then get worse for a while, and worse until I croak (never better)." Initially, Lou denied treatment—listening to his body, which he thought was saying it was ready to die. But the rest of Lou was not. Although he had reached a point where his health would not improve, Lou hoped it would stabilize "long enough that I can still accomplish a thing or two."[112]

However, Lou's health became so poor that he was unable to leave his apartment for a week. Lou's family and friends rallied around him, preparing meals, cleaning and attending to his needs. "I think it scares both me and them to see me this way," he confessed in his journal. "I've had several cries these past few weeks—just looking at myself in the mirror scares me, paper-thin flesh hanging on small pointy bones. I'm a walking skeleton." As letters and phone calls poured in, Lou noted with a bit of astonishment that "all the female-to-males who have benefited from my work in the community are coming forward and telling me things like, I'm their hero!"[113]

Lou was not mistaken in referring to an FTM community. Over the past several years, thousands of FTMs around the world had found and stayed in contact with one another through correspondence, organizations and publications, benefitting greatly from an infrastructure that Lou worked tirelessly to help build. And his fellow FTMs were not mistaken in identifying Lou as a hero. He had faced and overcome many challenges, and in the face of death (the only challenge that Lou could not overcome), he gave his life to helping other FTMs thrive in theirs.

It was his work on behalf of FTMs that gave meaning to Lou's life. This work made him want to live. And he did so for an astonishing four years after his AIDS diagnosis—three years longer than statistics at the time said he should. After his relationship with Keith ended, sex and romantic relationships took a backseat to Lou's FTM activism. He poured all of his heart and soul into creating a world where FTMs could be their authentic selves. In private, Lou struggled with his AIDS diagnosis, but in public he bent it to his will. In the eyes of gender professionals, Lou's AIDS diagnosis gave him gravitas, for AIDS was considered a gay disease. And Lou's AIDS diagnosis gave him an almost superhuman drive and focus when it came to FTM advocacy, organizing and scholarship. In just four short years Lou accomplished more than most activists do in a lifetime.

ENDNOTES: CHAPTER 6

1. Sullivan Journal, 7 January 1987, box 1 folder 14, LGS Papers.

2. Sullivan Journal, 21 December 1986, box 1 folder 14, LGS Papers.

3. Maryellen Sullivan Hanley, interview by author, 23 June 2007, San Francisco, tape recording, in author's possession.

4. Sullivan Journal, 21 December 1986, box 1 folder 14, LGS Papers.

5. Sullivan Journal, 7 January 1987, box 1 folder 14, LGS Papers.

6. Maryellen Sullivan Hanley interview.

7. Sullivan Journal, 7 January 1987, box 1 folder 14, LGS Papers.

8. Sullivan Journal, 22 March 1986-1 April 1986, box 1 folder 14, LGS Papers.

9. Meredith May, "Gay Men's Chorus Carries On: A Quarter-Century after the Start of the Epidemic, the Group Has Suffered the Deaths of 257 Members," *San Francisco Chronicle* (4 June 2006): E6.

10. Stryker, *Transgender History*, 113-114.

11. Sullivan Journal, 7 January 1987, box 1 folder 14, LGS Papers.

12. Lou Sullivan to Paul Walker, 30 January 1987, box 3 folder 121, LGS Papers.

13. Paul A. Walker to Lou Sullivan, 5 February 1987, box 3 folder 121, LGS Papers.

14. Paul Walker to Lou Sullivan, 1 September 1988, and Paul Walker to Lou Sullivan, 28 November 1988, box 3 folder 121, LGS Papers.

15. Sullivan Journal, 7 January1987, box 1 folder 14, LGS Papers.

16. Michael L. Brownstein interview.

17. Sullivan Journal, 7 January 1987, box 1 folder 14; 16 February 1987, box 1 folder 15, LGS Papers.

18. Sullivan Journal, 20 January 1987, box 1 folder 14, LGS Papers.

19. Sullivan Journal, 19 February 1987, box 1 folder 15, LGS Papers.

20. Michael L. Brownstein interview.

21. Sullivan Journal, 11 October 1988, box 1 folder 15, LGS Papers.

22. Michael L. Brownstein interview. During his 2007 interview, Brownstein guessed that he had operated on up to 3,000 FTMs. He would have easily surpassed that number by the time of his 2013 retirement.

23. Sullivan Journal, 14 March 1987, box 1 folder 15, LGS Papers.

24. Sullivan Journal, 3 March 1987, box 1 folder 15, LGS Papers.

25. Sullivan Journal, 25 January 1987, box 1 folder 15, LGS Papers.

26. Sullivan Journal, 1 February 1987, box 1 folder 15, LGS Papers.

27. Sullivan Journal, 11 January 1987, box 1 folder 14, LGS Papers.

28. Sullivan Journal, 16 July 1987, box 1 folder 15, LGS Papers.

29. Sullivan Journal, 11 January 1987, box 1 folder 14, LGS Papers.

30. Sullivan Journal, 16 January 1987, box 1 folder 14, LGS Papers.

31. Randy Shilts, *And the Band Played On* (New York: St. Martin's, 1987), 76, 98.

32. Stryker and Van Buskirk, 94.

33. Sullivan Journal, 24 September 1987, box 1 folder 15, LGS Papers.

34. Sullivan Journal, 20 January 1987, box 1 folder 14, LGS Papers.

35. Sullivan Journal, 13 February 1987, box 1 folder 15, LGS Papers.

36. Sullivan Journal, 16 February 1987, box 1 folder 15, LGS Papers.

37. Sullivan Journal, 24 March 1987, box 1 folder 15, LGS Papers.

38. Sullivan Journal, 9 March 1987, box 1 folder 15, LGS Papers. The government paid all of Lou's medical bills through Medi-Cal, and he received Supplemental Security Income and State Disability Insurance.

39. Sullivan Journal, 16 June 1987, box 1 folder 15, LGS Papers.

40. Sullivan Journal, 13 February 1987, box 1 folder 15, LGS Papers.

41. Sullivan Journal, 16 January 1987, box 1 folder 15, LGS Papers.

42. Sullivan Journal, 3 February 1987, box 1 folder 15, LGS Papers.

43. Sullivan Journal, 22 April 1987, box 1 folder 15, LGS Papers.

44. Sullivan Journal, 16 June 1987, box 1 folder 15, LGS Papers.

45. Sullivan Journal, 30 June 1987, box 1 folder 15, LGS Papers.

46. Sullivan Journal, 16 June 1987, box 1 folder 15, LGS Papers.

47. Sullivan Journal, 22 January 1988, box 1 folder 15, LGS Papers.

48. Sullivan Journal, 2 February 1988, box 1 folder 15, LGS Papers.

49. Sullivan Journal, 28 March 1988, box 1 folder 15, LGS Papers.

50. Jim Dickey, "The Transformation of Bobby Cordale: How a Midwestern Girl Who Felt Trapped as a Female Became a Man—and a Victim of the AIDS Epidemic," *San Jose Mercury News* (7 May 1988): pages unknown.

51. Sullivan Journal, 3 February 1987, box 1 folder 15, LGS Papers.

52. Sullivan Journal, 9 March 1987, box 1 folder 15, LGS Papers.

53. John-Manuel Andriote, *Victory Deferred: How AIDS Changed Gay Life in America* (Chicago: University of Chicago, 1999), 174.

54. Sullivan Journal, 20 March 1987, box 1 folder 15, LGS Papers.

55. Sullivan Journal, 10 April 1987, box 1 folder 15, LGS Papers.

56. Sullivan Journal, 13 April 1987, box 1 folder 15, LGS Papers.

57. Sullivan Journal, 10 April 1987, box 1 folder 15, LGS Papers.

58. Sullivan Journal, 17 June 1987, box 1 folder 15, LGS Papers.

59. Sullivan Journal, 30 June 1987, box 1 folder 15, LGS Papers.

60. Sullivan Journal, 29 August 1988, box 1 folder 15, LGS Papers. See also box 7, folder 258: Aerosol Pentamidine: Participation as Human Subject in Study of, LGS Papers.

61. Andriote, 91.

62. Andriote, 107-109.

63. Sullivan Journal, 5 October 1988, box 1 folder 15, LGS Papers.

64. Sullivan Journal, 19 December 1987, box 1 folder 15, LGS Papers.

65. Cleve Jones qtd. in Andriote, 366.

66. See Benjamin Heim Shepard, *White Nights and Ascending Shadows*, particularly quotes from Cleve Jones.

67. Andriote, 2.

68. On lesbians and AIDS see Lillian Faderman, *Odd Girls and Twilight Lovers: A History of Lesbian Life in Twentieth-Century America* (New York: Penguin, 1991), 292-299.

69. The BESTD Clinic was originally named the Gay Peoples Union Venereal Disease Clinic and was founded in the fall of 1974.

70. "AIDS Project Forming New Corporate Parent," *InStep* (19 December 1985-22 January 1986): 8.

71. Alyn Hess to Lou Sullivan, 12 April 1987, box 3 folder 96, LGS Papers. An individual with ARC exhibits manifestations of AIDS but has not yet developed major immune function deficiency.

72. Sullivan Journal, 17 July 1988, box 1 folder 15, LGS Papers.

73. Ira B. Pauly, *Female to Gay Male Transsexualism: Part IV (One Year Later)* (Reno: Department of Psychiatry & Behavioral Sciences, University of Nevada School of Medicine,[1990]).

74. Sullivan Journal, 23 March 1988, box 1 folder 15, LGS Papers.

75.   Sullivan Journal, 17 April 1988, box 1 folder 15, LGS Papers.

76.   Sullivan Journal, 22 April 1988, box 1 folder 15, LGS Papers.

77.   Sullivan Journal, 20 June 1989, box 1 folder 15, LGS Papers.

78.   Sullivan Journal, 11 July 1987, box 1 folder 15, LGS Papers.

79.   Sullivan Journal, 1 March 1987, box 1 folder 15, LGS Papers.

80.   Sullivan Journal, 1 March 1987, box 1 folder 15, LGS Papers; Ron to [Lou Sullivan], undated, box 4 folder 172, LGS Papers.

81.   Small Guys & Fans, 1 September 1987, box 4, folder 172, LGS Papers.

82.   Sullivan Journal, 4 October 1987, box 1 folder 15, LGS Papers.

83.   Sullivan Journal, 2 November 1987, box 1 folder 15, LGS Papers.

84.   Sullivan Journal, 30 November 1987, box 1 folder 15, LGS Papers.

85.   Sullivan Journal, 2 November 1987, 5 November 1987, box 1 folder 15, LGS Papers.

86.   Sullivan Journal, 9 December 1987, 21 December 1987, box 1 folder 15, LGS Papers.

87.   Sullivan Journal, 7 November 1987, box 1 folder 15, LGS Papers.

88.   Sullivan Journal, 21 December 1987, box 1 folder 15, LGS Papers.

89.   Sullivan Journal, 22 April 1987, box 1 folder 15, LGS Papers.

90.   Ibid.

91.   Sullivan Journal, 6 November 1990, box 1 folder 16, LGS Papers.

92.   Sullivan Journal, 10 November 1988, box 1 folder 15, LGS Papers.

93.   Sullivan Journal, 28 November 1988, box 1 folder 15, LGS Papers.

94.   Sullivan Journal, 5 December 1988, box 1 folder 15, LGS Papers.

95.   Sullivan Journal, 24 July 1987, box 1 folder 15, LGS Papers.

96.   Sullivan Journal, 15 October 1989, box 1 folder 15, LGS Papers.

97.   Sullivan Journal, 16 December 1988, box 1 folder 15, LGS Papers. On December 16, 1988, Lou and Jerry joined 250 others in an ACT UP San Francisco demonstration outside of a local NBC affiliated station. The demonstration was orchestrated in response to an episode of the drama *Midnight Caller* titled "After It Happened." The storyline of the episode "After It Happened" hinged on a bisexual man with AIDS who was intentionally infecting others with the virus. Despite the protestors' demands, the show still aired. However, the station aired a thirty-minute news special following the episode in which community leaders and city public health officials expressed their concerns about the

episode's content. The station also referred viewers to the San Francisco AIDS Foundation, and stated "San Francisco is a role model in AIDS education and has set the standard for effective and humane public policy." For more information on the episode, see: Stephen Tropiano, *The Prime Time Closet: A History of Gays and Lesbians on TV* (New York: Applause Theater and Cinema Books, 2002): 101-103.

98.   Sullivan Journal, 27 May 1989, box 1 folder 15, LGS Papers.

99.   Sullivan Journal, 28 May 1989, box 1 folder 15, LGS Papers.

100. Sullivan Journal, 25 June 1987, box 1 folder 15, LGS Papers; Flame Sullivan interview; John Blum, communication with author, 4 December 2009.

101. Sullivan Journal, 25 June 1987, 27 June 1987, box 1 folder 15, LGS Papers.

102. Sullivan Journal, 27 June 1987, box 1 folder 15, LGS Papers.

103. Sullivan Journal, 11 July 1987, box 1 folder 15, LGS Papers.

104. Sullivan Journal, 25 June 1987, box 1 folder 15, LGS Papers.

105. Sullivan Journal, 27 June 1987, box 1 folder 15, LGS Papers.

106. Sullivan Journal, 10 March 1989, box 1 folder 15, LGS Papers.

107. Sullivan Journal, 29 June 1989, box 1 folder 15, LGS Papers.

108. Sullivan Journal, 31 March 1989, box 1 folder 15, LGS Papers.

109. Sullivan Journal, 17 July 1989, box 1 folder 15, LGS Papers.

110. Sullivan Journal, 20 June 1989, box 1 folder 15, LGS Papers.

111. Sullivan Journal, 19 July 1989, box 1 folder 15, LGS Papers.

112. Sullivan Journal, 28 April 1989, 19 July 1989, box 1 folder 15, LGS Papers.

113. Sullivan Journal, 27 July 1989, box 1 folder 15, LGS Papers.

Chapter

FTM

Reflecting upon his life while ringing in 1990 on New Year's Eve, Lou wrote:

> …"thankful" is not really what I am feeling. What I <u>am</u> feeling is amazed, inspired, relieved, amused. Here I am, long after I ever imagined…. I feel like a sneaking spy, somehow able to observe the daily surroundings I was supposed to have missed. Often I think to myself, "So if I <u>had</u> died like I was supposed to, <u>this</u>… THIS is what I would be missing!" And it makes every little event joyfully amusing to me. So <u>this</u> is what I am supposed to have missed… Each day is a blessing and a special moment. How lucky I am to be Lou Sullivan![1]

Lou lived out his final days with an enviable awareness of and appreciation for life. He had pulled through his health crisis in the summer of 1989 and would astound everyone by pulling through several more health crises over the next two years. Lou continued to pull through because there was still more work that he needed to do.

Lou would eventually die three months before his 40th birthday. Far too young by our standards, but Lou was at peace when he died because he felt that he had accomplished everything that he set out to do. By the time that he died, Lou had published two books, transformed gender professionals' understanding of FTM gender identity and sexuality, organized FTM individuals around the world into a community, and helped start the modern-day trans movement. Perhaps most importantly, Lou inspired everyone who knew or knew of him to live their lives fully and authentically.

Autobiography Apprehension

In Lou's first journal entry after receiving his AIDS diagnosis, he wrote that his "main thoughts were completing my Jack Garland story and publishing you, diary."[2] Lou desperately wanted to leave behind a record of gay FTMs so that others would not feel the same sense of isolation he had, and believed that completing these two projects would do so. He did not know if he would ever leave the hospital alive, and the hospital graciously permitted Lou to bring in his word processor from home to work on his projects.

As soon as Lou was diagnosed with AIDS, he began transcribing his journals in earnest. Lou had long used his journals as a site for reportage, not just reflection and confession. He dutifully reported significant events in his life, and had toyed with the idea of publishing his journals for the past decade. Throughout his life Lou revisited past journal entries to better understand present situations and to generally make sense of his life. Within his journals lay a comprehensive case study of a gay FTM, and this was important because no case studies of gay FTMs existed at the time— let alone one so articulate and detailed.

As Lou became more conscious of recording his thoughts and experiences for an imaginary audience—especially after his AIDS diagnosis—his entries became more journalistic but no less candid. Like most individuals confronting their mortality he wished to leave a legacy, but Lou never suffered from delusions of grandeur and had always been committed to living as honestly as possible. He did not wish to present himself as a hero, but rather to leave behind an historical record of his life and experiences.

Publishing his journals was one life goal Lou set for himself that he failed to meet. It was likely a combination of Lou's lifelong struggles with insecurity, the consciousness of his fallibility, his historian's bent, and his aversion to sensationalism that prevented Lou from publishing his journals before he died—despite the encouragement he received from others. But there was also the important role that death itself plays in one's life story, and while he lived there remained events, thoughts and experiences for Lou to document.

The nearest thing to an autobiography that Lou published was a June 1989 article for *The Advocate* titled "Sullivan's Travels: A Transsexual Talks About His Life As A Woman Wanting To Be A Gay Man."[3] On at least two occasions, *The Advocate* declined Lou's offers to write articles for them. It took them several years to embrace the idea of an article about gay FTMs.

Eventually they reached out to Lou as a result of his involvement with the GLBT Historical Society, and he was ecstatic to write about gay FTMs for the "largest gay publication in the U.S., if not the world."[4]

Originally, Lou titled his article "Female-to-Gay Male Transsexuals" and was shocked to see the printed version edited into more of a "personal exposé" about him. The text of the article itself remained educational and true to what Lou had written, but he was unhappy with its sensationalistic presentation. Lou was frustrated that much of his text had been cut to make room for three large images of pre-transition photographs of him. And the front cover of the magazine advertised Lou's article with the headline "TRAPPED! I Was a Gay Man in a Woman's Body," which bothered him.[5] Lou was tired of trans people being tabloid fodder and feared people discounting him as such. But despite *The Advocate*'s tampering, his article was well received and brought more gay FTMs out of the woodwork.

THE CASE FOR GARLAND

After taking some time to settle into life as a PWA, Lou began contacting literary agents about publishing his biography of Garland. The literary agents he contacted turned down Lou's manuscript, saying they found the work intriguing but there was no market for it.[6] Transsexuals and transvestites had become more visible in American culture, but this visibility was confined to talk shows, tabloids and pornography, and was largely salacious and sensationalistic. Convincing others that trans people had a history—and one worth reclaiming—was an uphill battle. But a battle that Lou was more than willing to fight. And had been fighting for some time.

Members of the GLBT Historical Society were ready and willing to be Lou's comrades in arms in the battle to reclaim trans people from history. In addition to continuing his work on the Historical Society newsletter, Lou also became the secretary of the Archives Committee in July 1987. In light of his AIDS diagnosis, Lou found his thinking shifted a bit at times from archival volunteer to archival donor. On more than one occasion Lou wrote "I fancy [my collection] to be one of the best female-to-male collections about," and "I'm going to be proud to donate all this stuff to the Historical Society after I get killed."[7]

Eric Garber, a founder and board member of the Historical Society, offered to introduce Lou to a representative from Alyson Publications—"a gay publication looking especially for gay history works"—in the hopes that they might be interested in publishing Garland's biography.[8] Garber was very supportive of Lou's work, and even stepped in to help Lou with an issue of the Historical Society's newsletter that put Lou's research front and center.[9]

At Garber's urging, Lou's March 1987 Historical Society article on Garland spanned the entire front page of the issue, and not only included information about Garland but also explained why Lou had undertaken the task of writing his biography. Lou began by telling the readers that he first learned of Garland when attending Allan Bérubé's presentation of "Lesbian Masquerade," and included portions of his review of the presentation printed in "*The Gateway*, the Bay Area's transvestite/transsexual publication" wherein Lou emphasized the important role that recovering transvestite and transsexual history can play in "accepting ourselves." Lou then explained that his "gay sensibility" told him that the "crossdressing female-to-male" Garland was a "man-loving man" about whom he desperately wanted to know everything.[10] Concluding his article, Lou spoke of the GLBT Historical Society in terms of offering an all-inclusive space:

> I joined the Historical Society primarily to glean ideas and learn about available resources from others who have searched for our history…. Our history must not be lost, and this belief has kept me active in the Historical Society. Females have dressed and lived, passing as men, throughout the past and even in today's "liberated" society approach sex reassignment centers to ease their adjustment into the men's world.[11]

Eric Garber took the initiative and spoke with Sasha Alyson himself on Lou's behalf. Alyson founded Alyson Publications, which was the largest independent publisher of gay and lesbian books until the mid-1990s. According to Garber, Alyson was "quite interested" and promised to give Garland's biography "a fair reading."[12] However, when Lou reached out to Alyson, he simply received a form letter stating they had not evaluated Lou's work because they were all booked up until 1989 and that Lou should resubmit his material then.[13]

Lou feared he would no longer be alive by the time Alyson Publications could consider his work, so he contacted other publishing companies. The mainstream companies Routledge & Kegan Paul and Beacon Press respectively "[did] not feel it is a project we can pursue for our list" and "found that it would not be appropriate for our list," wishing Lou "every success in making suitable publishing arrangements."[14] Lou was also rejected by the women's presses, leading him to observe that "The mainstream press thinks it's a gay story, but the men's press thinks it's a woman's story, and the women's press thinks it's a man's story."[15] As a result, no one would publish his book.

Lou was beginning to despair when he received a phone call from the president and co-founder of Naiad Press, a cisgender lesbian named Barbara Grier. Lou was surprised by the call because initially Naiad Press had sent him a form letter rejecting his book, saying they were a press "for, by and about lesbians." However, Grier told Lou "she's <u>so</u> excited about my Garland story and it <u>must</u> be published, but that they couldn't publish it," and encouraged him to contact Alyson. Lou explained the situation with Alyson and said he could not wait until 1989 to publish his manuscript because he had been diagnosed as having AIDS. Lou asked whether the reason Naiad could not publish his manuscript was because Garland was not a lesbian or because Lou was a man. When Grier said it was the latter, Lou explained that he was a gay FTM.

> That really threw her for a loop!... She said I should be writing my <u>own</u> story…. [Grier] said these stories <u>must</u> be published and I should give her a few days to think about this, but that if they decided they couldn't publish it, she "knows <u>everybody</u>" and if I'd like, she'll help me find someone who <u>will</u> publish it.[16]

Once again, despite some of his FTM contemporaries' experiences to the contrary, Lou received much needed validation and support from someone who identified as a lesbian and a feminist. Grier contacted Sasha Alyson, who claimed it was a "total error" that Lou had been sent the form letter, and told Grier that he too was very excited about Lou's work.[17]

Alyson contacted Lou, who quickly sent him portions of his manuscript. Shortly thereafter Alyson sent Lou a letter saying: "After looking over the sample material you sent for the [Garland] biography and talking to several people about it, I'm convinced that it would make a wonderful addition to our list and would like to offer you a contract."[18] When Lou received the news, he was so overwhelmed that tears welled up in his eyes.

> To actually see this wonderful story and those beautiful pictures all together in a fine book—I am so proud!... If I

can just last long enough, if I can just live long enough to see this book—I'll be fulfilled! I just want it in libraries all over, so when someone, like I was at age 21, is searching the libraries for mention of a female-to-male, there Garland will be—proud and beautiful! I am so lucky!... I am truly actualizing all the dreams I had for myself while young, i.e., to be a man, to be a gay man, to be a published writer. That is why I feel at peace with my impending death. It's OK.[19]

Lou worked very hard on the manuscript, sending the first full draft to Alyson in August 1988.[20] It took a little over a year for Lou and Alyson to agree on a version of the manuscript, and Lou congratulated himself on living long enough to see Garland's biography through to completion.[21] Eric Garber from the Historical Society scheduled a book signing party for Lou at "San Francisco's finest gay bookstore, A Different Light on Castro Street" to correspond with the May 1990 publication date.[22]

On the whole, *From Female to Male: The Life of Jack Bee Garland* met with favorable reviews.[23] Reviews in the trans press were unanimously favorable, while those in the gay and lesbian press were mixed. What is more, the reviews of *From Female to Male* published in the gay and lesbian press were divided in their readings of Garland as either an FTM or a "passing woman" who lived as a man to experience male privilege (as opposed to living as a man because he identified as a man).

Joan Nestle, who co-founded the Lesbian Herstory Archives in 1975, wrote a unique review in that she referred to Garland as a passing woman, but also lauded Lou's "interpretation of Garland's life" for being an "original contribution to our history."

> Because [Garland] constantly sought out the company of men, was so dedicated to her masculine identity, and because she risked so much and was so comfortable in her male self, Sullivan asserts that Garland was a transsexual in a time when only dress and not the body itself could be transformed into another sex.... What Sullivan has preserved in this book is the record of the indomitable spirit of Jack Bee Garland. Hers is a spirit that challenged us to rethink what we think we know about gender and our own history.[24]

Kate Bornstein, on the other hand, characterized Garland as "one blatantly out female-to-male." At the time, Bornstein was an openly lesbian MTF gaining local acclaim as a performance artist, and she would go on to become one of the best-known trans people of the early 2000s for her ability to make people rethink gender through humor. As Bornstein saw it, *From Female to Male* was "blazing the trail for a very brave minority to come out and be counted."[25]

The publication of Garland's biography caused Lou to feel "so overwhelmed with pride" that he cried. "[I]t's not just that I'm proud of my work," he explained, "but that it's so wonderful to see this incredibly beautiful person, my Jack Bee Garland, finally honored with a book of his life—a permanent tribute for generations to come. He came so close to being forgotten forever."[26] Nearing the end of his life, Lou wrote in his journal that: "Though it is Garland's story, it tells about me… it explains my reality for future generations of female-to-gay males."[27] For though the details of their lives differed dramatically, Lou felt like the core experience of what it meant to be a gay FTM transcended time and place.

From Vagrant Subject to Viable

As Lou faced his own extinction, rectifying the denial of gay FTM existence became his mission. On some level, Lou perhaps feared that he served as the best example of the viability of gay FTM identity, and that all knowledge of being a gay FTM would die with him. He spent nearly a decade trying to educate medical professionals about gay FTMs before the first signs of an institutional shift began. In July 1987 at the Tenth HBIGDA Symposium, psychiatrist Dr. Dorothy Clare of London presented the findings of her research project on what she termed "transhomosexuality" in FTMs.[28] If symposium attendees missed Clare's presentation, they learned about her findings in Dr. Ira Pauly's presidential address.[29] Predictably, once an esteemed and properly-credentialed professional dared proclaim the existence of gay FTMs, others in the field of gender dysphoria followed suit.

In fact, according to Paul Walker, after the 1987 HBIGDA symposium gay FTMs were suddenly the hot topic in the field of gender dysphoria, with professionals clambering to do research and publish works on the subject. Walker phoned Lou after the symposium to see if he would be interested in working with Dr. Eli Coleman of the University of Minnesota Program in Human Sexuality and then-doctoral candidate Walter Bockting, both of whom would go on to become leaders in the field of gender dysphoria and lead long, distinguished careers.

> I answered Yes! of course!! Told Walker I'm <u>SO GLAD</u> that we, the female-to-male gay men, are being recognized and that a big fear of mine is that I will die before the gender professionals acknowledge that someone like me exists, and then I really <u>won't</u> exist to prove them wrong.... So I am so so delighted this is finally happening, and deep down am proud to have been one of the ground-breakers who can honestly report I've never wavered in my desire to be a gay man—and I've done a hell of a good job at reaching my dream, through no help from the so-called experts.[30]

Less than two weeks later, Lou met with Coleman and Bockting.[31] He served as an interview subject for their research project on gay and bisexual FTMs and connected them with other FTMs he knew in Wisconsin, Illinois, Virginia, Connecticut and California.[32]

One month after their interview, Coleman called Lou asking his permission to discuss his case with Dr. Ray Blanchard, who was planning his own research project on gay FTMs and wanted information about Lou.[33] Blanchard was a psychiatrist who worked at the Clarke Institute's gender program in Toronto and knew Lou's fellow FTM activist Rupert Raj. When asked, Lou "of course" granted Coleman permission to discuss his interview with Blanchard, and thought: "I'm going to have all these 'experts' vying for the right to do a 'case report' on me and I hope they <u>all</u> do so that other F→M gay men will not search the literature for a mention of someone like themselves in vain (as I did)."[34] After learning of Blanchard's interest in Lou's case, Coleman and Bockting decided to publish Lou's interview as its own case study apart from their larger study of gay and bisexual FTMs, which would take some time to publish. Coleman asked Lou to inform other gender professionals that they were publishing his case study. "Ha! ha!" Lou wrote in his journal. "All of a sudden these docs are scrambling to be the first to publish my existence."[35] Now when Lou told gender professionals that he was a gay FTM, they listened.

Lou was not only an articulate, well-informed and likable interview subject. He was also the only gay FTM who had AIDS. In fact, he was the only FTM known to have AIDS, which made him a highly desirable interview subject. In their article "'Heterosexual' Prior to Sex Reassignment,

'Homosexual' Afterwards: A Case Study of a Female-to-Male Transsexual," Coleman and Bockting claimed that Lou's AIDS diagnosis was "a very unfortunate conclusion to this case study."[36] However, both the gender professionals "scrambling" to tell his story and Lou himself capitalized on his AIDS diagnosis and used it as a means of encouraging professionals in the field of gender dysphoria to think differently about FTM transsexuals, specifically the variation of sexual orientations that existed among FTM transsexuals.

Although Coleman and Bockting were listed as authors, the article was a collaborative effort between them and Lou. In the text Coleman and Bockting allowed "L.S." to speak for himself by including many direct and lengthy quotes. In addition, Coleman sent the article to Lou for his input before submitting it for publication.[37] Lou greatly appreciated the respect accorded him by these gender professionals, and when sending back the article with his requests and proposed corrections, Lou wrote, "It is my wish, Dr. Coleman, that you receive 'credit' for first publishing on the female-to-gay-male."[38] This was a big compliment coming from a man who had spent so many years searching and yearning for any such publication. The article, published in the *Journal of Psychology and Human Sexuality* in early 1989, served Coleman and Bockting well in their careers.

To help the Canadian Dr. Blanchard with his research project on gay FTMs, Lou responded to two solid pages of questions.[39] One of the questions Blanchard posed to Lou was whether contracting AIDS had caused him to regret transitioning. Lou had more or less asked himself the same question weeks earlier while sitting in the Castro bar Moby Dick's one summer evening, surrounded by "young lean smiling boys."

> I've come all this way, gone thru this whole change.... Now what? My future compressed into a shortened time slot. Most dead in 2 years. Some live for 5. What have I been striving toward?... Oh! to be "NORMAL." To be a mere victim of my lust, instead of having orchestrated my desires, my place here.... Yet it's been worth all the years just to be in this bar, here, now, with AIDS, and to be a man among men. Not to have to wonder if they think I'm a female... that I know is no longer an issue. To be included, however voyeuristically, however theoretically, in the society of men who can only openly proclaim their ardor for other men— as those within this bar—I have gladly endured these years

and these trials. It may be "the love that dare not speak its name" but it is surely the love that endures, that persists against all condemnation, even through the threat of death, of "AIDS," a love that cannot die; to me, this is the only REAL love.[40]

Now, Lou told Blanchard: "No, I have never regretted changing my sex, even for a second, despite my AIDS diagnosis, and in some twisted way feel that my condition is proof that I really attained my goal of being a gay man—even to the finish, I am with my gay brothers." He then told Blanchard that in the limited time he had left in this world, Lou was concentrating on helping other FTMs, which included educating gender professionals about gay FTMs.[41]

CAUGHT ON TAPE

Shortly after interviewing with Coleman and Bockting and submitting his responses to Blanchard, Lou boarded a bus for Reno, Nevada to interview with Dr. Ira Pauly. The timing was such that Lou missed out on attending the Second National March on Washington for Lesbian and Gay Rights in Washington, D.C., where the Names Project AIDS Memorial Quilt was publicly displayed for the first time. The march was held on October 11, 1987, and thereafter October 11 has been celebrated as National Coming Out Day. Lou knew what a big deal the march would be, but his thinking that "I'll be of much better use going to Reno to educate Pauly" proved correct.[42]

By the time that Lou reached out to Pauly, offering to meet with him, Pauly had three decades of experience in diagnosing gender dysphoria. In 1974, Pauly published "Female Transsexualism: Parts I and II" in the *Archives of Sexual Behavior*, thus establishing himself as the leading expert on FTM transsexuals.[43] Despite his expertise, it was not until the 1987 HBIGDA symposium that gay FTMs made it onto Pauly's radar. Contrary to expectations, Pauly was ecstatic about being contacted by Lou. He not only told Lou that he would very much like to meet with him, but that "Since I have not seen a person in your circumstance before, I would appreciate the opportunity to learn from you."[44] Thus Lou headed to the University of Nevada, Reno School of Medicine to interview with Dr. Pauly.

Ira Pauly had interviewed many transsexuals over the course of his career, but he found Lou to be exceptional and stopped Lou minutes into their interview to ask if he could videotape it. Pauly told Lou "that I was one of the most eloquent he's ever talked with and that he would show this video many places and educate a wide audience, getting my message across that the female-to-male gay man does exist and can live successfully."[45] Lou believed that the videotape would reach a much broader audience than an article could, but he was unaware of the profound impact that the medium itself would have in conveying his story and challenging perceptions regarding the construction of his identity.

Due to the power of visual representation, this videotaped format served to normalize Lou as a transsexual subject in ways that a case study published by accredited professionals in medico-scientific journals could not. Furthermore, this medium allowed Lou to literally speak for himself. For his part, Pauly did not edit out any of their interview, and in the videotape Dr. Pauly, the former college football player with a PhD in psychiatry, came across as the intellectual equal of Lou, a slight gay man with effeminate mannerisms whose formal education ended with a high school diploma. But more than that, Lou effectively came across as the expert of his own identity.

As was standard for psychologists in the field, Pauly devoted a good deal of time to Lou's childhood and adolescence during their interview. Doing so served as a means for medical professionals to supposedly locate the "truth" of individuals' gender dysphoria in their developmental years. But time and again Lou refuted Pauly's archetypal transsexual narrative. And as the tape progressed, Lou continued offering his own theories regarding the evolution of his gay FTM identity, causing Pauly to interject, "You're better at this speculation than I am," to which Lou laughingly responded, "I've thought about it so hard for so many years."

At the end of the interview, when Pauly asked, "What are the things you want to leave us with?" Lou answered:

> I feel an urgency to have this story told so that I don't have to feel that I'm going to die and there's going to be more female-to-males coming to gender clinics and being told there's not such a thing as a female-to-male gay man and it can't be done and you can't do it—like they told me. I want the gender profession to know that it can be done and it has been done and there are others out there that feel the way that I do. And that—most solidly I guess I

want to state that I think I portray that sexual preference and gender identity are two totally different phenomena. That because someone feels male does not necessarily mean they're going to be attracted to females. That your self-perception is far different—how you feel about yourself is a different matter than who you want to sleep with or who you want to have sex with.

"Rest assured this story will be told," Pauly told Lou.[46]

After taping the interview, the two men spent more time speaking in Pauly's office and he invited Lou to return in three months to make an additional videotape.[47] In January 1988 they filmed a second interview, which Pauly titled *Female to Gay Male Transsexualism: II—Living with AIDS*. The first videotape had addressed Lou's transsexual narrative and enabled him to speak about his own identification. The second videotape elaborated on Lou's sense of himself as a gay FTM and also delved into his experiences as a gay FTM PWA.

During the second interview, when Pauly said, "You paid a high price for your preference for the male role," and asked, "Was there ever a point in time when you had thought about going back to your female status?" Lou said that he could not think of living any way other than as a man. "I would not have felt like I spent my time in any kind of enjoyable way other than what I did." He stated that even without the benefits of hormones and surgeries he would have crossdressed in order to pass as a man, just as FTMs had throughout history. Furthermore,

> I feel kind of privileged to know that my time is limited and that I have a certain amount of time to get my affairs in order, and to make sure that I've contributed my story and what I can to society before I die. In a way I don't even feel bad about having AIDS. In a way I feel it's almost a poetic justice…[48]

Journaling about the experience later, Lou wrote that he felt proud because, "I truly feel I've made a dent with these gender professionals now, and no longer need we hear there's no such thing as a female-to-male who wants to be a gay man."[49]

As promised, Pauly shared the videotapes far and wide. One of the screenings occurred at the annual meeting of the American Psychiatric

Association (APA). Lou attended this screening in May 1989 and participated in a question and answer session afterwards. He had expected the
100-150 psychiatrists in the audience to be antagonistic, and was pleasantly
surprised to find them empathetic. At the end of the session Lou was met
with thunderous applause, and he continued to receive compliments afterwards. On the whole Lou found the experience "really uplifting."[50] Pauly
also screened the interviews at the 1989 HBIGDA biennial symposium
and—as at the APA meeting—they "received enthusiastic applause."[51]

In the two years since the last HBIGDA symposium, gay FTMs had gone
from a hot topic to a proven fact, courtesy in large part to Lou's contributions to the research of Ira Pauly, Eli Coleman and Walter Bockting. At the
symposium, Coleman and Bockting presented "Homosexual and Bisexual
Identity Development in Female-to-Male Transsexuals" based upon the
case histories of nine Dutch and seven American FTMs. In addition to
screening his interviews with Lou, Pauly also presented "Preference of
Female-to-Male Transsexuals," using what he had learned from his association with Lou to begin a discussion among professionals about separating
the diagnosis and treatment of gender identity from (hetero)sexuality.[52]

Lou helped Pauly begin fleshing out his argument for this separation
during their third videotaped interview, which they conducted just prior
to the 1989 symposium. By the time of their third interview, Pauly had
come to a place where he could overtly state that gay FTMs were "just as
deserving of sex reassignment surgery" as their straight counterparts. Lou
concurred by stating:

> My gender identity—who I think I am—has nothing to
> do with what I'm looking for in a sexual partner. I think
> that these two things have been equated—that "Well,
> it's normal to be heterosexual, and if we're gonna make
> somebody better that means we have to make them hetero-
> sexual"—I hope that's out.

Pauly stated that since meeting Lou he had heard of a number of
other gay FTMs, and observed that as soon as gender professionals began
acknowledging the existence of gay FTMs, others began looking for and
finding subjects who identified as such. Lou responded by saying that the
gay FTMs he knew disguised their sexual orientation for fear of being
denied treatment. When Pauly said that now it seemed hard to understand why someone's sexuality should matter in regards to undergoing sex

reassignment, Lou interrupted, "or any other facet of their lifestyle—any other way they want to live their life shouldn't play into that." Both agreed that the primary consideration should be one's gender identity.

In this third interview Lou also compared his coming out as a PWA to coming out as trans. When Pauly asked Lou whether or not he was open about his AIDS diagnosis, Lou answered:

> Like the transsexual issue, I feel that people are afraid of this and have preconceived notions that are incorrect because they've never met someone like that. They've never met somebody with AIDS so they feel like "Oh God what if there's somebody in the room with AIDS? That would just be awful." And once that happens—once they meet somebody who has AIDS—it's no big deal. So I think it's really important that people do talk about it, be out front about it, try to educate…. I feel like I spent so many years trying to figure out what was going on inside of my head and trying to find a place in society that I felt comfortable in where I could understand what was going on that for me, once I find that niche, to me it's such a joyous kind of a situation that I just don't see any reason to hide it. I don't see any reason to make up a story that isn't true and try to hide my feelings because it took me so long to figure them out in the first place.[53]

Lou conducted a fourth and final videotaped interview with Pauly the following year. Toward the end of the interview (which views like an epilogue to the first three), Pauly told Lou that he was impressed by "the courage [Lou] had shown, and the tremendous spirit and positive coping with what is clearly a terminal illness," and that Lou had "shown us… how to utilize our time on earth as constructively and as positively as possible." Pauly choked up when concluding the interview, telling Lou that he wanted him to know that "for me this has been an important experience and you've been more than just another subject for me to write a paper about and… I'd like to say thank you."[54]

For Drs. Pauly, Coleman, Bockting, Brownstein, Pomeroy, Fraser—for every gender professional who opened up himself or herself to knowing Lou—he became more than a subject or patient. And their views on what it meant to be trans were forever changed. More importantly, their understanding of what it meant to be human was forever changed—changed by this courageous person who had defied all odds to live as authentically as possible, and would die a happy man as a result.

FTM Get-Togethers and FTM Newsletter

Lou was committed to ensuring that all FTMs could live as authentically as possible, whatever that meant for them. World-renowned trans advocate and author Jamison Green would always remember one of Lou's "pet peeves" as being "that it wasn't right for anyone to judge whether someone else's expression of masculinity was 'correct,' no matter what kind of body was doing the expressing."[55] Green began attending Lou's FTM Get-Togethers in the summer of 1988, around the same time as Loren Cameron and Max Valerio, both of whom would also go on to become published authors.[56] The group of get-together attendees was diverse not only in terms of gender presentation, but race, class, education level and sexual orientation as well.[57]

Lou hosted the FTM Get-Togethers quarterly until he died, and attendance ranged from 20-35 people. He hosted the first in December 1986, just weeks before his AIDS diagnosis, but due to illness and completing his bottom surgery Lou was not able to host another until September 1987. For the fall 1987 get-together, Lou shared Bérubé's slideshow with the nine FTMs in attendance, who "learned quite a bit about our history from the slide/tape show on Bay Area women who passed as men in the early 1900's."[58] For Lou, the realization that others like him had existed throughout history had done a lot to validate his identity and alleviate his sense of isolation, and he was excited for the opportunity to help bring other FTMs to this same realization. Lou reiterated the value of history in the recap of this get-together that he published in the quarterly *FTM*, "a newsletter for the female-to-male transsexual and crossdresser," which he first unveiled in September 1987.[59]

Lou illustrated the importance of history again in the spring 1989 issue of the *FTM* newsletter. In that issue, the recently deceased jazz musician Billy Tipton was given front-page coverage. Tipton had lived fifty years as a man, and Lou identified him as "one of our grandfathers," telling his readers:

> Sometimes we neglect to remember the many FTMs who
> have done, or are doing it on their own. Tipton lived in

a time when there were no gender counselors, no doctors to prescribe hormones, no surgeons to perform chest or genital surgery. If you wanted to live as a man, you just had to make do with what you had.... We owe a tribute of thanks to him for living the way he felt most comfortable, having the wisdom to understand what he had to do, and doing it. Men like Billy Tipton prove that we, as FTMs, are not a bizarre recent phenomenon—that throughout history there have been females who knew deep down that they were men, and did whatever they had to do to live their lives honestly.[60]

Lou was well aware of the difficulties of identifying and living as an FTM in the 1980s, but he believed that historical perspective enabled one to recognize the benefits of the present.

Also, through his coverage of Tipton, Lou implied that FTMs had a history—an important notion for an identity-based community. However, it is important to note that Tipton—like a number of the historical figures Lou identified as FTM—only became known to Lou because of the news coverage he received upon his death, when it was "discovered" that he had female embodiment. Individuals like Tipton had lived as men, not as FTMs. *FTM* was not only a recent category, but also a different way of being in that it involved a certain level of ongoing disclosure that those before had not engaged in. Lou's generation differed from their predecessors in their embodiment of maleness. At the same time that science and medicine made it easier to look male, FTMs like Lou were publicly acknowledging their female pasts and presenting an FTM version of maleness.

Back in the fall of 1987, when Lou began the newsletter, he initially planned on printing it for FTMs in the area who might attend the get-to-gethers, and so gave recaps of the get-togethers front-page coverage. In the first issue of *FTM*, Lou introduced the get-togethers in this way:

We all remember our first steps during our transitions, our need to talk to others who felt the same way, and the joy of learning we weren't the 'only ones.' The FTM Get-Togethers give us an opportunity to meet and learn from others who understand, and to be there for those who seek answers and advice.[61]

Although it was designed for local FTMs, Lou quickly began distributing the newsletter to all of his contacts. As a result, the get-together recaps also had the potential to serve as models for those FTMs across the country and around the world who were interested in organizing their own groups. However, during that first year of compiling materials, writing articles, then pasting up the newsletter on the old *GPU News* typesetter to print, Lou considered *FTM*'s sphere of influence as extending to the state of California at best. Its reach and influence would surpass Lou's wildest imagination.

Lou doubled the size of the newsletter for the spring 1988 issue, and by the fourth issue, published in June 1988, Lou had become the editor of "the only newsletter exclusively for the female-to-male transvestite and trans-sexual."[62] This distinction owed in part to the discontinuation of Rupert Raj's *Metamorphosis*. Raj ceased publication of *Metamorphosis* because he could no longer afford all of the time and energy that he was giving to peer support on a voluntary basis.[63] Luckily, Lou received enough money from Social Security Disability and the occasional odd job to do trans advocacy, educating, counseling and writing on a full time basis. Despite his initial frustrations at having to go on Disability—receiving money from Social Security because he had AIDS—it became a blessing. Raj graciously shared his *Metamorphosis* contacts list with Lou, and the two men continued to stay in touch.[64]

The June 1988 issue of *FTM* premiered the "FTM 'Male' Box," which became the most effective means of helping alleviate readers' sense of isolation. In this section, Lou began printing some of the correspondence he received from individuals around the world, including Brazil, Canada, England, Japan and the Netherlands. Lou printed letters from individuals whose only contact with other FTMs was through Lou and the newsletter, from individuals around the United States and in other countries who were working to establish their own support groups, and occasionally from gender professionals Lou knew and sent the newsletter to. Regardless of which letter or where the letters came from, their FTM authors all addressed similar topics: access to and quality of medical services, community organizing and/or connections with other FTMs, and the legal status of FTMs.[65] Through these letters readers not only saw that they were not alone. They could also imagine themselves part of a vast FTM international communication network and envision themselves part of a broader movement.

Sometimes corresponding was not enough. Lou published letters from an FTM named Daniel and his wife Nancy wherein they expressed feeling isolated because of Daniel's being trans. Within a matter of months the couple moved from Hawai'i to the Bay Area and attended the fall 1988 FTM Get-Together. The newsletter had not only proven a lifeline for them, but also suggested that San Francisco offered a welcoming and supportive environment.

Lou reported on Daniel and Nancy's move in the get-together recap. He did not typically mention attendees by name, but in this newsletter he mentioned several. In addition to Daniel and his wife, Lou mentioned David, who had just moved to San Francisco from Europe, and Chris, "an old timer from the Bay Area who escaped to Oregon for a while and is now back."[66] In his mention of these individuals, Lou was encouraging the migration of other FTMs and their loved ones to San Francisco, which remains a mecca for trans people to this day.

As editor of *FTM*, Lou printed and researched information relevant to his readership, and included announcements about events from around the world and various research projects underway. He also continually solicited and published articles from other FTMs. Despite the breadth of his knowledge about FTM transvestites and transsexuals, Lou was committed to giving other FTMs a voice, and through his get-togethers and newsletter he enabled other FTMs to speak with one other about what it meant to be an FTM. They did so not only through their letters in the "FTM 'Male' Box," but also through lengthier articles that theorized FTM identity, discussed romantic relationships and offered practical advice—all from the perspective of individuals discussing their personal experiences. Lou published articles by authors whose ideas challenged or contradicted not only other authors', but his own ideas, too. The pages of *FTM* presented the dynamism of FTM identity and demonstrated that diversity and solidarity could exist simultaneously within the burgeoning FTM community.

With the December 1988 issue, which he distributed to those in attendance at the January 1989 FTM Get-Together, Lou expanded the *FTM* newsletter to eight pages. Cognizant of his expanding readership, especially in light of the discontinuation of *Metamorphosis*, Lou began the newsletter by answering the question "What is FTM?"

> We are an informal group of female-to-males, in varying stages of the female-to-male continuum, from those who just like to dress up once in a while, to those who have lived as men for over a decade. The FTM mailing list has reached 100 names, with the majority in California,

but also reaching FTMs across the country, as well as in England and New Zealand and Canada.

FTM hosts Get-Togethers every three months for female-to-males and their guests only, in order that we might exchange information and socialize with others who understand what we are feeling.[67]

Based on member feedback, the January 1989 FTM Get-Together featured a panel of FTMs' significant others.[68] According to the get-to-gether recaps printed in the *FTM* newsletter, FTMs' significant others had attended the get-togethers for at least a year. Although the group was open to FTMs of all sexual orientations, the majority of FTM individuals attending the get-togethers expressed attraction to women.[69] Cisgender wives and girlfriends of these heterosexual-identified FTMs regularly attended the FTM Get-Togethers. Few, if any, of the gay FTMs who attended the get-togethers were in committed relationships, and cisgender men rarely attended, except as guest speakers.

Lou provided a space for those with loved ones who were FTM to find support, to find others who understood and could provide information and community. He printed letters in the "FTM 'Male' Box" from people like Janet. In her letter, Janet stated that she and her FTM partner read and re-read all of the issues of *FTM*. She also wrote: "I'd love to hear from other partners… I've felt really isolated in my ups and downs [regarding her partner's transition] even though [he] and I are real open between us."[70] Another letter came from Judy, who sought "partners of FTMs" with whom to correspond. "I am not a transsexual, am comfortable being a woman, but I am attracted to FTMs and need to define my place, my self-discoveries and open a path to a wonderful future in the FTM world… since that is where I believe I belong."[71]

Lou not only printed letters from significant others seeking others with FTM significant others, but also letters from those seeking FTM partners. For example, in the December 1988 issue of *FTM*, Lou printed a letter from Claudia, a cisgender woman who sought FTMs with whom to correspond, and stated, "For your information, there are women out here who would like to get to know you. Either for romance or just to make friends…. I will answer all correspondence."[72] Several months later Lou acted as best man at the wedding of Claudia and Jeremiah, an FTM who had responded to Claudia's posting.[73] Future issues featured additional postings from cisgender women. There were also postings from FTMs seeking romantic partners, which included cisgender women, cisgender men, MTFs and other FTMs. During Lou's term as editor, only one posting appeared from a cisgender man seeking an FTM partner.

Lou recognized and appreciated the significant role that FTMs' loved ones played in their lives and how their lives, in turn, were impacted by having FTM loved ones. He was also conscious of the fact that many FTMs and their significant others had previously been active members of the lesbian community, where they had been equal members.[74] And Lou had spent his formative activist years in Milwaukee's gay liberation movement where he experienced all-inclusiveness as a community strength. As a result, Lou saw and treated significant others and other loved ones as members of the FTM community.

According to Lou, "an eager audience" attended the January 1989 FTM Get-Together featuring a panel of wives and girlfriends of FTMs. Topics included the sense of loss people experience when their loved one transitions, and the changes to social identity and sexuality that people with FTM partners have to navigate when their loved one transitions. Lou also noted in the recap that the "female partners put forth some excellent advice to FTMs."

> When asked the most important thing they had to say to FTMs, this is what they replied: Be who you are, not some macho stereotype. Keep communicating and be honest with your partner; don't withdraw or hold your feelings in. Trust what you are becoming; trust that it will draw people to you, not repel them; and trust that it will bring to you what you need.

Lou concluded this get-together recap in *FTM* by thanking the panel participants for "sharing so much with us" and said, "We hope the panel will be a springboard in extending peer support to all female partners of FTMs."[75] Sadly, while FTM support groups would follow the example set by Lou's FTM Get-Togethers in many regards, this was rarely one of them.[76]

At the time, leading experts in the field of gender dysphoria had only begun considering the viability of FTMs being gay, and Lou lacked enough representation for a panel of gay FTMs, let alone cisgender men whose partners were FTM. So he followed the get-together spotlighting cisgender women with straight-identified FTM partners by featuring Dr. Walter Bockting, an expert who could speak to the existence and experiences of gay and bisexual FTMs. Bockting had recently published his co-authored case study of Lou and was wrapping up his broader research project with co-author Dr. Eli Coleman. His discussion of "Homosexual and Bisexual Identity Development in Female-to-Male Transsexuals" at the spring 1989 FTM Get-Together helped Bockting prepare for the presentation he gave at the HBIGDA symposium a few months later. The get-together was well attended, with one FTM coming all the way from Seattle.[77]

Over the next year, FTMs continued to travel from Seattle to attend Lou's get-togethers in San Francisco. In the fall of 1990, Lou was able to return the favor by traveling to Seattle for an "F-M Gathering." The nineteen who attended were not only familiar with Lou but expressed their admiration for him, which he somehow found surprising.[78] By this time Lou Sullivan was known by FTMs around the world—or, perhaps more accurately, his works were. And none of his works were better known among FTMs than his *Information for the Female-to-Male Crossdresser and Transsexual*, which continued to serve as bible, how-to manual and friend for countless FTMs.

In late 1989, Lou contacted the Ingersoll Gender Center in Seattle about publishing a third edition of his *Information for the Female-to-Male Crossdresser and Transsexual*. According to Lou, they were "ECSTATIC," and Ingersoll founder Marsha Botzer personally told him "how glad they are to publish it!"[79] It would be published as a "regular paperback book" rather than in booklet form like the first two editions.[80] In March 1990, future groundbreaking author Jason Cromwell, then an Ingersoll FTM support group facilitator, delivered a proofreading copy to Lou when he and three other FTMs came down from Seattle to attend the spring FTM Get-Together, and he later informed Lou that there were 150 advance orders.[81]

Lou added three new chapters in the third edition, one of which was titled "Female-to-Gay-Male Transsexuals." The other two new chapters were titled "Leaving the Lesbian World" and "Transsexuals and Children." The third edition also contained an "exhausting bibliography of all books, films, medical journal articles, etc. on the subject of female-to-males dating from 1919 to the present," and photos of FTM surgical procedures. An elder Billy Tipton graced the cover of the third and final edition.[82] When Lou received a final copy from Ingersoll, he described it as "<u>beautiful!</u>" and said "I can't find one fault with it."[83] The January 1991 FTM Get-Together—Lou's last—was a "book signing party" for his third edition of *Information for the Female-to-Male Crossdresser and Transsexual*.[84]

The penultimate FTM Get-Together that Lou hosted was in Milwaukee in the summer of 1990.[85] Through his correspondence with FTMs and gender professionals in the area, Lou knew that the only FTM peer support meetings in Milwaukee were hosted by (cisgender) gender professionals from the Pathways Counseling Center Transgender Program. Furthermore, though these meetings may have been offered for peer support, they were nonetheless a requirement for "all Program participants who have sexual reassignment as a goal," as opposed to being voluntary.[86]

Lou hosted the get-together at his childhood home—a space free from gender professionals in which individuals could discuss matters of relevance to FTMs without having to worry about what they said impacting their ability to physically transition. Lou's mother was very supportive of his hosting the get-together and pleased when another FTM's mother joined her in attending.[87] In total, eight FTMs attended, including one from Madison, Wisconsin, one from Iowa, two from Chicago ("who are lovers"), and another from rural Illinois. Writing about this "Historic Midwest FTM Get-Together" in the *FTM* newsletter, Lou hoped that "our brothers from the Midwest" would continue to stay in contact with each other.[88] In fact they did, and several FTMs from Milwaukee even regularly attended meetings in Chicago before michael munson founded FORGE in 1994—a Milwaukee-based organization for those on the transmasculine spectrum and their significant others, friends, family and allies, that munson has run with his partner Loree Cook-Daniels since 2000.[89]

This visit to Milwaukee proved to be Lou's last. He was able to revisit places of his youth like UWM and what used to be the Garde, and he met his old friend Eldon for dinner.[90] Sitting in the childhood bedroom that he had shared with his now-deceased sister Kathleen, Lou wrote: "This house and this city still seem to me to be 'home' although I would never want to live here again and nothing draws me here." He shared the sentiments of many people who leave their childhood homes for places where they feel a greater sense of opportunity and freedom to be who they are. "San Francisco is not 'home,'" Lou wrote, "but it amuses and keeps me in awe and I love living there."[91]

Home was not only where Lou spent his childhood, but where he came of age. Where he first began discovering who he was, first fell in love, first belonged to a community. Time and place were inextricably linked. Lou could not return to that time and—by extension—that place. Nor did he want to, for while Lou had grown up and come of age in Milwaukee, it was in San Francisco that he became a man. And it was in that time and place—

San Francisco at the height of the AIDS epidemic and the beginning of the trans movement—that Lou made a place for himself in history.

THE REALITY OF AIDS

Lou's health alternately ground him to a halt and spurred him into action. And Lou alternated between wanting medical intervention to prolong his life and accepting that he had a terminal illness. In the spring of 1989 Lou experienced ongoing chest pains and fever. He received a physical exam from Dr. Harry Hollander, director of the UCSF Medical Center AIDS Clinic, who ruled out the usual opportunistic infections of pneumocystis carinii pneumonia, tuberculosis and cytomegalovirus, and ordered a CT scan for Lou.

In addition to trying to identify the cause of Lou's chest pains, Hollander also noticed something unusual with Lou's spleen. The doctor spoke privately with a nurse, who returned to the examination room and told Lou:

> they'd continue to do tests to find out what's the matter, but even if they did identify the problem, chances are they won't be able to treat it anyhow and that's "the reality of AIDS." She said I should begin to make preparations for when I can't take care of myself—do I want to get on a waiting list for a hospice, or do I want to go in to the hospital, or just stay home and let it happen. She assured me they'd make sure I was "very comfortable" with morphine or whatever, that I wouldn't suffer any pain. But I need to think of how to arrange for when I need 24-hour care, and can I coordinate family and friends to care for me? So that's "the reality of AIDS."[92]

One week later Lou's CT results came in saying that he had lymphadenopathy, and that the chest pains he was experiencing were the result of swollen lymph nodes along his sternum. He also had an enlarged spleen and a "thickening of the small bowel" that the doctors at the AIDS Clinic suspected might be cancerous.[93]

After further tests the doctors concluded that Lou did not have cancer, but they were unsure what he did have and proposed taking more tests. However, Lou was tired of the process and no longer cared why he was sick.[94] He accepted that no matter how many tests they ran on him, it would not personally help Lou to know what specific ailments he had, for the ultimate problem was that he had AIDS and there was no cure for that. After years of agreeing to be an experimental subject—first for gender professionals and later for AIDS researchers—Lou declined to be a guinea pig for the sake of science. Lou told the doctors and nurses at the UCSF Medical Center AIDS Clinic: "I don't want to put myself through a lot of pain if I'm just going to die anyway. That I want to do it easy and peacefully."[95]

In addition to wanting to die peacefully and avoid unnecessary pain, Lou wanted to make his remaining time as meaningful as possible. Once, Lou had the time, energy and health to help improve the lives of others by being both an active agent for change and a passive scientific subject. But accepting that he had an incurable and fatal disease, one that soon confined Lou to his home most of the time, entailed prioritizing what he found to be the most meaningful use of his remaining time. Lou's top priority became FTM outreach. He devoted the majority of his time to corresponding with FTMs, speaking with them by telephone and meeting with them in person. Lou also continued to research and write about FTMs, and to speak about them to cisgender audiences when his health allowed. But for Lou, nothing was more powerful or rewarding than personal connection, and he always made time for his fellow FTMs.

Sexuality had always been a key component of Lou's talks about being FTM, and after his AIDS diagnosis Lou found himself in the unique position of educating others about AIDS and the trans community. On several occasions, Lou gave talks at the Institute for Advanced Study of Human Sexuality on the topic of "The Transgender Community and AIDS."[96] Though well-versed in AIDS-speak pertaining to gay men, the lack of trans-specific AIDS resources meant that Lou had to offer his own speculations as to why trans people might be at risk of contracting the disease.

Lou found that his speculations rang true with members of the trans community. He shared them at the spring 1990 FTM Get-Together and printed them in the summer 1990 *FTM* newsletter recap of the get-together.

> I think the [trans] community is at very high risk for
> AIDS for a number of reasons, particularly because we all
> know how hard it is to get sex partners. We have special
> circumstances with our bodies, then go through a tense
> courtship after finally attracting someone, and you don't

want to throw any obstacles in the way. If someone is going to be nice to us, touch us and love us, we don't want to say "no." We're so desperate for physical contact that we throw caution to the wind and say to ourselves, "Well, it's just this one time…it'll be OK…."

I think we're at a mental disadvantage because we have such problems with our bodies in the first place. Our bodies aren't something we want to care for or nurture. We've struggled with our bodies, they don't function for us correctly, the surgeries are lousy… we live our lives with a negative body image which prevents us from taking care of ourselves because we're so busy adjusting ourselves. It's a self-esteem problem.

Another problem, as Lou saw it, was that FTMs and MTFs may experience "psychological barriers" with using safer sex items like dental dams and condoms, respectively, and stated that, "Something none of this safe sex information addresses is our individual unique body statuses." Lou encouraged his fellow FTMs to overcome these barriers and be vigilant in their safer sex practices. Sterling, Lou's co-presenter at this FTM Get-Together, showed attendees how. He was a long-time member of Lou's FTM support network who had been working at the San Francisco AIDS Foundation for a number of years.[97]

Lou's was one of the first and most widely heard voices expounding upon the causes and effects of AIDS infection within the trans community. The psycho-emotional causes that Lou identified proved to be part of a myriad of factors that put the trans community disproportionately at risk. Other factors included social stigma, economic disadvantage, healthcare barriers and lack of educational resources.

Unfortunately, Lou would not live to see an influx of AIDS funding not only help the trans community combat the virus but also strengthen the trans community as a result. AIDS funding employed people to engage in community outreach, create and disseminate educational materials, and facilitate support groups. Trans people not only benefited by being the recipients of these resources; with AIDS funding trans people could find employment doing the kind of work that Lou had only been able to do voluntarily—and only on a full time basis once he had to leave the workforce due to AIDS. Ironically, the same deadly virus that killed Lou would prove an unwitting impetus that carried on his legacy of empowering the trans community.

I'M GONNA SIGN OFF HERE NOW

Amidst the pain and degradation of a devastating disease, Lou found cause to "feel lucky to have AIDS." His AIDS diagnosis "forced people to act on their feelings and tell me <u>now</u> what they feel, as tomorrow it might be too late."[98] Dying from a terminal disease allowed Lou to experience being honored for his contributions as opposed to his simply being memorialized upon death.

On May 12, 1990 ETVC, the most prominent trans organization in the Bay Area at the time with more than 200 members, hosted an honorary luncheon for Lou in recognition of his contributions to the trans community. In the publicity flier for the event, ETVC described Lou as a "leading organizer/activist, writer and theorist in the gender community, and one of the primary spokesmen for female-to-male transsexuals." The luncheon began with its ETVC organizer reading letters from people across the country who praised Lou and often mentioned how much *Information for the Female-to-Male Crossdresser and Transsexual* meant to them. As the organizer informed the audience, "everyone across the world in the [trans] community knows the name Lou Sullivan."

Next, people took turns commending Lou, claiming there would be "no movement" were it not for him and offering detailed explanations as to why. Those commending Lou included Paul Walker and Lin Fraser, who testified to Lou's instrumental role in transforming gender professionals' understanding of the relationship between gender identity and sexual orientation or, more accurately, the lack thereof. According to Lou, the speakers "went on and on… I mean, I know I've been an 'activist' and have contributed in several ways to the emerging [trans] movement—but, no! These people were saying there would be no movement had it not been for me!" When it was Lou's turn to speak he cut it short because he was too overwhelmed with emotion. Later, reflecting on the event in his journal, Lou declared: "How wonderful that life has taken me so high."

The day after the ETVC luncheon, Lou had his book signing for Garland's biography at A Different Light bookstore. The manager of the bookstore claimed that Lou's book signing "was probably one of the most successful they've ever had."[99] Several months later, *From Female to Male: The Life of Jack Bee Garland* was still on display in the front window of A

Different Light, and the manager eagerly ordered copies of Lou's *Information for the Female-to-Male Crossdresser and Transsexual* once the third edition was in print.

It was very important to Lou to ensure that people had access to the information in his *Information for the Female-to-Male Crossdresser and Transsexual,* and making it available via the bookstore and San Francisco Public Library, "which [housed] the only special gay/lesbian collection in a library in the world," was a task that he was determined to complete before he died. In fact, one of Lou's final outings was to A Different Light and the library, where he donated two copies of *Information for the Female-to-Male.* Of the outing, Lou said that "I wasn't sure I'd be able to get through it," especially after he fell down while trying to climb up the few stairs in the entry way to his apartment.[100]

When Lou celebrated his 39th birthday on June 16, 1990, he had a backyard barbeque, and guests included his sister Maryellen and FTM friend Denis, both of whom were now providing him with regular care-giving services. Lou felt "like the luckiest guy," but also felt "deep down" that this birthday would be his last.[101] And he was correct. At the time, only one in five people lived three years after receiving their AIDS diagnosis, and he was six months beyond that point.[102] Lou knew that he was on borrowed time and appreciated the gift of each moment.

In September 1990, Lou was hospitalized with tuberculosis and a second bout of pneumocystis carinii pneumonia. In the hospital, Lou noted, "Everyone has questions about my female-to-male status and I try to reassure them I'm glad to answer their questions, as I think—especially the medical profession—needs to be educated about this."[103] Lou lined up his "first-string care providers" and was released after spending nine days in the hospital.[104]

Five days after being released, Lou was readmitted to the hospital. During those five days, the only thing that Lou wrote in his journal was an entry dated September 26, 1990 that read: "I weigh 88 lbs. and can't remember ever feeling worse."[105] Before being diagnosed as having AIDS, 5'7" Lou had weighed, on average, 125 pounds. Several days later Lou wondered why he had sought medical intervention, believing he "probably would have died" from dehydration had he not been readmitted.

> You know how I always say, when the time comes for me to die naturally, that I just want to lay there peacefully and let it happen. Now I'm wondering about my conviction....

[W]hy did I rush off to the hospital? I believe it's because I know it's NOT the end for me yet.... As it is, in a few simple steps, I'm on the mend and I believe my quality of life is still worth the effort.[106]

When Lou was readmitted to the hospital he had the opportunity to educate another doctor about gay FTMs. After laughing at the doctor when he asked Lou whether he had any prostrate problems, the two began discussing Lou's surgeries, and the doctor "took a good look during the general examination." The doctor then asked Lou if he could ask him a personal question: "Why did you want to change?"

I said because it was too weird being a female—that I'd be in a room full of women and feel totally alienated, like "What are these people <u>talking</u> about?" But when I was in a group of guys and passing as another guy, I felt completely comfortable and it all made sense.... [I] briefly described how the gender clinics spurned me because I wanted to live (and was living) as a gay man. And that's how I got AIDS.

After writing about this interaction in his journal, Lou wrote: "I feel so proud and so good about myself being able to relate this remarkable and joyous life I've had to this young eager and attractive doctor. I feel like someone who's done something important and worthwhile with his life and I hold my head high."[107] Lou's weight increased to 98 pounds and he was released from the hospital in early October.[108]

Lou's health held steady at best. In early January 1991 he wrote of having a "very traumatic day" in which he collapsed on the sidewalk and could not get back up. "I was so horrified and humiliated," Lou wrote. "I can't walk anymore."[109] For the past six months, with the aid of his father's cane, Percocet and blood transfusions, Lou had retained some mobility.[110] But now even that painful and limited mobility was largely gone.

Lou had spent nearly thirty years researching homosexuality, transvestism and transsexuality. He now began researching death and dying. Lou did not fear death per se. "I just feel I'll be stepping into a new place of existence... one that, in all likelihood, will be just as interesting, if not more so, than the one I'm in now."[111] But Lou feared "being needy." He found it difficult to ask for help and to trust that someone would be there to help him.[112] His sister Maryellen reminded Lou that she had offered to be there many times before, but he had rejected the idea. Lou was now "so thankful" and "so relieved" to know that he would not be alone during his final transition.[113]

On February 15, 1991, Lou wrote in his journal that something weird had happened to him that morning.

> Awoke at 8:45 a.m., felt as usual went back to sleep. At 9:30, Maryellen came over and I was soaked through with sweat and truly "delirious," the only word I can think that describes what I felt. I was floating away. Felt I was no longer grounded in this world. I couldn't bring myself back to earth and I really thought, hey, this is it... I'm dying. Maryellen immediately realized it and called [the nurse], telling her I was "weird." Because I didn't want to go into the hospital, they immediately initiated arrangements to get me hospice care. I simply nodded out, seemingly in a dream, unable to move.

Lou saw it as a "Godsend" the way in which his nurse practitioner and sister Maryellen had cared for him. By that night Lou was feeling "a lot like I have been lately—back to earth."

> I'm incredibly weak, my feet and legs still very swollen, I can't eat much substantial, my mouth is very dry. I don't know if this is the beginning of the end, or just another bad phase, but it does seem to have been a steady decline since getting out of the hospital in early October. I feel peaceful and accepting, and reassured there'll be someone there for me.[114]

Several things happened between Lou's near-death experience and his actual death, suggesting that there were some loose ends that his soul wished to tie up before departing.

Lou began his journal entry, dated February 27, 1991, with: "Changes are occurring daily, so quickly that I can hardly keep up with developing adaptations to the obstacles these deteriorations in my body present." This journal entry would prove to be Lou's last. Lou required assistance with showering and used a commode in his bedroom because it was too difficult to walk to the bathroom. Lou also required assistance with applying anti-fungal ointment to the rashes on his torso and legs, and his FTM friend Denis obliged. For two weeks Lou's average temperature had been

94 degrees, and the nurse informed Lou that his systems were shutting down.[115]

In his final entry, Lou recorded meeting with Willie Walker from the GLBT Historical Society and Jamison Green, meetings which would be integral to securing his legacy. Less than six months after receiving his AIDS diagnosis, Lou had decided to donate his historical research and rare manuscripts to the Historical Society, and ultimately bequeathed not only his research materials and rare manuscripts, but also his magazines, video-tapes, audiotapes, photographs, published and unpublished writings, corre-spondence, various organizational materials and journals. This meeting with Walker to secure and finalize the donation of Lou's materials left him "feeling very at peace and reassured that my work will be preserved."[116]

When Jamison Green visited Lou, they discussed logistics regarding the *FTM* newsletter and FTM Get-Togethers. While Lou was in the hospital, Green had successfully hosted the fall 1990 get-together, which Lou viewed as "an opening dress rehearsal… because I'm quickly losing the energy to do it any more."[117] Lou soon felt "confident that [the group] has a life of its own and will continue to happen even after I'm unable to coordinate it."[118]

During their last meeting, Lou provided Green with peer counseling tips and gave him the contact information for all of the FTMs with whom he corresponded. After Green had left, Lou wrote: "I feel much relieved that it'll be in good hands and survive."[119] Interestingly, Lou used "it" in reference to his international communication network, newsletter and get-togethers, suggesting that Lou perceived these as parts of a greater whole—an organizational body comprised of an international community of self-identified FTMs who were connected through the newsletter, corre-spondence, meeting attendance and—perhaps most importantly—a shared sense of identification. This body was referred to as FTM. Under Green's leadership, Lou's FTM would become FTM International.[120]

After writing about the status of his health and of meeting with Green and Walker, Lou then wrote:

> I've been scheduled to speak on a panel at the gay writers' conference Out/Write on writing as a sexual minority (TV/ TS) within a sexual minority (homosexual) this coming Sunday, but I've begged off. It'll just be very hard to get there on Sunday morning (my worst time of the day), plus I haven't anything prepared. But [Willie] Walker's going to assist me in the wheelchair to be able to attend the keynote

address Friday night given by one of my favorite authors,
John Rechy....

This was immediately followed by the poignant "I'm sure there's a lot more I should be writing here, but I'm gonna sign off here now"—the last thing that Lou ever wrote.[121]

ENDNOTES: CHAPTER 7

1. Sullivan Journal, 31 December 1989, box 1 folder 15, LGS Papers.

2. Sullivan Journal, 7 January 1987, box 1 folder 14, LGS Papers.

3. L. Sullivan, "Sullivan's Travels: A Transsexual Talks About His Life As A Woman Wanting To Be A Gay Man," *The Advocate* 526 (6 June 1989): 68-71.

4. Sullivan Journal, 31 December 1989, box 1 folder 15, LGS Papers.

5. Sullivan Journal, 21 May 1989, box 1 folder 15, LGS Papers.

6. Sullivan Journal, 18 April 1987, box 1 folder 15, LGS Papers.

7. Sullivan Journal, 24 June 1987, 24 April 1987, box 1 folder 15, LGS Papers.

8. Sullivan Journal, 24 April 1987, box 1 folder 15, LGS Papers.

9. Sullivan Journal, 24 March 1987, box 1 folder 15, LGS Papers. After Lou's AIDS diagnosis, Garber regularly assisted him with publishing the newsletter.

10. Sullivan, "Members' Work in Progress," 1.

11. Sullivan, "Members' Work in Progress," 5.

12. Eric [Garber] to Lou [Sullivan], 18 June 1987, box 4 folder 141, LGS Papers.

13. Sasha Alyson to […], 21 September 1987, box 4 folder 141, LGS Papers.

14. Christine Babick to Louis G. Sullivan, 21 October 1987, and The Editors to Louis G. Sullivan, 26 October 1987, box 4 folder 142, LGS Papers.

15. "Another FTM Book in the Works," *FTM* 4 (June 1988) in Rawlings-Fein, 11.

16. Sullivan Journal, 7 November 1987, box 1 folder 15, LGS Papers.

17. Sullivan Journal, 23 November 1987, box 1 folder 15, LGS Papers.

18. Sasha Alyson to Louis G. Sullivan, 4 March 1988, box 4 folder 141, LGS Papers.

19. Sullivan Journal, 7 March 1988, box 1 folder 15, LGS Papers.

20. Sullivan Journal, 29 August 1988, box 1 folder 15, LGS Papers.

21. Sullivan Journal, 31 December 1989, box 1 folder 15, LGS Papers; Louis Sullivan, *From Female to Male: The Life of Jack Bee Garland* (Boston: Alyson, 1990).

22. Sullivan Journal, 17 January 1990, box 1 folder 15, LGS Papers.

23. See box 4 folder 143, LGS Papers.

24. Joan Nestle, "The richness of Lesbian and Gay history," *Seattle Gay News* (4 May 1990): page unknown.

25. Kate Bornstein, "What Makes a Man a Man?" *Bay Area Reporter* (24 May 1990): page unknown. Lou reprinted this review and one from Rupert Raj in the *FTM* newsletter. See "From Female to Male: The Life of Jack Bee Garland," *FTM* 12 (June 1990) in Rawlings-Fein, 68-69.

26. Sullivan Journal, 26 February 1990, box 1 folder 16, LGS Papers.

27. Sullivan Journal, 9 April 1990, box 1 folder 16, LGS Papers.

28. Walter O. Bockting, Eli Coleman and Harold I. Lief, "Letters to the Editor: A Comment on the Concept of Transhomosexuality, or the Dissociation of the Meaning," *Archives of Sexual Behavior* 20.4 (August 1991): 419-421.

29. Ira Pauly to Louis G. Sullivan, undated, box 3 folder 114, LGS Papers.

30. Sullivan Journal, 30 July 1987, box 1 folder 15, LGS Papers.

31. Sullivan Journal, 1 August 1987, 9 August 1987, box 1 folder 15, LGS Papers.

32. Louis G. Sullivan to Eli Coleman, 24 August 1987, box 2 folder 88, LGS Papers.

33. Sullivan Journal, 21 September 1987, box 1 folder 15, LGS Papers and Ray Blanchard to Louis G. Sullivan, 8 September 1987, box 2 folder 85, LGS Papers.

34. Sullivan Journal, 21 September 1987, box 1 folder 15, LGS Papers.

35. Sullivan Journal, 26 September 1987, box 1 folder 15, LGS Papers.

36. Eli Coleman and Walter O. Bockting, "'Heterosexual' Prior to Sex Reassignment – 'Homosexual' Afterwards: A Case Study of a Female-to-Male Transsexual," *Journal of Psychology and Human Sexuality* 1.2 (February 1989): 77.

37. Eli Coleman to Lou Sullivan, 29 December 1987, box 2 folder 88, LGS Papers.

38. Lou Sullivan to Eli Coleman, 16 January 1988, box 2 folder 88, LGS Papers.

39. Ray Blanchard to Louis G. Sullivan, 8 September 1987, box 2 folder 85, LGS Papers.

40. Sullivan Journal, 15 August 1987, box 1 folder 15, LGS Papers.

41.   Louis G. Sullivan to Ray Blanchard, 1 September 1987, box 2 folder 85, LGS Papers.

42.   Sullivan Journal, 2 September 1987, box 1 folder 15, LGS Papers.

43.   Ira B. Pauly, "Female Transsexualism: Parts I and II," *Archives of Sexual Behavior* 3.6 (November 1974): 487-525.

44.   Ira Pauly to Louis G. Sullivan, undated, box 3 folder 114, LGS Papers.

45.   Sullivan Journal, 12 October 1987, box 1 folder 15, LGS Papers.

46.   Pauly, *Female to Gay Male Transsexualism: I – Gender & Sexual Orientation.*

47.   Sullivan Journal, 12 October 1987, box 1 folder 15, LGS Papers.

48.   Ira Pauly, *Female to Gay Male Transsexualism: II – Living with AIDS* (Reno: Department of Psychiatry & Behavioral Sciences, University of Nevada School of Medicine, 1988).

49.   Sullivan Journal, 13 January 1988, box 1 folder 15, LGS Papers.

50.   Sullivan Journal, 10 May 1989, box 1 folder 15, LGS Papers; Pauly, *Female to Gay Male Transsexualism: Part IV (One Year Later).*

51.   "Surprise Guest Speaks at September's FTM Get-Together," *FTM* 10 (December 1989) in Rawlings-Fein, 49.

52.   "Surprise Guest Speaks at September's FTM Get-Together"; Pauly, *Female to Gay Male Transsexualism: Part IV (One Year Later)*; Rupert Raj-Gauthier, "Eleventh International Symposium on Gender Dysphoria: An Insider's Report," *FTM* 11 (March 1990) in Rawlings-Fein, 61.

53.   Pauly, *Female to Gay Male Transsexualism: Part III.*

54.   Pauly, *Female to Gay Male Transsexualism: Part IV (One Year Later).*

55.   Jamison Green, *Becoming a Visible Man* (Nashville: Vanderbilt University, 2004), 59.

56.   Green, 56. Green recalled meeting Loren Cameron at the June 1988 FTM Get-Together, and said the two "soon became friends." Max Valerio also describes his impressions of the first get-together he attended, in October 1988, in his autobiography. See Max Valerio, *The Testosterone Files: My Hormonal and Social Transformation from Female to Male* (Emeryville: Seal, 2006), 108-111. In his book, Loren Cameron photographed some of the men he met through the get-togethers—including Green and Valerio—though he does not explicitly state in

the book where he met his subjects. See Loren Cameron, *Body Alchemy: Transsexual Portraits* (San Francisco: Cleis, 1996).

57. Green, 56-58. In terms of race, Green says that "transsexual-identified men [who were] Latino, white, Hawaiian, black, immigrants from Europe, the Middle East, India, China, and Malaysia [all] drifted in and out" of the group.

58. "Dr. Michael L. Brownstein to Speak at Female-to-Male Get-Together #4," *FTM* 2 (December 1987) in Rawlings-Fein, 3.

59. "Dr. Michael L. Brownstein to Speak at Female-to-Male Get-Together #4," and "Welcome to Our First Issue!" *FTM* 1 (September 1987) in Rawlings-Fein, 1.

60. "A Final Tribute to Billy Tipton," *FTM* 7 (March 1989) in Rawlings-Fein, 25-26.

61. "Welcome to Our First Issue!"

62. "FTM Newsletter," *FTM* 4 (June 1988) in Rawlings-Fein, 10.

63. Rupert Raj, "Important Notice to Currently Paid-Up Members," "Not 'Quitting the Game' – Just Switching Sides," box 3 folder 116, LGS Papers.

64. Lou Sullivan to Rupert Raj, 15 May 1988, box 3 folder 116, LGS Papers.

65. See "FTM 'Male' Box," *FTM* 9 (September 1989) in Rawlings-Fein, 42-43; "FTM 'Male' Box," *FTM* 10 (December 1989) in Rawlings-Fein, 50-51. See additional letters from van Aerle and Tysoe-Calnon in "FTM 'Male' Box," *FTM* 9 (September 1989) in Rawlings-Fein, 42-43. Green discusses his impressions on these letters in *Becoming a Visible Man*, 60-63.

66. "Another Big Turnout at Our Fall '88 Get-Together," *FTM* 6 (December 1988) in Rawlings-Fein, 17.

67. Ibid.

68. "Winter '88 Get-Together: A Panel of Wives/Girlfriends of FTM's," *FTM* 7 (March 1989) in Rawlings-Fein, 27.

69. Green, 58.

70. Janet …, "Dear FTM," *FTM* 5 (September 1988) in Rawlings-Fein, 15.

71. Judy, "FTM Networking," *FTM* 6 (December 1988) in Rawlings-Fein, 19.

72. Claudia, "FTM Networking," *FTM* 6 (December 1988) in Rawlings-Fein, 19.

73. Sullivan Journal, 2 June 1988, box 1 folder 15, LGS Papers.

74. Special thanks to Loree Cook-Daniels for her insights into and experiences regarding the challenges of going from a lesbian activist to an FTM's significant other. See Loree Cook-Daniels, "Oral History Interview with Loree Cook-Daniels, January 30, 2011," *Milwaukee Transgender Oral History Project*, http://collections.lib.uwm.edu/cdm/ref/collection/transhist/id/5.

75. "Winter '88 Get-Together," *FTM* 7 (March 1989) in Rawlings-Fein, 27.

76. One notable exception is Milwaukee's FORGE which, since its inception in 1994, has always included significant others, friends, family and allies as members.

77. "Our Spring 1989 FTM Get-Together and Upcoming Summer Social," *FTM* 8 (June 1989) in Rawlings-Fein, 33.

78. Sullivan Journal, 3 September 1990, box 1 folder 16, LGS Papers.

79. Sullivan Journal, 30 November 1989, box 1 folder 15, LGS Papers.

80. Sullivan Journal, 3 September 1990, box 1 folder 16, LGS Papers.

81. Sullivan Journal, 22 March 1990, 3 September 1990, box 1 folder 16, LGS Papers. See Jason Cromwell, *Transmen & FTMs: Identites, Bodies, Genders & Sexualities* (Urbana and Chicago: University of Illinois Press, 1999).

82. "Information for the Female to Male Crossdresser and Transsexual," *FTM* 14 (December 1990) in Rawlings-Fein, 81.

83. Sullivan Journal, 8 December 1990, box 1 folder 16, LGS Papers.

84. Sullivan Journal, 22 January 1991, box 1 folder 16, LGS Papers.

85. "Historic Midwest FTM Get-Together," *FTM* 13 (September 1990) in Rawlings-Fein, 78.

86. Institute for Psychosexual Health, "Milwaukee Transgender Program"; Gretchen Fincke and Charles Kiley to Participants in the Milwaukee Transgender Program, box 3 folder 102, LGS Papers.

87. Sullivan Journal, 15 July 1990, box 1 folder 16, LGS Papers.

88. "Historic Midwest FTM Get-Together."

89. michael munson, "Oral History Interview with michael munson, April 25, 2011," *Milwaukee Transgender Oral History Project,* http://collections.lib.uwm.edu/cdm/ref/collection/transhist/id/27. FORGE is one of the longest-running trans support groups in the nation.

90. Sullivan Journal, 19 July 1990, box 1 folder 16, LGS Papers.

91. Sullivan Journal, 15 July 1990, box 1 folder 16, LGS Papers.

92. Sullivan Journal, 11 April 1989, box 1 folder 15, LGS Papers.

93. Sullivan Journal, 19 April 1989, box 1 folder 15, LGS Papers.

94. Sullivan Journal, 28 April 1989, box 1 folder 15, LGS Papers.

95. Sullivan Journal, 20 June 1989, box 1 folder 15, LGS Papers.

96. Sullivan Journal, 5 November 1987, 10 November 1988, box 1 folder 15; 22 March 1990, box 1 folder 16, LGS Papers.

97. "Spring Get-Together Focuses on FTMs and AIDS," *FTM* 12 (June 1990) in Rawlings-Fein, 65, 67; Sullivan Journal, 22 March 1990, box 1 folder 16, LGS Papers.

98. Sullivan Journal, 13 May 1990, box 1 folder 16, LGS Papers.

99. Ibid.

100. Sullivan Journal, 12 February 1991, box 1 folder 16, LGS Papers.

101. Sullivan Journal, 16 June 1990, box 1 folder 16, LGS Papers.

102. Sullivan Journal, 2 July 1990, box 1 folder 16, LGS Papers.

103. Sullivan Journal, 13 September 1990, box 1 folder 16, LGS Papers.

104. Sullivan Journal, 19 September 1990, box 1 folder 16, LGS Papers.

105. Sullivan Journal, 26 September 1990, box 1 folder 16, LGS Papers.

106. Sullivan Journal, 1 October 1990, box 1 folder 16, LGS Papers.

107. Sullivan Journal, 27 September 1990, box 1 folder 16, LGS Papers.

108. Sullivan Journal, 1 October 1990, 4 October 1990, box 1 folder 16, LGS Papers.

109. Sullivan Journal, 8 January 1991, box 1 folder 16, LGS Papers.

110. Sullivan Journal, 3 August 1989, 7 August 1989, box 1 folder 15, LGS Papers.

111. Sullivan Journal, 22 January 1991, box 1 folder 16, LGS Papers.

112. Sullivan Journal, 2 February 1991, box 1 folder 16, LGS Papers.

113. Sullivan Journal, 5 February 1991, box 1 folder 16, LGS Papers.

114. Sullivan Journal, 15 February 1991, box 1 folder 16, LGS Papers.

115. Sullivan Journal, 27 February 1991, box 1 folder 16, LGS Papers.

116. Ibid.

117. Sullivan Journal, 16 September 1990, box 1 folder 16, LGS Papers.

118. Sullivan Journal, 22 January 1991, box 1 folder 16, LGS Papers.

119. Sullivan Journal, 27 February 1991, box 1 folder 16, LGS Papers.

120. As of printing, FTM International has members in 18 countries and serves as the largest transmasculine organization in the world.

121. Sullivan Journal, 27 February 1991, box 1 folder 16, LGS Papers.

CHAPTER

8

LOU'S LEGACY

E arly in the morning on her birthday, Lou's sister Maryellen received a call. It was March 2, 1991, and Lou's roommate called to inform her that he was not responding. Maryellen rushed over to Lou's apartment where she found him lying in bed and gasping for air. She phoned Lou's hospice nurse, who informed Maryellen that Lou was going to die that day. Maryellen tidied up Lou's bedroom as he would have liked it, then climbed into bed with him for several hours. She knew that Lou needed permission to die—that he needed someone to tell him that he had done all that he was meant to and that it was time to move on. So Maryellen repeatedly uttered: "It's okay. You can go," while she held and loved on her brother—her best friend. As Lou drew his last breath, Maryellen "felt a physical change in her body," and she described it as "a very simple, pure and actually beautiful passing."[1] Maryellen considered Lou's dying in her arms on her birthday to be a special bond, and she cherished the experience for the rest of her life.[2]

In typical Lou Sullivan fashion, he had made all of the arrangements for his cremation and funeral services. Lou was saddened to use his father's inheritance for this occasion, which was a far cry from the joy of bottom surgery that his father's inheritance had also financed. But it had comforted him to know that everything was arranged and paid for in advance, making things easier for others.[3]

Two weeks after his death, Lou's family and closest friends spread his ashes in the San Francisco Bay and then joined approximately 100 people for a celebration of Lou's life.[4] Those at Lou's memorial service represented "several different community sub-groups," including the San Francisco Sex Institute, the GLBT Historical Society, ETVC, and of course FTM.[5]

The following month the 17th FTM Get-Together served as another memorial service for Lou. Approximately forty people attended, including gender professionals. Those in attendance "spoke of the impact Lou had on their lives and the sense of loss they felt without him."[6] The spring 1991 issue of *FTM* read like a tribute to Lou, with the front page devoted to Lou and his passing. Letters poured into the newsletter from FTMs around the world mourning the loss of Lou, and appeared not only in the spring 1991 issue but also that year's summer issue as well.

In a dedication ceremony on August 11, 1991, a panel made for Lou on behalf of the FTM organization he founded became part of the Names Project AIDS Memorial Quilt.[7] Lou's panel was the first made for an FTM, and was included among the thousands memorializing gay men who had succumbed to the disease. Lou's pink AIDS Memorial Quilt panel reads:

LOU SULLIVAN

3-2-91

one man who made a difference

you are missed – ftm[8]

———————◆———————

Lou devoted countless hours to researching and writing about transsexual and gay issues, to finding speakers for our Get-Togethers, to public speaking on the FTM experience, to phone calls from the curious and the desperate, and to writing letters to FTMs, researchers and service providers from all over the world who were and are interested in gender issues. He was every bit as much a pioneer as the historical figures he loved so much to study. He was instrumental in changing the opinion of the medical establishment on the existence of the female-to-gay male transsexuals.... He didn't judge us. He was a role model for many of us. He was there for us. He knew he was dying of AIDS, and still he served his community.... It is my fervent hope that we will continue in the spirit of brotherhood, in the best sense of the word.

—James [a.k.a. Jamison Green]
"From the Editor," *FTM* 15 (April 1991)[9]

Lou made a tremendous difference in the lives of those who knew him and knew of him, and as a result he continues to make a difference in the lives of trans people and those who know them today. At the end of his life, Lou was credited for the role he played in fostering the trans movement. That movement would gain great momentum in the years right after his death and seemingly explode onto the mainstream scene a generation later. Lou's legacy is the work that he did to help lay the foundation for the trans movement. He did so by articulating and advocating for FTM existence (particularly gay FTMs), validating and supporting FTMs through relationships and connecting FTMs with one another, and by establishing an all-inclusive community.

EXISTENCE

> Lou was the first female-to-male transsexual I met. At the time he faced an uphill struggle for recognition. Of course, that didn't stop him. That was Lou. He didn't let others dissuade him from what he knew to be true about himself.... Female-to-male transsexual identity is still one of those things people don't want to see and whose reality people try to deny. It is Lou's legacy and success that he has made that denial that much harder to do.
>
> —Jill
> "Tribute to Lou Sullivan," *FTM* 16 (July 1991)[10]

As a member of the FTM community I feel the loss of a dedicated man who worked tirelessly in networking with other FTM transsexuals and in educating professionals, especially in the area of gay FTMs. Ten years ago I had a rare condition that no one knew anything about. I was afflicted with two seemingly diametrically opposed conditions of FTM transsexualism and male homosexuality.... [A]fter I met Lou and established a friendship with him, I was able to begin the process of accepting my own sexual orientation. I am very thankful that Lou had the courage to speak out and reveal his sexual orientation in order to network with others.... I will always remember Lou for the great humanitarian that he was. He worked tirelessly for establishing an FTM community, a newsletter and a resourceful information manual for the FTM. He was always willing to be helpful. The FTM community should never forget Lou... Let us not let the memory of him ever die.

—Joseph
"FTM Male Box," *FTM* 16 (July 1991)[11]

Lou spent his entire life fighting to exist as a man, specifically a man who loved other men. Lou knew who and what he wanted. He came of age when identity-based movements transformed U.S. society. He embraced the gay liberation movement and longed to embrace gay men. Lou also came of age when medical professionals began transforming unprecedented numbers of trans people's bodies to align with their gender identities. He felt blessed to live in a time when such feats were possible and felt cursed to be denied them.

Lou knew that he wanted gay men and that he wanted to transition, but searched long and hard for evidence that someone like him existed—that someone like him *could* exist. Lou looked in community. He was welcomed with open arms by a number of communities (i.e., at the Garde and in GPU and GGG/G) but struggled to find others like himself. Lou looked in the medical literature and found nothing on gay female-to-male transsexuals. On the contrary, the medical literature reflected the belief of gender professionals that if a person assigned female at birth expressed desire for men, that person should not undergo physical transition and therefore could not be transsexual.

Perhaps because of the difficulty and loneliness of his journey, Lou went to great lengths trying to document his existence as a gay FTM. Lou personally documented his existence in his journals, articles, correspondence and speaking engagements, and had others document his existence in case studies, interviews and public exhibits. As a result of Lou's tireless efforts, sexual orientation is no longer a barrier to transition; gay men can simply transition.

Lou's Herculean achievements were rooted in the simple, humble desire to save others from undergoing the struggles that he had—the struggles of articulating his identity, advocating for his existence, and suffering in isolation. Lou first found others like himself in the annals of history. How fitting that Lou become an historical figure himself, etched into the bedrock of time, providing a foundation for trans men who trod the Earth after his departure from it.

But what if Lou's identity had not been a battleground, his sexual orientation not a rampart to transitioning? Would Lou have still been a founder of the trans movement, a seminal historical figure? Or would he have simply transitioned, a thread in the tapestry of human existence as opposed to a panel of the AIDS Memorial Quilt?

RELATIONSHIPS

> I live 3,000 miles away from San Francisco, in New England, and yet Lou was the most special friend I have ever had. Lou was my first validator as an FTM. Because of him, I became able to identify myself openly as an FTM TV. Before Lou, I had no language for my man-soul and absolutely no support.... Lou's gift to me was voice and visibility for my identity. It was space in the world for my man-soul to live. Lou's death was a tremendous loss for me. Some mornings I wake up and ask myself, "Was it me who died?"
>
> —Bet
> "FTM Male Box," *FTM* 16 (July 1991)[12]

The depth and breadth of Lou's relationships with other FTMs was remarkable. Whether writing, speaking on the phone, or meeting in person, Lou always gave people his full and undivided attention. His hand-written letters were lengthy, detailed and personal. Phone calls could last hours. And sometimes in-person meetings could extend into sleepovers. Lou always made time for other FTMs—as much time as they needed. And he loved and cared for each of them as if they were lifelong friends, even if they only had one interaction. Lou gave this time, love and care to hundreds of FTMs.

For the vast majority of Lou's correspondents, callers and counselees, he was the first FTM they met. For many of them, Lou was the only FTM they knew. And Lou validated the existence of every single one of them, no matter who they were nor where they fell on the transmasculine spectrum. Lou understood well how much easier it is to see oneself when someone else sees you. He was a ready mirror for these FTMs, introducing himself by way of recounting his FTM narrative and inviting theirs. If Lou did not share their experience, he mentioned other FTMs who did. Lou connected FTMs with one another and with other resources (books, therapists, movies, surgeons, etc.) that helped empower individuals to embrace who they were. These relationships served as the crucial bridge from "I exist" to "We exist."

Where would those FTMs be today without Lou's friendship? Would all of the transsexuals have transitioned? Would the transvestites have subscribed to the gender binary? Would they have come together as a community? Would there still be a community today if Lou had not emphasized and modeled the importance of personal relationships?

COMMUNITY

> I can't call you up, but I can talk to you in my own way, and try to keep your goals and dreams alive in the FTM group you brought into being, through the special friends I have made by coming into that community.... [N]o matter what your personal feelings or preferences were (and you were not shy about sharing them, which was quite refreshing), you kept a spirit of openness for the group. That openness has led to the continuing growth and learning between TSs, TVs, significant others, friends wanting to know more, and gender [professionals] all with interest in FTMs.... I am glad you had the courage to come out publicly as a trans-sexual and as a gay man. For all of us, whether in the gay or [trans] communities (or not), the world is a better place because of you. Thank you for the personal encouragement to "be who you are and have fun with it," and for being my friend.
>
> —Francis
> "In Remembrance," *FTM* 15 (April 1991)[13]

As we all are aware, we've lost a pioneer…. I've decided that I am only one of many of us who can, should and will carry the torches.

—Jason Cromwell
"FTM Male Box," *FTM* 16 (July 1991)[14]

Lou's FTM Get-Togethers and *FTM* newsletter were made possible by the relationships he fostered with other FTMs, and out of the get-togethers and newsletter, community grew. Community exists because of the willingness to be supportive of others, because of the willingness to effect change because of care for another. Through the get-togethers and newsletter, Lou amassed a group of individuals who connected as a result of their shared identity and were inspired to take action by and for FTMs. They began making change first by speaking and connecting with each other, then with their loved ones, then acquaintances, and finally strangers.

Several individuals who found both themselves and community in Lou's FTM became trans leaders, educators, authors, counselors and organizers. They expanded awareness about what it means to be trans and created more space to be trans. They honored Lou's memory by being public figures, coming out—as he had—in an effort to garner greater FTM visibility. They actively exposed broader audiences to FTM existence to improve the existence of FTMs. These activists and those who followed their lead changed the minds of mainstream Americans.

But most of the FTMs Lou knew were not activists. They did not take to stage or print. Coming out was difficult for them—as it is for most trans people today—for they were private people who simply wanted to go about living their lives in safety and comfort. It took tremendous courage for these FTMs to come out to those with whom they had personal relationships. But doing so is what changed mainstream Americans' hearts.

To mainstream Americans, trans people seem like a 21st century phenomenon. Though they are not, their level of visibility is. Such visibility would not have been possible without activists like Lou fighting for their existence, establishing relationships and forging community; without their doing all of the behind-the-scenes work that enabled trans people—and their movement—to seemingly appear out of nowhere, causing us all to consider the nature of gender.

To trans people, mainstream Americans' consciousness of and compassion for trans people is phenomenal. The immense value of trans allies cannot be overstated. How to understand such a swelling in their ranks? These supporters have gone through an evolution similar to that which spawns movements: They became aware that trans people exist, got to know (and care about) trans people through relationships, then became agents for change. Through the everyday courage of trans people living their truth and sharing it with others, trans allies had the opportunity to support them. And by transforming their worlds, the world itself is changing.

As stated on his AIDS Memorial Quilt panel, Lou was indeed "one man who made a difference." Against all odds, he discovered and actualized who he was and empowered countless others to do the same. In the process he helped us to discover that perhaps the most difficult and most significant thing that we do in this life is dare to be who we are. May you, dear reader, find the courage to be who you are. The world will be better for it.

ENDNOTES: CHAPTER 8

1. Maryellen Sullivan Hanley interview.

2. Maryellen Sullivan Hanley, "FTM 'Male' Box," *FTM* 16 (July 1991) in Rawlings-Fein, 98. Sadly, Maryellen died from cancer in 2012. Only two of the six Sullivan siblings remain alive: Flame and Bridget.

3. Sullivan Journal, 29 April 1988, box 1 folder 15, LGS Papers.

4. Maryellen Sullivan Hanley interview; Kevin…, "In Memoriam," *FTM* 15 (April 1991) in Rawlings-Fein, 89.

5. Kevin…, "In Memoriam."

6. "17th Get-Together Marks Lou's Passing," *FTM* 16 (July 1991) in Rawlings-Fein, 97.

7. "Lou's Panel Part of Names Project Quilt," *FTM* 17 (October 1991) in Rawlings-Fein, 109.

8. The panel was made by an FTM named Jeff, and a photograph of it can be found in box 1 folder 2, LGS Papers.

9. James [a.k.a Jamison Green], "From the Editor," *FTM* 15 (April 1991) in Rawlings-Fein, 94.

10. Jill …, "Tribute to Lou Sullivan," *FTM* 16 (July 1991) in Rawlings Fein, 99.

11. Joseph …, "FTM Male Box," *FTM* 16 (July 1991) in Rawlings-Fein, 98.

12. Bet …, "FTM Male Box," *FTM* 16 (July 1991) in Rawlings-Fein, 98-99.

13. Francis, "In Remembrance," *FTM* 15 (April 1991) in Rawlings-Fein, 91.

14. Jason Cromwell, "FTM Male Box," *FTM* 16 (July 1991) in Rawlings-Fein, 99.

Sources Cited

"AIDS Project Forming New Corporate Parent." *InStep* (19 December 1985 – 22 January 1986): 8.

Andriote, John-Manuel. *Victory Deferred: How AIDS Changed Gay Life in America.* Chicago: University of Chicago, 1999.

Anspacher, Carolyn. "Sex Change Uproar in Emeryville." *San Francisco Chronicle* (7 August 1976): 1.

Armstrong, Elizabeth A. *Forging Gay Identities: Organizing Sexuality in San Francisco, 1950-1994.* Chicago: University of Chicago, 2002.

Bailey, Robert W. *Gay Politics, Urban Politics: Identity and Economics in the Urban Setting.* New York: Columbia University, 1999.

Benjamin, Harry. *The Transsexual Phenomenon.* New York: Warner, 1966.

Bérubé, Allan. *Coming Out Under Fire: The History of Gay Men and Women in World War Two.* New York: The Free Press, 1990.

Bockting, Walter O., Eli Coleman and Harold I. Lief. "Letters to the Editor: A Comment on the Concept of Transhomosexuality, or the Dissociation of the Meaning." *Archives of Sexual Behavior* 20.4 (August 1991): 419-421.

Bornstein, Kate. "What Makes a Man a Man?" *Bay Area Reporter* (24 May 1990): page unknown.

Boyd, Nan Alamilla. *Wide-Open Town: A History of Queer San Francisco to 1965.* Berkeley: University of California, 2003.

Brondino, Steven M. and Jamakaya. Milwaukee Pridefest exhibit. *History in the Making: Milwaukee's Gay and Lesbian Community.* Milwaukee, Wisconsin, June 1997.

Brownstein, Michael L. Interview by author, 31 March 2007, Milwaukee. Tape recording. In author's possession.

Burke, Sue. "Milwaukee Has 1st Gay Radio Program, Newspaper in Early 1970s." *Wisconsin Light* (9 February 1989 – 22 February 1989): 12.

Cameron, Loren. *Body Alchemy: Transsexual Portraits.* San Francisco: Cleis, 1996.

Coleman, Eli and Walter O. Bockting. "'Heterosexual' Prior to Sex Reassignment – 'Homosexual' Afterwards: A Case Study of a Female-to-Male Transsexual." *Journal of Psychology and Human Sexuality* 1.2 (February 1989): 69-82.

Cromwell, Jason. *Transmen & FTMs: Identities, Bodies, Genders & Sexualities.* Urbana: University of Illinois, 1999.

D'Emilio, John. "Gay Politics and Community in San Francisco since World War II." In *Hidden from History: Reclaiming the Gay and Lesbian Past*, ed. Martin Bauml Duberman, Martha Vicinus and George Chauncey Jr., 456-473. New York: Meridian, 1990.

Denny, Dallas. "Transgender Communities of the United States in the Late Twentieth Century." In *Transgender Rights*, ed. Paisley Currah, Richard M. Juang and Shannon Price Minter, 171-191. Minneapolis: University of Minnesota, 2006.

Dickey, Jim. "The Transformation of Bobby Cordale: How a Midwestern Girl Who Felt Trapped as a Female Became a Man—and a Victim of the AIDS Epidemic." *San Jose Mercury News* (7 May 1988): pages unknown.

Doylen, Michael. "Gay Liberation Organization at UWM (GLO-UWM)." *Wisconsin GLBT History Project*, http://www.mkelgb-thist.org/organiz/act_pol/gay-lib-org.htm.

"Editorial," *GPU News* (December 1972): 2.

Elving, Ron. "Science Delayed Grief, but Lent Comfort, Too." *The Milwaukee Journal* (24 October 1978): 1.

Faderman, Lillian. *Odd Girls and Twilight Lovers: A History of Lesbian Life in Twentieth-Century America.* New York: Penguin, 1991.

Fisk, Norman M. "Gender Dysphoria Syndrome—The Conceptual-ization that Liberalizes Indications for Total Gender Reorientation and Implies a Broadly Based Multi-Dimensional Rehabilitative Regimen." *The Western Journal of Medicine* 120.5 (May 1974): 386-391.

Fox, Margalit. "Stanley H. Biber, 82, Surgeon Among First to Do Sex Changes, Dies." *New York Times* (21 January 2006), http://www. nytimes.com/2006/01/21/national/21biber.html.

FTM 1-16 (September 1987-July 1991). In *FTM Newsletter, 1987-1992,* ed. Martin Rawlings-Fein, 1-104. San Francisco: FTM International, Inc., 2005.

FTM Informational Network, http://www.ftminfo.net/jude.html.

Garber, Eric. "A Spectacle in Color: The Lesbian and Gay Subculture of Jazz Age Harlem." In *Hidden from History: Reclaiming the Gay and Lesbian Past*, ed. Martin Bauml Duberman, Martha Vicinus and George Chauncey Jr., 318-331. New York: New American Library, 1989.

"The Gay Peoples Union Collection." *University of Wisconsin Digital Collections*, http://digicoll.library.wisc.edu/GPU/.

"Gay Perspective Now Aired 8:30 P.M." *GPU News* (October 1971): 1, 5.

"GPU Ball…" *GPU News* (February/March 1974): 14-15, 29.

"G.P.U. Publishes New Newspaper." *GPU News* (October 1971): 1.

Green, Jamison. *Becoming a Visible Man.* Nashville, TN: Vanderbilt University, 2004.

Hanley, Maryellen Sullivan. Interview by author, 23 June 2007, San Francisco. Tape recording. In author's possession.

Hoffman, Martin. *The Gay World: Male Homosexuality and the Social Creation of Evil.* New York: Basic Books, 1968.

International Transgender Day of Remembrance, http://www.transgen-derdor.org/.

James Groppi Papers, 1956-1989. "Biography/History: James Groppi Papers, 1956-1978." *Archival Resources in Wisconsin: Descriptive Finding Aids,* http://digicoll.library.wisc.edu/cgi/f/findaid/findaid-idx?c=wiarchives;view=reslist;subview=standard;didno=uw-whs-mil000ex;focusrgn=bioghist;cc=wiarchives;byte=102610936.

Laub, Donald R. and Norman Fisk. "A Rehabilitation Program for Gender Dysphoria Syndrome by Surgical Sex Change." *Plastic and Reconstructive Surgery* 53.4 (April 1974): 388-403.

Lin Fraser, linfraser.com.

Louis Graydon Sullivan Papers. 91-7. The Gay, Lesbian, Bisexual, Transgender (GLBT) Historical Society.

Martino, Mario with harriet. *Emergence: A Transsexual Autobiography.* New York: Crown Publishers, 1977.

May, Meredith. "Gay Men's Chorus Carries On: A Quarter-Century after the Start of the Epidemic, the Group Has Suffered the Deaths of 257 Members." *San Francisco Chronicle* (4 June 2006): E6.

Meeker, Martin. "Archives Review: The Gay and Lesbian Historical Society of Northern California." *Journal of Gay, Lesbian, and Bisexual Identity* 4.2 (April 1999): 197-205.

Members of the Gay and Lesbian Historical Society of Northern California. "MTF Transgender Activism in the Tenderloin and Beyond, 1966-1975: Commentary and Interview with Elliot Blackstone." *GLQ: A Journal of Lesbian and Gay Studies* 4.2 (1998): 349-372.

Meyerowitz, JoAnne. *How Sex Changed: A History of Transsexuality in the United States.* Cambridge: Harvard University Press, 2002.

Milwaukee Mss 233 (Donna Utke Papers, 1971-1991). University of Wisconsin-Milwaukee Libraries. Archives Department.

Milwaukee Mss 240 (Gay Peoples Union Records, 1971-1984). University of Wisconsin-Milwaukee Libraries. Archives Department.

Milwaukee Mss 256 (Eldon Murray Papers, 1938-2007). University of Wisconsin-Milwaukee Libraries. Archives Department.

Milwaukee Transgender Oral History Project, http://collections.lib.uwm.edu/cdm/search/collection/transhist.

Murray, Eldon. Interview by author, 12 February 2005, Milwaukee. Tape recording. In author's possession.

Nestle, Joan. "The richness of Lesbian and Gay history." *Seattle Gay News* (4 May 1990): page unknown.

"Obituary—Willie Walker." *Bozeman Daily Chronicle* (9 October 2004), http://bozemandailychronicle.com/articles/2004/10/10/obituaries/walker.txt.

Pauly, Ira B. *Female to Gay Male Transsexualism: I – Gender & Sexual Orientation*. VHS. Reno: Department of Psychiatry & Behavioral Sciences, University of Nevada School of Medicine, 1988.

Pauly, Ira B. *Female to Gay Male Transsexualism: II – Living with AIDS*. VHS. Reno: Department of Psychiatry & Behavioral Sciences, University of Nevada School of Medicine, 1988.

Pauly, Ira B. *Female to Gay Male Transsexualism: Part III*. VHS. Reno: Department of Psychiatry & Behavioral Sciences, University of Nevada School of Medicine, [1989].

Pauly, Ira B. *Female to Gay Male Transsexualism: Part IV (One Year Later)*. VHS. Reno: Department of Psychiatry & Behavioral Sciences, University of Nevada School of Medicine, [1990].

Pauly, Ira B. "Female Transsexualism: Parts I and II." *Archives of Sexual Behavior* 3.6 (November 1974): 487-525.

Pomeroy, Wardell. "The Diagnosis and Treatment of Transvestites and Transsexuals." *Journal of Sex and Marital Therapy* 1.3 (Spring 1975): 215-225.

Prosser, Jay. *Second Skins: The Body Narratives of Transsexuality*. New York: Columbia University, 1998.

Raj, Rupert. "Information for the Female-To-Male." *Metamorphosis* 3.5 (October 1984): 7.

Ramsey, Allen. "The Student Strike and Later Protests, 1970-1975." *Vietnam War Protests at the University of Wisconsin-Milwaukee*, http://guides.library.uwm.edu/content.php?pid=85020&sid=633131.

Raymond, Janice. *The Transsexual Empire: The Making of the She-Male*. New York: Teachers College Press, 1994.

Rechy, John. *City of Night*. New York: Grove, 1963.

Reed, L.G.S. "Letter to the Editor." *Bay Area Reporter* (26 May 1983): page unknown.

Rivera, Sylvia. "Queens in Exile: The Forgotten Ones." In *Genderqueer: Voices from beyond the Sexual Binary*, ed. Joan Nestle, Clare Howell and Riki Wilchins, 67-85. Los Angeles: Alyson, 2002.

Roderick, Kevin. "Questions on Prop 64: Clearing the Confusion." *Los Angeles Times* (29 October 1986), http://www.aegis.org/news/Lt/1986/LT861002.html.

Schwamb, Don. "Alyn Hess." *Wisconsin GLBT History Project*, http://www.mkelgbthist.org/people/peo-h/hess_alyn.htm.

Schwamb, Don. "Donna Utke." *Wisconsin GLBT History Project*, http://www.mkelgbthist.org/people/peo-u/utke_donna.htm.

Schwamb, Don. "Eldon Murray." *Wisconsin GLBT History Project*, http://www.mkelgbthist.org/people/peo-m/murray_eldon.htm.

Screaming Queens: The Riot at Compton's Cafeteria. DVD. Directed by Victor Silverman and Susan Stryker. San Francisco: Frameline, 2005.

Shepard, Benjamin. "Sylvia and Sylvia's Children: A Battle for a Queer Public Space." In *That's Revolting!: Queer Strategies for Resisting Assimilation*, ed. Mattilda, a.k.a. Matt Bernstein Sycamore, 97-111. Brooklyn: Soft Skull, 2004.

Shepard, Benjamin Heim. *White Nights and Ascending Shadows: An Oral History of the San Francisco AIDS Epidemic*. London: Cassell, 1997.

Shilts, Randy. *And the Band Played On*. New York: St. Martin's, 1987.

Shilts, Randy. *The Mayor of Castro Street: The Life and Times of Harvey Milk*. New York: St. Martin's Press, 1982.

Streitmatter, Rodger. *Unspeakable: The Rise of the Gay and Lesbian Press in America*. Boston: Faber and Faber, 1995.

Stryker, Susan. "Portrait of a Transfag Drag Hag as a Young Man: The Activist Career of Louis G. Sullivan." In *Reclaiming Genders: Transsexual Grammars at the Fin de Siècle,* ed. Kate More and Stephen Whittle, 62-82. London: Cassell, 1999.

Stryker, Susan. *Transgender History.* Berkeley: Seal, 2008.

Stryker, Susan and Jim Van Buskirk. *Gay by the Bay: A History of Queer Culture in the San Francisco Bay Area.* San Francisco: Chronicle Books, 1996.

Sullivan, Flame. Interview by author, 5 March 2006, Milwaukee. Tape recording. In author's possession.

Sullivan, L. "Sullivan's Travels: A Transsexual Talks About His Life As A Woman Wanting To Be A Gay Man." *The Advocate* 526 (6 June 1989): 69-71.

Sullivan, Lou. "Lesbian Masquerade: some lesbians in early san francisco who passed as men." *The Gateway* (July 1979): no pages given.

Sullivan, Lou. "Letter to the Editor." *Metamorphosis* 2.3 (June 1983): 8.

Sullivan, Lou. "A Transvestite Answers a Feminist." In *The Transgender Studies Reader*, ed. Susan Stryker and Stephen Whittle, 159-164. New York: Routledge, 2006.

Sullivan, Louis. *From Female to Male: The Life of Jack Bee Garland.* Boston: Alyson, 1990.

Sullivan, Louis. *Information for the Female-to-Male Crossdresser and Transsexual*, 2d ed. San Francisco: Zamot Graphic Productions, 1986.

Sullivan, Louis G. "A Biography of Jack Bee Garland (a.k.a.) Babe Bean." *Metamorphosis* 6.4 (July-August 1987): 18-20.

Sullivan, Louis G. "Members' Work in Progress: A Biography of Jack Bee Garland AKA Babe Bean." *San Francisco Bay Area Gay & Lesbian History Society Newsletter* 2.3 (March 1987): 1, 5.

Sullivan, Sheila. "Looking Toward Transvestite Liberation." *GPU News* (February/March 1974): 22-23, 25-26.

Sullivan, Sheila. "Looking Toward Transvestite Liberation." In *The New Gay Liberation Book: Writings and Photographs about Gay (Men's) Liberation*, ed. Len Richmond with Gary Noguera, 147-153. Palo Alto: Ramparts Press, 1979.

Sullivan, Sheila. "Review: Emergence: A Transsexual Autobiography by Mario Martino with Harriett. Crown Publishers, Inc., New York, 1977. $10." *GPU News* (February 1978): 17-18.

Sullivan, Sheila. "A Transvestite Answers a Feminist." *GPU News* (August 1973): 9-11, 14.

Taylor, Michael. "Edward Falces—Surgeon Dedicated to Pro Bono Medicine." *San Francisco Chronicle* (2 January 2005): A-23.

TransGender San Francisco, http://www.tgsf.org.

Tropiano, Stephen. *The Prime Time Closet: A History of Gays and Lesbians on TV.* New York: Applause Theater and Cinema Books, 2002.

Valerio, Max Wolf. *The Testosterone Files: My Hormonal and Social Transformation from Female to Male.* Emeryville, CA: Seal Press, 2006.

University of Wisconsin-Milwaukee Libraries. *March on Milwaukee Civil Rights History Project*, http://www4.uwm.edu/libraries/digilib/march/index.cfm.

Weston, Kath. "Get Thee to a Big City: Sexual Imaginary and the Great Gay Migration." *GLQ: A Journal of Lesbian and Gay Studies* 2 (1995): 253-277.

What Sex Am I? VHS. Directed by Lee Grant. USA: Joseph Feury Productions, 2005.

Wisconsin Cartographer's Guild. *Wisconsin's Past and Present: A Historical Atlas.* Madison: University of Wisconsin, 1998.

WPATH (World Professional Association for Transgender Health), http://www.wpath.org/site_page.cfm?pk_association_webpage_menu=1351&pk_association_webpage=4655.

"You Can Help Preserve Lesbian and Gay History!': A Brief History of the GLBT Historical Society." *San Francisco Bay Area Gay and Lesbian Historical Society Newsletter* 1.3 (March 1986): 5.

Made in the USA
Columbia, SC
02 October 2018